Pebbles on the Path

Pebbles on the Path

A Medium's Journey into the Spirit World

Patricia Gagliardo

Dear Sue,
God Bless You - and
we love & miss you -
Love,
[signature]

Writers Club Press

San Jose New York Lincoln Shanghai

Pebbles on the Path
A Medium's Journey into the Spirit World

Published by Writers Club Press
an imprint of iUniverse.com, Inc.

For information address:
iUniverse.com, Inc.
620 North 48th Street, Suite 201
Lincoln, NE 68504-3467
www.iuniverse.com

ISBN: 0-595-12299-X

Printed in the United States of America

Dedication ▶

This book is dedicated in loving memory to
my beloved cousin, Crystal, my sister, my friend.
A special thanks to my son, David, his wife, Denise, and to
my wonderful grandson, Michael, for their love and support;
and to my husband, Gene, and all members of the Unity.

—Patricia Gagliardo

~ ~ ~

And special mention to Vincent,
for his guidance in the writing of this book.
'My mission in life is to turn one spirit
closer to God-consciousness.'

—Brother Vincent

Epigraph ▶

"I saw it with my own two eyes and I still don't believe it! Scratches appeared on both of Ms. Gagliardo's hands and then disappeared! The girls were found just as she described them and their hands were bound with wire!"

—Detective Tom Williams, Wheeling, WV

"Ms. Gagliardo said we would find something in Lincoln Cemetery, and we did. She led the tracking dogs to a child's bloody windbreaker and T-shirt."

—Arthur Langford, Councilman, Atlanta, GA

"Our police department has used Ms. Gagliardo very successfully, through her psychic abilities we were able to close previously unresolved cases. I am satisfied with the fact that she is a true psychic. I can personally vouch for her integrity, honesty and moral character and would and have referred her to other police agencies in the country."

—Lt. Lawrence Fawcett, Coventry, CT

"Pat Gagliardo is regularly consulted in homicide cases when all other available leads have been exhausted. I am at a loss to explain the phenomenon she possesses, however, the information received is credible and a solving factor in several cases. This officer will always remain indebted to Ms. Gagliardo for her assistance"

—William C. Gavitt, Deputy Chief, NLPD, CT

"Many people view psychics as frauds or someone who makes absurd predictions, as evidenced by numerous tabloid magazines and phony 900 number associations, and while this may be true in many cases, there are those, such as Ms. Gagliardo who use their ability for the good of mankind. I was formally the news Director for one of Connecticut's largest radio news staffs and became familiar with Patricia Gagliardo's involvements and successes. She has gained the respect of law enforcement agencies around the country. Her efforts have been recognized in various national publications and broadcast news programs. I have personally changed my own opinion of the word "psychic" concerning Ms. Gagliardo."

—*Dennis MacCarthy*

"This program has been a highlight of the year for our student body. I had the opportunity to speak with the student who had a private reading with you. She stopped by my office the following day and couldn't stop talking about how accurate you were and how she was going to make some changes in her life to improve it.

She shared with me how comfortable you made her feel and how trusting she was of you. The program Board chairwoman has already said that she wants to do this program again next year. Again, thank you so much for a fantastic program and best wishes."

—*Shawn A. Anderson, Director of Student Life,*
Albertus Magnus College, New Haven, CT

"I've been going steadily to you for the past 15 years and it's amazing how accurate your readings have been. Everything you have predicted has come through, and I highly recommend anyone to come and see you so that they can get a better perspective on life and sort out any problems they may have. You are an amazing woman and I have the highest respect for you."

—*Tove Prue, Norwich, CT.*

Contents ▶

Foreword ▶

When Pat asked me to write the foreword for this book, I was quite flattered. However, I declined, telling her that I thought writing the foreword was a privilege given to a notable person with a title, to which she replied, "It is, that's why I chose you. You're my friend." This gesture is typical of Patricia Gagliardo…she makes people feel important and recognize their self-worth.

It seems as though I've known Pat forever. As children, we attended the same church and knew of each other through catechism classes and church events. It wasn't until the late seventies that our paths crossed again, this time at Veterans School where I was a teacher and Pat transported our students. We briefly renewed our acquaintance, but the most contact that we had with each other usually involved a bus incident with one of my students. During this time, I had quite an interest in psychic phenomena and had enrolled in classes given at our local junior high school. I had already completed the spring session and decided to take it again in the fall. When I entered the class on the first night, I was surprised to see Pat. She introduced me to her husband and sister-in-law and I commented that it was pretty neat to see that we both had an interest in psychic phenomena. She immediately told me, in no uncertain terms, that *she* didn't believe in any of this nonsense—it was her husband who had lovingly manipulated her into attending the classes. 'So much for that', I thought and sat down.

I was quite taken aback when, at the break, Pat approached me and asked if I saw lightning bolts shooting out of the instructor's fingers. I truly thought she was kidding so I made a flip remark. She seemed quite emphatic about what she saw, but didn't pursue it with anyone else. The incident left me puzzled—only thirty minutes before, she told me she didn't believe in any of this nonsense, and now she's telling me that she was seeing lightning bolts shooting out of someone's fingers? Quite frankly, I thought maybe she had driven one too many busloads of screaming kids home from school that day.

It turned out that the proverbial joke was on me. During the second half of that first class and in the weeks to follow, Pat would have the most amazing meditations that always seemed to reveal something profound. When she held the instructor's watch and described her house in front of the whole group, we were truly astonished, as was she. It was obvious that she possessed an ability that the rest of us could only dream about.

At school, Pat and I managed to visit for a few minutes each day, talking excitedly about what was happening to her. Although she was truly amazed by all that was taking place, she didn't seem to share in the joy and excitement that many of us felt for her. Instead, she seemed plagued by the question of why she could do these things and other members of the group couldn't. Despite these feelings, she didn't shy away. Instead, she seemed to make it a quest. It was during one of these 'quests' that she called to tell me that she had purchased Tarot cards, and wanted to know if I would be willing to experiment with her. Of course, I agreed. I believe it was on that day that our friendship was cemented. Out of all the members of our class, she picked *me* to trust as her first person to read for.

What happened on that first day with me has occurred daily with others over the past twenty-two years—detailed accurate information, but always with a focus to guide you in the right direction or help you in some way. All this from a woman who, in the beginning, never saw herself as 'good enough' or 'worthy' to accept the gifts that God had planned for her. I have been with Pat from the very beginning and have witnessed many of her challenges as well as her successes. It has been an exciting trip watching her career branch off into many successful directions, but what has been more rewarding is watching her evolve into the confident, compassionate woman, who is credible in every sense of the word, and takes pure and simple joy in helping others.

While Pat will make everyone think I did her a huge favor by spending so much time working with her on this book, the very opposite is true. Two weeks prior to the inspiration for this book, my beautiful mother passed away. Although she had many serious illnesses over the past few years, her death came as a shock because, to the amazement of her doctors and everyone, she always had this uncanny ability to bounce back with renewed strength and faith. Her death left me devastated. She was not only my mother, but she was my best friend with whom I spent a lot of time. How was I ever going to get through this? Although many refer to it as coincidence, we know that it's divine intervention that comes to the rescue when you need it most, and that is exactly what took place with Pat's phone call asking for my help. Still emotionally overwrought, I agreed to help her, even though my heart wasn't in it. I should have known from the very beginning that this was exactly what was needed to help me through my grief. In the beginning, reading and editing each night seemed to give me a purpose and a place to be…I was so grateful. As the book progressed, Pat shared many of Brother Vincent's spiritual messages, which brought great comfort and peace to me. Through these messages, many of my questions were answered and many of my fears were put to rest. I was coming to rely on them and couldn't wait to leave school and race over to Pat's to see what she had written that day. What started out as merely a book, has developed into a source of spiritual comfort that I want to keep with me forever.

Pebbles on the Path is so spellbinding that you will want to read it from cover to cover in one sitting. At the same time, it is like an old friend that you will keep coming back to for the comfort that it brings. So many others, like me, are at a time in our lives where we are experiencing losses, questioning the meaning of our lives, or are simply searching for spiritual guidance and something to believe in. *Pebbles on the Path* is a book that will fill these needs.

— *Susan Reardon*

Preface ▶

There are several reasons behind my writing this book, but the primary inspiration began with a visit from my cousin, Alan, of Burbank, California. In early January of this year, 2000, Alan came out and spent two weeks with me. In the course of his visit, he attended our Unity group. Alan was moved by his experience of peace and the knowledge that we all shared with him concerning the spirit world. He told me that he had been on a spiritual quest for several years. What he had experienced in that one evening had answered so many of his questions, that he asked me, 'Why haven't you shared your experiences and knowledge in a book?'

I gave Alan's suggestion some serious thought. I began to reflect over the past thirty some years of my life—my own previous skepticism, cynicism and frustrations. I thought of the emotional, mental and physical obstacles that I had faced and eventually overcame by faith and perseverance. I began to think of all the people, maybe even you, that could relate to some of these same conflicts and challenges that I had faced. I felt that by sharing the knowledge of why tests and trials are important for spiritual growth that perhaps it may help to answer some of your questions as well. I thought of my family, clients, friends, and other encounters with people that have benefited from these spiritual enlightenments.

You may think it is a book of one woman's courage and strength, who lives a pious life. I wish that were a truth; it isn't. I have never viewed myself as a courageous person or having inner strength, and I am definitely not a saint. I am a woman that feels very blessed to have been given such gifts; and a second chance in this life to utilize them in helping my fellow man.

I hope I have conveyed by the factual events depicted in this book, a woman's story of humanness, gratefulness and compassion, and how the spiritual servants guide me along my path. It's a journey first, of a human being, subject to the same fallibilities and emotional challenges daily, as we all are, and second, as an instrument for spiritual intervention and a servant for mankind.

The Love of God and His Spiritual Guardians, love and support of close family and friends, has enriched my life. The writing of this book and the anticipation of it's publication, is the final pebble on my path, a gift back to God; to enlighten those who are seeking, bring open-mindedness to the skeptical, and to provide or restore faith in mankind.

In Love and Light,

Patricia Gagliardo

Acknowledgements ▶

I would like to take this opportunity to express my sincere appreciation and gratitude to all those who have encouraged, and stood by me through all of my endeavors. Without their continuous support and faith in my abilities, the material provided in this book would not have been possible.

To You, Lord, a very special thank you for sending me *Vincent* and *Bernard.*
Giving me these gifts and allowing me the privilege to be utilized as an instrument for Your Good Works, has made my life meaningful and rewarding.
I pray, with continued guidance, I'll always use them wisely.

To all the members of the Unity, a very special thank you for all the learning and experiences that we have shared over the years. In listening to me each week and offering your stories and encouragement has made the publication of this book a reality.

To my husband, Gene, who has been so supportive and has devoted endless hours at the computer, scanning, printing and preparing all the documents for this book.
A very special thank you.

To my family, Dave, Denise and *Michael,* whom I love more than life, I thank you for your love, support and encouragement. David, a special thank you for all that you had to endure in your youth and for your faith and support in all of my efforts.

To my Aunt Lorraine, Crystal's mother, whom I love and admire, a very special thank you for setting an example of selflessness, strength, and honesty. I will always treasure our friendship and your support.

To my cousin, Sam, thank you for your support in all of my efforts and for creating my website. Your laughter, teasing and love, I will always treasure.

To my sister-in-law Mary, whom I also love and admire, thank you for your editorial skills and the endless hours and expedience in which you have assisted in the production of this book.

To Carol Farrell and Nancy Brayman, to Carol, thank you for providing the transcription machine and your support. To Nancy, thank you for your transcription skills and taking the time out of your schedule to prepare the material necessary for the Atlanta chapter.

To Cheryl Vocatura and Marge Izbicki, thank you for the hours that you both have taken from your busy schedules to read each chapter, proofreading and offering your valuable and treasured comments.

To Alan Luzietti, my cousin, my friend and my Inspiration, there may be thousands of miles between us, but the bond and the love that we share can never be separated. Your enthusiasm, encouragement and continuous support, I will always treasure. I love you and I miss you.

To Susan, my valued friend, mentor and confidant, words cannot express my heartfelt appreciation and sincere gratitude for all of your support, your daily visits since January, reading, editing and advising. There are no words to describe what your friendship means to me. I love you.

1 ▶▶

The Interviews

It is October 4, 1979, Thursday night. Gene, (my husband), my cousin Ron's wife, Edie and I gather at our house to meditate. The same visions occurred, the man in uniform, the eagle, the cranes, the brick sidewalk, the buildings and a persistent urge to telephone my cousin, Sam, who at that time was a sergeant with the New London Police Department.

"I have to call him," I said. "I need to do something about these visions. Maybe I can help find that man, that Coast Guard guy that Sue told us about."

"If you feel that strongly about it, call him," Gene said, a concerned look on his face. "Just prepare yourself. Not everyone *believes,* you know."

"I know, especially Sammy. I'll be prepared for *his* remarks. Don't worry, hon." I smiled.

I walked over to the telephone and called Sam at home.

"Hey cuz! How are you?" he asked, calling me by his shortened version of the word cousin.

"I'm doing fine, thanks. I need to ask you something," I said a little hesitation in my voice. "Is the New London PD handling that missing person, the Coast Guard man who disappeared in April?" I asked.

"Not anymore, why?" he asked with a curious tone in his voice.

"Well, I-uh think I might be able to help locate him," I said, and quickly added, "I've been getting images in a meditation, that I think pertain to him."

"Oh yeah," he snickered. "Well, it's in the hands of the State's Attorney's office. If you call them and you tell them that you're seeing things, don't mention my name!" he laughed.

I was prepared for Sam's sarcasm, and I knew he loved me; he was just concerned about 'his reputation' and the ridicule he would probably receive. I ignored his comments and we chitchatted a few minutes about getting together for coffee.

We said our goodbyes and I hung up the phone and walked over to the dining room table and sat down. I told Edie and Gene the conversation.

"State's Attorney's office!" Gene remarked. "Nothing like going straight to the top!"

"I will ask for help," I smiled. "If it's meant to be, like everything else so far, I *know* I will get some *guidance*."

"Let me know what happens," Edie said, getting up and walking to the door.

"I will." I smiled, and we both said good night to her.

*   *   *

It is Friday morning, October 5th. I had just completed my first two school bus runs with my high school and junior high school students. I had about a 10-minute break before starting my route of grammar school children. I always parked the bus on the 'green' at Norwich Free Academy and waited there until it was time to leave. While I sat there, I reminisced over my telephone call with Sam and the meditations. I closed my eyes and silently whispered, "Please help me. Show me something that will tell me what I should do." Immediately, in my mind's eye, I saw a white truck with a sliding panel door in the rear of it, and an owl. "Will I *see* this? Is this a sign?" I mentally asked, and then opened my eyes.

During the entire run, I looked for the white panel truck and every time I stopped to pick up the children, I would look up into the trees for an owl before closing the door and starting off again. I didn't see either the truck or an owl. I dropped the children off at Veteran's School. Veteran's School is also where my friend, Sue, teaches 5th grade students.

I left the schoolyard and proceeded down Laurel Hill Avenue to the intersection of the viaduct. The light was turning from yellow too red. I stopped at the bottom of the hill at the light. I looked straight and a little to my right at the traffic that was approaching the viaduct from the other direction. The first vehicle that proceeded through the green light was a *large white truck.* As it passed in front of me and turned onto the bridge, I saw the *white sliding panel in the rear and also a picture of an owl with the words written, "Wise Potato Chips"!*

There it was!! The *confirmation* I needed to make the telephone call to the State's Attorney's office!

I drove directly home. I raced into the house and picked up the phone and dialed information for the number of the State's Attorney's office.

"State's Attorney's Office. Detective Viens," a man's voice said.

"Good morning. My name is Pat Gagliardo and I am calling because I think I can help you with a missing person." I said rapidly, feeling a bit anxious and nervous.

"What's your name again?" he asked.

I repeated my name and continued, "I think I can help with the missing Coast Guard man."

"Oh, and how do you think you can help us?" he asked.

"I am psychic and I do something called meditation and I have been getting these persistent images. If I give you some information, maybe that would be helpful." I rambled, changing my sentence in midstream, not wanting him to think I was crazy. "Do you know if there was any construction going on when he disappeared?" I asked, and explained about the cranes.

"Yes, I believe there was," he replied.

"I would like to describe the man I have seen. The man is kind of ruggedly built, brown hair a little grayish, and wears glasses. I see a light blue car, and him inside, slumped over the seat. Water, a lot of water." I said.

"Tell you what. Why don't you come to our office, we can show you around and take you to some of these water areas," he said with kindness in his voice.

"Okay. When would you like me to be there?"

"Well Monday is a holiday, Tuesday it will be hectic around here. How about Thursday the 11th," he said.

"What time would you like me to be there?"

"Let's say 10 in the morning. Do you know how to get here?" he asked.

"No. I don't" I replied.

"We are on Captain's Walk. Do you know where that is?"

"Yes. I am familiar with that area."

"Okay. We are next to the Karate school. There is a huge sign on the building where that school is. We are upstairs, 302."

"I have it, thank you. I will be there at 10 on the 11th."

"Okay and thank you," he replied and hung up.

I hung up the telephone and went into the kitchen to make a pot of coffee.

After I had poured myself a cup, I walked into the dining room and took the pad out of the hutch that had all the meditation notes written on it. As I flipped through the pages and I read the words, memories of the visions in the meditations flooded my mind. "I know you have let me see these things for a purpose," I reflected. 'Just like before when I saw the boat accident and bridge accident that had claimed the lives of all those people—Mt. Fuji explosion and a phone call Dennis had made telling me of a news clip that Ted Kennedy was thinking of running for the presidency, had all come to pass. "I *trust* you will guide me through this as well," I sighed.

I tried to put everything out of my mind. I would just keep 'faith' that everything would turn out the way it was intended to.

The day went by quickly. When Gene arrived home that afternoon, I told him about my conversation with Detective Viens.

"It's a huge responsibility, Pat," he said smiling at me. "But I agree with you, there has to be a reason for all the visions. You know I am behind you all the way, no matter what the outcome may be," he said, giving me a kiss and a hug.

The days went by. I had asked, Sam, my boss, for the whole day off on Thursday, as I had no idea how long I would be. I didn't tell him the reason I needed it off, just that it was 'personal'.

*   *   *

Thursday, October 11th. I chose a casual but attractive outfit to wear, blue slacks and a white and blue print long sleeve top to match. I would probably have to face some scrutiny and I wanted to make a good impression.

I made the trip to New London 'physically' alone. Gene would have accompanied me, but I told him it wasn't necessary, that I wouldn't be *alone.*

I left my house at 9:30 am. On the drive to New London, I whispered the Protection prayer and tried to keep myself as calm as possible. I approached the bottom of the hill at the traffic light, which was red, and I stopped the car. I would have to take a left onto Captain's Walk, when it *hit* me! In the center of Captain's Walk, the street was all 'red brick' and all the buildings were very close together.

I found a parking place approximately a block away from the address. I got out of my car, locked it, and proceeded to walk up the sidewalk, looking at the numbers on the building, and then I saw the Karate School sign.

I entered into the building next to it, 302. There was an elevator; I pushed the up button, the door opened quickly. My heart was racing now and I could feel my anxiety building. I glanced at the directory, State's Attorney Office-2nd floor. I pushed the button and took a deep breath trying to calm myself down. "How would I be greeted?" I wondered.

The elevator door opened to a brightly lit hallway. I walked down the hallway and I saw the numbers written in bold black on a glass door. The sign said, 'Walk In.'

A neatly dressed young woman came toward me.

"May I help you?" she asked, staring a little peculiarly.

"Yes, thank you. My name is Pat Gagliardo. I have an appointment with Detective Viens." I answered a bit nervously.

She walked toward another office door and I glimpsed at the clock above her desk and realized I was about 10 minutes early.

"Mrs. Gagliardo," her voice sounded. "They will see you now. Please follow me."

The office I walked into was very plain; no décor to speak of, yet upon entering the room a peaceful feeling replaced the anxiety that I had felt.

Two gentlemen were in the office. One man was slender in build and about average height with dark brown hair. The other gentleman was older, a bit heavier in build with lighter graying hair. Both of the men were wearing suits.

"How do you do?" The older gentleman asked in a very pleasant but authoritative voice. "I'm Ed Pickett. Please sit down and we'll get acquainted," he smiled. "This gentleman is Detective Viens."

"Thank you. It's nice to meet you both," I answered softly, feeling a little anxious again. "I am a little nervous, as I am sure you noticed." I smiled.

"Well that makes two of us. This is the first time I've met a psychic, just as it is your first time speaking to a detective," he chuckled, making me feel relaxed and at ease with myself.

"So tell me, Pat, just what is this psychometry business all about? And how do you think it can help us find Mr. Eastman?" he asked, settling back in his chair, and staring into my eyes.

"Well, I can try to explain how it works to the best of my knowledge. As for a scientific explanation of why or how it came about, I can't tell you. I can only speak of my own experiences," I answered, feeling my hands becoming moist and clammy from nervousness. "But I must be seeing these visions for a reason." I added quickly.

"Just relax," he smiled, with a matter of fact, but sincere note of interest and kindness in his voice, "Go on, and tell me the whole story."

"This is how it began. I do something on a daily basis called meditation. For about two or more weeks prior to our telephone conversation, during these sessions, I began to see visions. Each session the previous vision would appear followed by a new vision."

"Just a minute. You are losing me. Are you telling me that you are just sitting down or something and these things come to you?" he asked, with a curious frown on his face.

"Sort of," I replied, trying to find the right words to explain the phenomena. "I guess the best way to describe it is it's like a hypnotic state. In this trance-like state, pictures appear in my mental eye," I said, pointing to the center of my forehead.

"In my first vision, I saw a man in uniform in a slumped position. I didn't know if he was in the trunk of a car or over the seat of the car, a blue car. Then in another vision, the same man, and water. Then in another vision, the same man, the water and an eagle. Each time, a new picture would accompany the previous one. Do you understand?" I asked, now feeling relaxed and confident.

"I believe I am getting the drift. Continue. What did you do then?" he asked smiling at me.

"Well, I talked to my friend Sue about it. She thought it might be wise to check the papers, because she thought she had read something back in April about a missing person from the Coast Guard. When this man disappeared, I wasn't in the area then. My family and I were vacationing in Florida. After talking with Sue and having persistent images, I called my cousin who is in the New London Police Department and he told me your office was handling the case. That's when I called here."

"Hmm, I see. You told Detective Viens about a rope and something either in the trunk of the car or on the floorboard of the vehicle. Could you give me a little more detail on what exactly it was?" he asked, making a frown.

"Yes, that's correct. It looked like some kind of material wrapped around something else," I answered, making a gesture with my hands to indicate the size of the object. "I can't tell you what was inside, only that I felt it was metallic."

He smiled at the other detective and then said, "Okay, that's interesting. There's no way you could have known about the equipment he was carrying; that information was never given to the reporters. Would you like to see a picture of this man? Maybe by looking at it, you might come up with more details."

"I have more details to give you, other impressions that I have received in meditation. However, to help you locate him, I will probably have to hold an object that belonged to Mr. Eastman. Preferably an item he would have had close to him. That is how I perform psychometry," I stated with much certainty now and confidence.

"Come this way," he said, pointing to another door. "This is our library. Records and files are kept in here. I will also give you a credit card that belonged to the missing man," he said walking over to the filing cabinet. "Uh, to do the thing, psychometry, can you do this with anybody?" he asked not looking at me, his head down, searching through the files.

"I have so far. I have been doing it with people since last September," I answered, already knowing he would ask me to do a 'reading' for him.

"Ah, here it is," he said, as he took the folder out and walked over to the conference table. He searched through the folder and pulled out a picture of the man.

"This is our missing man, Richard Eastman, does he look familiar to you?" he asked as he handed the picture to me.

My heart nearly stopped when I took the photo from him and held it upright to my eyes. "Oh my God, I can't believe it," I whispered, my whole body shaking. Here *was* the man I had envisioned so often.

The uniform and description were identical in every detail. I was numb for a few seconds, upon realizing this photo was real and that I was seeing him physically and not mentally. "The eagle, the golden eagle, here it is on his hat!" I exclaimed, as I examined every inch.

"What about it?" Ed asked taken by my outburst.

"Well, during the visions, I always saw the eagle, but it wasn't attached to anything. I mean I didn't see it on a hat. I couldn't figure out why I saw it alone." I remarked, handing the picture back to him.

"Did you know the name of the boat he was on? It was also named the *Eagle*. Maybe that was it, huh? He was a very important man. Everyone, including the government, wants to find out what happened to him. He was working with some special top-secret radar equipment. The government, especially, wants to find him."

"I gathered he was a pretty important fellow when Detective Viens told me he was on a special assignment," I said, calming down again.

"Now, how can I be of assistance to you?" he asked, pulling a credit card out of the folder and placing it on the table. "This was in his wallet. Do you think you can get more information from it?" he asked, picking it up and handing it to me.

"It should be just fine. May I please have a pad and a pen to write down any impressions and information?" I asked.

"No problem. Is there anything else? Do you want to be alone?" he asked taking the items from his desk drawer and putting them next to me.

"Yes, it would be better, the quiet, but please don't go too far, there may be some questions that I will need answers to." I replied.

"I'll be in my office. If you need anything, give a call and I'll return," he smiled, and they both walked out of the room.

The credit card was cut in half and taped together in the middle. I wondered why it was like that. I decided that I would ask him later.

I took several deep breaths, closed my eyes, and asked God to please send His guides to help me. "Please help me," I whispered. "Guide me in the right direction. I know you have *led* me here for this specific purpose."

I opened my eyes again and picked up the card, holding it on the ends with both of my hands. I had only held the card for a few seconds when I perceived the following images.

The first thing I envisioned after the *colors* was a huge barge on the water. When that image faded, it was followed by an image of a seaplane. Then next, the light blue car again, the two cranes, and what looked like a dock, and an anchor rope. The eyeglasses and the eagle appeared too. "It's for sure he's in the water someplace, near a boat dock," I murmured to myself.

I wrote down all the information and went to the door to call Mr. Pickett.

"Would you come back in please?" I asked, tapping lightly on his office door.

"I'll be right with you," he answered, "There is another gentleman I would like you to meet."

I walked back over to the table and sat down and waited for the two men to come in.

The other gentleman that walked in with Mr. Pickett was younger, had light brown hair, very fit and was wearing a very flattering suit.

"This is Inspector Rainville," Ed said. He is also working on this case. He may be helpful, as he is quite familiar with some follow up work that has been done on the case," he smiled warmly.

"How do you do?" his deep but soft-spoken voice said.

"Nice to meet you, Mr. Rainville. I certainly hope this visit will prove fruitful," I smiled looking into his deep-set eyes.

As we all sat around the table, I took another look at this gentleman, "I don't think he believes in psychic phenomena," I thought to myself. "I wonder if he thinks this meeting is a waste of time?" I studied him carefully throughout the discussion of my reading from the credit card. I was soon to discover my 'feelings' about him were right.

"The information you have come up with could fit a number of places, I suppose," he said, looking over the piece of paper I had written my impressions on.

"Well," interrupted, Mr. Pickett, "I think we should drive around to a couple of areas. Would that help you, Pat?" he asked with a stern look on his face; yet it also held compassion.

"I think it will help, yes. Maybe if I were to see the area physically, I might get some vibration," I replied.

"Okay. Let's go," Ed said getting up and walking toward the door. I followed him and Mr. Rainville walked behind me.

We took the elevator down to the basement. It really gave me the willies walking through there. It was dark and had a musty smell. "I wouldn't come through here at night!" I said jokingly, "This place gives me the creeps!"

We left by a door, which led to the rear of the building, and into a parking lot. While Ed drove to the first possible area, I closed my eyes and allowed my impressions of the previous images to come back to my mind, as well as the impressions I had picked up from the credit card. I was piecing everything together in my mind, like a puzzle. A *voice* inside my head was saying, 'a ferry slip, seaplanes and the cranes; they are the key.'

"Pat, this is the 419 Club," Mr. Pickett said, parking the car directly across the street from it.

I looked at the little bar, and up and down the street. Just above the numbers 419, I saw a glass fixture protruding from the face of the building. Written on the glass was the word; FIRE, in red letters. Upon reading the word, I remembered that in one of the meditations I did see the word fire.

"I saw that in a vision, Mr. Pickett. Just the word fire-like I told you about the eagle. It makes sense to me now."

"Do you get any 'feelings' from this place? Can you tell us where he went from here? According to our reports this is the last place anybody had seen him. No one has heard from him since," Ed commented.

I began to sense something here. I decided I would hold back on these impressions until we observed some of the water areas.

"Do you know anything about the man's character or habits?" I asked, turning to look at both men.

"We know a few things from his roommate's point of view," answered Mr. Rainville. "Just an ordinary guy; used to like to have a few beers now and then. Nothing outstanding, he wasn't peculiar or hadn't any hang-ups that we are aware of."

"I see," I smiled. "Was he in the service a long time?" I asked, not really paying too much attention to his comments. Something was 'telling' me that the missing man was uptight. I also felt that he had been drinking in that bar a long time.

"Thirty years, and he was due to get out in the next couple of months," Mr. Rainville replied, breaking my train of thought.

"We're going to take you to Pequot Ave. There is a ferry slip over there. It isn't used anymore, but maybe you might 'feel' something there." Ed said.

He drove the car on a gravel area close to the water. There was a Chinese restaurant to the right of us, and to the left a brick building.

"What do you think of this place?" Ed asked as his eyes combed the area.

"I really don't 'feel' anything here, but it might make a difference if I walked on the dock." It was very windy and cold. I walked up the ramp, my eyes scanning the surroundings. Silently, I said a little prayer. "Please give me some sort of Sign." There was no response. I felt absolutely nothing. This couldn't be the area, the restaurant didn't fit, nor the brick building. I was 'sure' I would have seen both in the visions.

"No. I don't believe this is the place we're looking for, I'm not getting any vibrations here," I said climbing back into the car. "Funny thing though, as I was walking back, a lighthouse popped into my mind. I don't understand it, a lighthouse did not come into mind when performing the psychometry, or in any of the meditation imagery."

"A lighthouse, huh?" Mr. Rainville laughed. "Hey Ed, drive up to the lighthouse, the one up the road here!" he remarked, grinning.

"Yeah. Yeah. I know what you're getting at. We'll stop here, Pat, see if you get anything," Ed said, pulling into a gravel area.

There was a sandy area to the right of the gravel area and a lighthouse that was white with black trim. It stood out in the water just a few feet offshore. To the left of the car was a small house. "Maybe it's the watchman's quarters," I reflected.

This time all three of us got out of the car. It was really cold, especially here; the wind was coming up off of the water. "Why did you want to come here?" I asked, my hands and feet freezing. I knew they had something they weren't telling me.

"Take a walk down on the beach over there," Mr. Rainville said pointing to an open area of white sand.

"I don't feel or sense anything at all in this place either. What are you keeping from me?" I asked.

"Come on, I'll help you climb over the wall, down to the sand," he said, reaching for my arm.

"No, really, it's not necessary," I explained, wanting to get out of the cold and into the car. "Are you going to tell me the purpose of this escapade?" I asked, jokingly.

"All right, let's get into the car and I will tell you," he grinned, opening the car door.

"A little over a week ago, our office received an anonymous phone call. The caller said he had witnessed a man in uniform being buried here. According to the information, it would have been approximately two-hundred yards from where we were standing," he said, reaching for a cigarette. "I thought perhaps you might come up with the same details."

"I don't think so. Probably I was reading into *your* thoughts. It's possible, I've done so before." I smiled.

"Mr. Pickett," I continued, "let's just sit here a few minutes and try to piece this together. We should be looking for an area with this description. I remember seeing a long dock, a ferry slip, the eagle and the glasses, then the man in a slumped position, and the rope. Also the psychometry in your office provided a seaplane, the two cranes and a barge. "Does an area like that ring a bell?" I asked.

"Not right off hand. There are those kinds of things in a lot of areas around here," he smiled.

"All right let's try something else. We'll break it down piece by piece. Keep this in mind too—I might be seeing the area exactly as it was when he disappeared.

Things could be changed or different now. I am 'sure' the dock and ferry slip is the keys to finding him. This is the order of the visions: the dock, letting me know one is in the area, the ferry slip, then the man in the slumped position, and the rope. Then the psychometry provided the barge, the seaplane and the two large construction cranes. So I believe, in order to determine the right location, we have to find out what dock and ferry slip had a barge, two large cranes of construction and a seaplane at the time he disappeared. Do you understand what I am getting at?" I asked.

"Hey! Wait a minute!" Mr. Pickett exclaimed, putting a finger to his lips. "In March they were dredging down at the City Pier, and if I'm not mistaken there were two cranes down there. There is a long dock and the ferry slip is across from it."

"I think you're right about that, and it is the *only* area the seaplanes come into," Mr. Rainville said.

"Let's go!" Ed said, putting the car into drive. "You know, there was a big barge down there at that time too!"

We drove through downtown New London, passing the 419 Club once again. We approached a red light and turned right. As we drove over some railroad tracks and stopped the car in front of a large long dock, my eyes widened like a cat's. "That's the dock! I know it is!" I gasped, grabbing the dashboard and pulling myself closer to the windshield.

My heart and soul took in every inch of the place. I looked to the right and there was the ferry slip. Over to the left, was one crane. I knew this was the place!

"Do you want to get out?" Mr. Pickett asked, looking at my obviously ghost like face.

"Yes, I do," I stated bluntly. "I am going to walk right over there," I said, pointing a finger toward the ferry slip.

I still had Mr. Eastman's credit card in my coat pocket. I placed my hand in the pocket and held the card in my hand. "Please, give me a sign," I whispered, silently. I walked onto the ferry slip and approached the side closest to the water. Suddenly and without warning, my whole body began to tremble violently. I looked down into the water, unable to see a thing, but the shaking continued. The 'feeling' was like I was freezing inside my body. There were no outward signs of my trembling.

"Pat, are you all right?" Mr. Pickett asked, taking a hold of my arm. "You look as though you are seeing a 'ghost'!"

"He's down there," I said solemnly, pointing to the water. "That's where you will find him and the car."

"I believe you're wrong," stated Mr. Rainville. "You see the car has been spotted several times. "Want to go someplace else?" he asked with a very nasty and sarcastic tone.

The tone of his voice upset me. "He is being very critical," I thought. I knew he was skeptical, but he didn't have to be rude and sarcastic. "If that's true, why don't you have the car in your custody?" I asked, staring right into his eyes.

"We haven't been able to nail it yet. But we will, it's just a matter of time," he said smugly, as he turned and began to walk toward the car. "Not only that," he added, turning to face me, "but this area *has already been searched by divers.*"

"If that's true," I said, looking back at Mr. Pickett, tears welled in my eyes, "I guess I am sorry that I have wasted your time."

"I'll check into it," Ed said, smiling at me. "Come on, let's go back to the office, have a cup of coffee and talk about it."

On the short drive back to the office, my mind was in a terrible turmoil. Why was I shaking like that? Why did I see all those descriptions? If that area were already searched, why would it be that 'strong' of a feeling to me? I was really confused.

Once we were back at the office and we went into the library again, I really began to wonder if I had done the right thing by calling them.

Ed and I sat at the conference table with our cups of coffee, while Mr. Rainville stood near us.

"Uh, Pat?" Mr. Pickett asked, moving his chair closer to mine, "Could you do that psychometry on me?"

"I can try. However, I have sort of mixed emotions at this point. I just can't believe I received all that information for nothing." I said, confused.

"What do you want from me? My watch, ring, you name it, and I will give it to you," he smiled.

"I'll use your watch, normally an item closest to the skin provides the best pictures and information." I said flatly.

He took the watch from his wrist and handed it to me, while Mr. Rainville took a chair, sat down and glued his eyes on me. "He's hoping I'll make a bigger fool out of myself," I thought. "Maybe, just maybe this will turn out *right*."

I took a deep breath, and mentally I told myself to calm down, I felt a soothing presence of peace. The *colors* appeared and then dispersed; with my eyes closed I relayed this information. "The first thing I am seeing is a house, looks brownish in color. I am pretty sure it is on a dead-end street; either that or it's a turn around. There is an eagle or something that sticks out on a garage. I see a driveway with a can and some wood leaning on both sides of it. I suspect the driveway was just capped or tarred or something. Tell me Mr. Pickett, do you know a boy named Randy? Before you answer, let me explain why I asked. I see this young boy with you having a disagreement or something. Maybe he had run over the new driveway and you were scolding him for it." I said, opening my eyes to look at him.

"Incredible! Absolutely incredible!" he bellowed as he stood up from his seat. "Are you sure you don't know me?" he asked grinning and quite pleased. "Come on Dick, give her your watch!" he ordered.

It was very evident, he did not want me to hold anything belonging to him, but reluctantly he agreed.

"I don't know," he said, his eyes moving back and forth from Ed to me. "Oh what the heck," he said, taking off his watch and handing it to me. "Go ahead, tell me what you see," he smirked.

I did my normal procedure, and then described, "I am inside of a house, I can't see the color of it, but I can describe the room. To my left is a mantle; straight ahead is an archway leading into a dining room. By the way, there is a window in that dining room that looks out into a backyard, I think. I am sensing there is water there, I can't see it, but I feel it. The only thing visible from the window, is a fence, I also see a van in the driveway. I believe it's yours. You know there is something odd, funny I feel about you. I'm getting lots of speakers all around you. I am not quite sure why, yet. One more thing, your wife does something that requires her to wear a uniform." I said, opening my eyes. He was very anxious to take his watch away from me. He reached over and took it out of my hand.

"Yeah, she sure does!" beamed Mr. Pickett.

"Your wife does too, doesn't she?" I asked, smiling at him. "I forgot to tell you that before."

"Pat, I want to clear up something with you," Mr. Pickett said, pulling his chair over to mine again and patting me on the hand. "That boy Randy you spoke of, he's my neighbor's son. You were right about the argument, but it's because he threw an egg at my house. You really are incredible! My house you accurately described, right to the eagle on the garage. Here," he said, grabbing a piece of paper and a pencil. "Please write down the location again along with all the information."

"Sure, Mr. Pickett," I smiled, taking the items from him. "By the way, I can assure you, I never knew an Ed Pickett existed before today."

"I know, I was only kidding, and call me, Ed," he smiled.

"Your details were pretty good about my house, too, Pat." Mr. Rainville said, his jaw tight. "You were right about the window in the dining room. The only thing you can 'see' is the fence. It goes around my 'pool'. And I do drive a van, and our wives are nurses," he said, a quick grin on his face and then he left the room.

"Here it is, Ed." I said, handing him the paper. "My goodness it's after two already. If there is nothing else, I had better be going."

"No, nothing else," he replied, handing me my coat. "Pat. I want you to know, I will personally check out everything. Everything, I don't want you to worry about it and thank you," he smiled.

Now feeling much more confident, walking toward the door, I said, "By the way, when you check into everything, I believe you're going to find out Mr. Eastman was in that bar quite a long time, probably since early afternoon. And I really think what happened to him was an accident," I remarked, and walked out of the door.

"The readings went well, thank You, Lord," I whispered, opening my car door. "It's in their hands now, and Yours."

As I drove past the Coast Guard Academy, I allowed my thoughts of that day to subside. My mind began to reel backwards over the past year. "Only a year," I sighed and so much has happened and changed my life so drastically. What was it like before?" I kept thinking. "You, of all people, Ms. Skeptic of all time!" I laughed aloud. Then I put the realization in its proper perspective. As I stopped at a red light, I gazed up at the heavens above. "You knew I was skeptical, cynical and a borderline atheist, Lord, yet You gave me this gift. I *know* everything will turn out all right. One question, though," I began to cry, tears rolling down my cheeks. *Why me?*

2 ▶▶

Challenges

It is so difficult for me at times to remember what my life use to be like. Who I was, what *I* wanted to be when I grew up, what *my* goals were. When I look in the mirror and stare into the eyes of the woman's reflection looking back at me, I wonder, "Who are you? Why were *you* chosen…?"

It's July 1962 and it is really hot. I heard my mother's voice and what sounded like moaning from my dad and it woke me up.

I was sweating and my nightgown was sticking to my thirteen year old body. I walked out of my room and down the hallway into the living room.

My mother's voice was clearer now and I heard her saying, "It's probably what you had last night, Joe."

I looked over at my father who was lying sort of crooked on the couch. His face was a grayish color and he was rubbing his left arm feverishly, and he was crying.

"Daddy!" I yelled, running over to him. "What's wrong, daddy!" I cried, hugging him very tight. I was so scared. I *knew* something was very wrong with my father, and I just wanted to keep my arms around him.

Mom walked over to the little table, between the windows, and picked up the handset that rested on the telephone. "Santo, please come here right away." I heard her say.

In just a few minutes my brother, Santo, was driving in the driveway. I watched in total horror and disbelief as my brother came into the house and rushed over to the couch.

"Call Dr. A. right away!" he shouted, as he laid my father down and began pumping with his hands on my dad's chest.

The rest of the day is nothing but a blur. I remember the doctor coming into the house, my mother crying, and I remember running and running and crying and running some more.

I ran up to my Aunt Lorraine and Uncle Jim's house, dad's brother. Uncle Jim was in the backyard doing some yard work.

"Uncle Jimmy," I gasped, short of breath and through my tears. "Something is wrong with daddy! Please! Please come to my house!" I pleaded.

The smile on his face when he saw me immediately turned to a frown of worry and fear. He yelled to Aunt Lorraine, "Something's wrong with Joe! Patricia's here, I'm taking her back home to see what's going on!"

When we rounded the corner from Mt. Pleasant Street onto Peck Street, a sickening feeling took place in my stomach, as I could see the ambulance, parked in our driveway. I knew something was very wrong. I would not see my father again. I just knew it.

After the funeral things at home were not the same. It was now just my mother and me. My other older brother, Jim, was in the Navy and Santo, the oldest, was married and living down the street.

I had attended an all girl Catholic high school because my dad wanted me too. I liked the school well enough and had pretty good grades, but with the loss of my father, and a poor relationship with my mother, I developed a very negative *attitude*. It certainly wasn't my *intention* to become skeptical, critical, cynical and so bitter; it was largely due to circumstances beyond my control.

This was the worst summer of my life. My father's death had taken a very serious emotional toll on me, more than anyone realized, especially me. The loneliness I felt simply can't be described.

My dad was my whole life. We did everything together. He took me to church, my CYO classes, shopping and visiting family. He played games with me; he even brushed my hair every morning when I was a little girl, before I went to school. I felt so loved by him, so safe and secure. I was his 'baby' and he was my world.

My mother and I were never close. And after Dad's death, my relationship with her deteriorated beyond repair. She criticized everything I did. Nothing was ever good enough or right in her eyes. I tried so hard to please her, as hard as any 13 year old could. I desperately wanted affection, approval and acceptance from her. I had chores to do, dishes, keeping my room clean and laundry. If I didn't get something done just right, I was reprimanded for it. But for the things I did well, I never heard any praise either. My girlfriends went shopping with their moms, out to lunches, and other mother and daughter things. I never knew what that was like, and how I envied them!

When Dad was alive, I loved the summer! There were always picnics at the beaches! We would get together with some of the other families at Ocean Beach, or Devil's Hop Yard, or Rocky Neck. It was so wonderful! And our families used to visit on Sundays, after church. Now, this summer, everything came to an abrupt halt! Very rarely did someone stop by to visit. No more beaches, no more family, no more love; nothing! Why was this happening? My other older brother Jim was in the Navy and Santo, the oldest, had his own life. The only time I heard from Santo was when my mom called him to come over, when she was mad about something I did, and I would get reprimanded and punished, or if he needed me to watch my niece. Before summer was over, I hated my life, I didn't trust people, and forget about God. *Who*? He just didn't exist for me at all! Where did all the *prayers* get *me*? What about the religion classes at school, learning about God's Love and Mercy? What about my dad's devotion, making sure that we always attended Sunday Masses? Yeah right!

I was pretty ticked off and I absolutely refused to go back to *that* school the following September. My mother and I had quite a few battles over it. She wanted me to stay in the Catholic high school and I was determined that I was not going back. I went to the local high school. Shortly after school started, my downhill life really spiraled out of control.

I made friends with an older crowd. Girls my age were just too silly and immature. I met a girl, Marie, who was in her junior year and she had a driver's license! She started to pick me up in the mornings and take me home after school. We became very good friends. She had a relationship with her dad, just like I had with my mother. So we commiserated a lot.

We started hanging out together after school and on weekends. She smoked cigarettes, so I started smoking too. One day after school, when Marie drove me home, I invited her in. After she left, my mother demanded that I no longer see her. Well, that wasn't going to happen, so Marie and I ran away. Well, actually, she drove and we went to New York. We were gone three days.

When we got back, there was hell to pay! Santo was very ticked off and he and my mother wanted to place me in a home somewhere. I was all for it! Anything would have been better than living there anyway! I had to meet with the school guidance counselor. I remember my mother saying, "She just doesn't listen to me. I don't know what to do with her!" I wanted to scream out, "What about listening to me? Doesn't that count?" Later, there would be a determination of what they were going to do with me. As it turned out, I left home, but not the way *they* wanted me to.

A month before my sixteenth birthday, I met this very handsome and charming Southerner, who swept me off my feet. Jerry was seventeen. It was perfect. I wanted to get away from home and he wanted to marry me and take me to his home in Georgia. Three months later, Jerry and I were married and moved to his family's home in Toccoa, Georgia.

I thought finally I would be happy again. We would *love* each other and I would feel safe and secure. Jerry worked with his father in his construction company and I took classes to finish high school. We lived with his parents until we had enough money to refurbish the downstairs and build our own apartment. Jerry started drinking and he became abusive toward me, emotionally, mentally and sometimes, physically. It was a side of him, I hadn't known existed, and it was usually prompted by an argument with his father, Horace.

I also had to contend with his father who was a very controlling man. He was a self-made minister of a church that he and some friends had built on his mother's property, which was about four miles from where we lived.

Their religion was very different from what I was used to, having grown up a Catholic. Their religious beliefs and practices I found to be quite odd. The women didn't cut their hair, or wear make-up and they never wore slacks or long pants of any kind.

The religion was a Pentecostal faith. I just remember people referring to the religion as 'holy rollers'. In the church, people would start throwing their hands up in the air and strange words and sounds would be uttered by some of the parishioners. Some would even jump over the pews.

I didn't want to attend the church services, but was commanded by Horace, "As long as ya'all live in this house, ya'all will be there!" He frightened me. He would physically, emotionally and mentally abuse his wife, Frances, who was so sweet and kind. I knew he would treat me the same way!

Shortly after we moved into our apartment downstairs. I had to face another shocking blow! Unbeknownst to me, Jerry had gotten into some trouble prior to his coming to Connecticut and he was now going to have to pay for it! He would be going to prison! The prison was located in Milledgeville, Ga., which was 300 miles away! He would be gone 10 months to a year! I would have to live with his parents!

Horace also dictated to me. Since he and Frances worked, and I didn't, I was told, "You can help out by doing the housework and preparing dinner." So, that ended the classes.

It was a horrible and frightening 11 months. I felt so trapped! We visited Jerry once a month, on Saturdays. It was a long drive and there was always some kind agitation between Horace and Frances. I would sit silently in the backseat, never saying a word.

I couldn't believe that Jerry was in such a place with hardened criminals! He and some other boys had stolen rims and hubcaps! This place was filled with murderers, rapists and all kinds of violent people!

As the separation from Jerry grew longer, Horace began to make advances toward me. He would say things like, "You need a real man in your life. A man that can give you things, and treat you right. A man to take you places and show you off," he would say smiling. "A man like me."

I wouldn't answer, or look at him; I would go downstairs and lock my doors. I was so frightened of him. I would lie in bed at night and wonder why *he* wasn't the one suffering! If God did exist—where was the *justice*? How could this *man of God*, who was such a hypocrite, go unpunished? I found most of the members of that church, including another preacher friend of his, Preacher Biggs, all to be hypocrites! I didn't trust anyone! It was like living in a nightmare—one that I couldn't wake up from!

Then the day I dreaded happened! Horace came home early from work, before Frances got in. I was preparing dinner. He snuck up behind me while I was at the counter in the kitchen, chopping okra, a long green vegetable that we fried with yellow squash. He threw his arms around me and tried to kiss me! I screamed, turned around and ran to the other side of the kitchen table; the long thick silver blade from the knife shaking in my hand.

"Get away from me, Horace!" I yelled. "Leave me alone!" I pleaded, as tears poured from my eyes.

"Ya know ya want it!" he sneered, and headed around the table toward me.

I ran around the table and flew out of the back door. I ran right across the road, never looking to see if any cars were coming. I ran up the long dirt driveway of our neighbors yard, the Davenport's, and I was screaming at the top of my lungs for help!

Hazel, an older woman, who didn't work, came out onto her back porch and ran toward me.

"What on earth is the matter child?" she asked, hugging me.

I told her what had happened and she took me inside of her house. Her husband, Leonard, who was retired, was there too. I heard them whispering in the kitchen, while I was still shaking and sitting on the living room couch. A phone call was made, and the next thing I knew, Jerry's Aunt Blanche, was driving up the dirt road.

I was given refuge at Blanche's home. I didn't know her very well. She didn't visit with us much at all. I was leery to stay with her, but I really didn't have a choice, and Jerry was coming home in about a week! No one was going to tell him the truth about why I was at his aunt's house, for his own good. Right after he came home, within a couple of days, we moved to Atlanta, one hundred miles away. Blanche loaned us the money to get away. Only I *knew* the real reason behind it.

Blanche confided to me that Horace was used to having his own way. "He has a lot of power down here. He knows all the right people. Even has the Sheriff, Wilmer Shirley, in the palm of his hand. Ya'all just need to move far away from him. He got his own brother's wife pregnant. If Jerry were to find out he tried having his way with you, there'd be a killing over it for sure!"

Shortly after we moved, I wanted to continue with school, but money was an issue, as we never had enough. As it turned out, within three months, I became pregnant! I was so delighted! Jerry seemed very happy too. My beautiful son, David, was born shortly after my 18th birthday. I had a very difficult delivery. Unbeknownst to the obstetrician, one of my pelvic bones was cracked and bent, causing an obstruction for the birth. My water had to be broken, and excessive force of forceps had to be used in bringing David into the world. He was born with a birth capit, (which looks like a boil, that covered his entire head) and I had to remain in the hospital a few extra days. With the birth of my son, and Jerry seemingly doing better, only drinking a few beers on the weekends, I was starting to let my defensives down some. I wanted to get a part time job and help out with expenses. Jerry was reluctant, but he finally agreed. Things were starting to look up, and we were even talking about buying a lot someday so he could build a small house on it for all of us.

Then another blow! When my son was 22 months old, Jerry was killed in an automobile accident! I was completely distraught, overwhelmed with sadness, despair and totally disillusioned. I telephoned my mother, at the request of my brother Jim, with whom we had stayed in contact by mail, and asked her if I could move back home, temporarily. She had a grandson now; maybe she would want to have an active part in *his* life.

I wasn't surprised by her answer. Somehow I expected it. She said no. In the interim, she had married the man who stood up for me at my baptism. I won't refer to him as a Godparent, because he never was. He was now my stepfather and he liked things the way they were, and said that I couldn't move back there. That was that.

I returned to my home state of Connecticut anyway and settled in New London, a couple of towns away from Norwich. I worked two jobs to provide a home for my son and myself, as an aide working in a nursing home during the day, and illegally tending bar in a family owned restaurant/bar, four evenings a week. I was desperate so I lied about my age to get the job.

I grew up in a hurry. A lot of guys made passes at me, and I quickly came to believe that such things as love, honesty, and trust just didn't exist! They were after one thing and one thing only; their self-satisfaction! Life was truly teaching me more and more everyday about bitterness, skepticism, distrust, insecurity and anger! It grew inside of me like a cancer. I just wanted to love someone! I wanted love in return! It wasn't going to happen! I finally decided to get out of the 'dream world' I was in and face the facts. Life was a bitch and you just needed to take from it what you could!

Within two years, I met and married my second husband, Dennis, and moved with him to his family home in Danbury, CT. It wasn't a great marriage right from the beginning. I couldn't trust, and I had built chains so thick around my heart, no one was going to break through them. But I wanted a father for my son; and a brother or sister for him, so he wouldn't know the loneliness I felt. I didn't want him to have to suffer the way I did. I was not prepared for all of the emotional, physical pain, and sadness that was *still* ahead of me.

My second child, another son, Richard, was born. Richard's delivery was also very difficult and, as a result, I developed a blood clot in my leg that separated and traveled up to my lung, causing a pulmonary embolism. I was placed on blood thinners and had to make several trips a week to the hospital's clinic to monitor the dose of the medication, coumadin.

Within the first six months of his life, I began to question Richard's emotional growth and learning capacity. I didn't mean to compare him to David, but the differences were far too extreme. Richard was examined but the results were not conclusive. After many years, the eventual diagnosis was autism. Despite the diagnosis, Richard grew to be loving and sensitive with a great depth of compassion. Today he functions quite well. He is independent and still maintains his loving, sensitive and compassionate nature.

In May of 1972, another shocking blow came! At 2 am on the morning of May 12th, I received a telephone call from my brother Santo's wife, Joan. She was informing me that my brother, Jim, had *died in a fire*! It was in our family home.

Jim and I hadn't seen each other often, but we remained very close. We continued to exchange letters and phone calls while he was in the Navy and phone calls once he moved back to the family home in southeastern Connecticut.

I was numb and in total shock. We immediately packed some things, took the boys to my husband's parents and drove the two hours to Norwich.

The fire was contained to Jim's apartment, which was upstairs in the house on Peck Street. I walked over to our neighbor's, the Boron's, and spoke with Mr. Boron. He was very obviously distraught, as he tried to explain how he entered through the front door and up the stairs to help

Jim. He couldn't. The tremendous heat and smoke made it impossible. I thanked him and we held each other and cried.

Jim's death wrought much more sadness in me and escalated all of my negative emotions. Life just wasn't the same. Of my immediate family, he was the only one I *really* talked to. How I missed him! I became so unhappy and very depressed.

Dennis thought a move away might help. We packed up the VW bus and headed to California. I worked nights and he worked days. I received my GED in the meantime, but I was terribly homesick for Connecticut, and I really didn't like California.

As it turned out, there was a terrible earthquake, and though the epic center was 60 miles away, we felt it where we lived in Sun Valley. Two weeks later we packed up and headed back to Connecticut. We settled near Dennis's family in Danbury.

While we were here, I learned how to drive a bus and I became a school bus driver. It was easier to have Richard with me, than to try to find adequate childcare.

Dennis and I argued a lot, and finally after six months, I took the boys and moved back to my hometown of Norwich and Dennis moved into his parent's home in Ridgefield.

Eventually we divorced. There was a great school called RESCUE, for children with problems such as Richard had. The school was located a couple towns away from Ridgefield. It wasn't an easy decision to make, giving up custody of Richard to Dennis, but I knew it was the right and best thing for him. It was such a heartbreaking loss for me! I knew Dennis and his parents also adored Richard and the school would give him the best care for his special needs.

My son, David, and I moved into a small but cute apartment in the city of Norwich. I went back to driving school bus, so I could be with him more. On his days off, I would be off too. I made several friends that were also drivers.

I dated a couple of men, but my heart wasn't really in it. I just wanted to try and have some fun in my life, for a change. But there wasn't much of that.

Within two years I met Gene, my present husband of 25 years. When we first met I was very cautious, my emotions were well guarded and I couldn't trust. I had had enough hurts and disillusionment in my life and I was in no hurry to add anymore.

It was a mutual decision that we would live together first and make sure our lives would be compatible before even considering marriage. Gene worked very hard and was very responsible, and we got along together well.

Approximately two and a half years later, we were married. Just when I started to feel comfortable and my life seemed content, crisis struck again!

I still worked part time as a school bus driver and attended Huntington Institute for classes in business. I really enjoyed driving for the school children. On most of the bus runs I had, my children were really great. I always talked and joked with the students and they would share with me some of their stories, private lives, and involvements.

At the end of every school year most of the drivers got together and decided on a place to go for the day. This particular year it was decided that we would go to Rocky Point Amusement Park, in Rhode Island.

I had developed a close friendship with three of the female drivers, Jan, Karen, and Verline. On the ride back home, in the school bus, all of us were sitting together joking and talking. I wasn't aware that I had been rubbing the top of my leg, but I do remember that my leg was aching.

Gene worked rotating shifts and this night he was on the second shift. Verline had arranged babysitting for my son, David, so she offered to pick him up and bring him to my home. The events of that night are still somewhat hazy to me, however, the conversations that I had had afterwards with all the people involved helped me to piece the puzzle together.

I remember walking in the door of my mobile home and having a very sharp pain in my chest that took my breath away. I recall stumbling toward my bedroom and the next thing being in the hospital emergency room. I didn't know then, how, who or why, I was there; it was learned afterwards, it was by Guardian Angel intervention…

I could hear voices that sounded very muddled and distant. I saw an outline of a man standing over me and he was talking, but his words were not audible to me. I remember him touching and looking at my leg and though his lips were moving, I could not make out what he was saying. In a few moments an outline of a woman was near me in a white uniform. She rolled me over, gave me an injection and soon I just felt very relaxed. The voices seemed to fade almost completely away and the pain in my chest was easing up.

I don't know how much time passed, but I remember opening my very heavy eyes, seeing two men and hearing loud voices shouting. "Don't you know what a milk leg is?" I heard one man say. "Get this woman to x-ray immediately!" The next thing I know I am being wheeled on a gurney through a dimly lit corridor, a woman walking next to me and she is holding my hand.

"Pat. Do you remember me?" she asked, whispering. "My name is Ruth. I am a private duty nurse. I know your brother, John." John is the name my brother, Santo, used most of his adult life. It is his middle name. As far back as I can remember his colleagues referred to him as S. John.

I was listening to her words, but really didn't know who she was. "Don't become alarmed now," she said soothingly. "They are going to put you where they can keep a closer eye on you." I remember thinking, "Who is going to put me where; why?" Ruth's involvement is more Guardian Angel intervention, which also comes later.

I was so heavily medicated that I was unconscious for two days. When I came to, my husband was standing over me. His handsome face was an ashen gray color and he had tears in his eyes. When he saw that I had opened my eyes, he smiled a nervous smile.

"What's wrong, Gene?" I asked in a very low hoarse type whisper.

"Honey," he said, gently squeezing my hand in his, and his voice shaking, "You have a blood clot that is close to the main vessel to your heart.

Please just stay calm and don't try to move around. The doctor has given you some medication called heparin and it is going to dissolve it."

I tried opening my eyes as wide as I could and saw both my arms strapped with all kinds of tapes and IV's. The top of my left thigh had something a little heavy and warm resting on top of it, and my chest felt like a vice grip was on it. It was very difficult to talk; it seemed to take every bit of my energy from me. I wanted desperately to tell my husband that I *had seen* my father and my brother, Jim, and they both were *talking* to me! And how happy it made me feel! I remember how ecstatic I felt because I *knew* they were alive! They hadn't left me! When Daddy said, "You have to go back, Patricia," I kept crying, "No. No. I want to stay with you and Jimmy!" "We will always be with you," he said smiling, and then he and Jim turned away and walked into a beautiful bright and soothing mist. Jim looked exactly like I remembered him, he was a very handsome man, he had very dark brown hair, ocean blue eyes and a han- dlebar mustache. He was 27 years old when he died, and he looked just the same. Daddy did too. He was 46 when he died. He had all of his dark almost black hair, he had a little bit of a paunch and he was handsome. I was trying to talk, but couldn't. A nurse came in, gave me a shot and I drifted off into sleep again.

I remained in Intensive Care for four days and then I was placed in a two-bed ward. A heating pad remained on my leg and I was given many injections in my right arm. I now had only one IV and it was in my left hand. The pain in my chest was easing up and the aching in my leg was just about gone, but my right arm was swelling and beginning to turn very black and blue. Within a few days my entire right arm, from the top of my shoulder and underneath my armpit to a little way around my back and down to my fingertips, was completely black and deep purplish in color. I started to cry and became very alarmed.

When Dr. Rousseau came in, my husband expressed his concerns about my arm, and demanded to know what happened. A nurse had told Gene that I had banged my arm while in intensive care. Gene was livid! We both knew that was impossible since I was asleep nearly my entire stay there. Dr. Rousseau admitted that a mistake had been made, but in the interim my life had been saved. The nurses had been giving me my heparin injections in my arm causing all the capillaries under my skin to break. The blood filling up under the skin caused the swelling and the discoloration. Heparin injections were only to be administered through the abdomen or the clavicle. The nursing administrator came into my room and boldly asked me if I intended to sue the hospital. We didn't. Gene and I were just grateful that my life had been saved. My arm stayed swollen for months and the discoloration lasted for over a year.

While still in the hospital, the crisis having passed, I was now able to have visitors; among them Ruth and Verline.

Gene and I were talking, when Verline entered into my room.

"Well I gotta tell you!" she laughed, after giving me a hug and telling me she was happy to hear that I was going to be all right. "You scared the you–know-what out of me!" she continued, shaking her head back and forth. "When I told the other drivers the story about that night, they were all pretty amazed that I knew it was your voice on the phone, when I only heard the word, 'Help!'" she said, smiling and looking at me and then to Gene.

"What are you talking about, Verline?" I asked, with some confusion in my voice.

"The night I brought you here!" she said flatly. "I figured I'd stay for awhile at Kathy's, and let Dave play with her kids a little longer, while she and I had coffee, but when the phone rang, I was closer to it, so I picked it up and heard your cry for help. She kept Dave for me and I flew over to your house!" she said, looking at me very curiously. "Don't you remember that I drove you to the hospital?" she asked.

"No," I answered, and quickly added, "I don't even remember picking up the phone, and you didn't give me Kathy's phone number. You were going to, but I don't remember you writing it down and giving it to me."

"Hmmm, well I *must* have. I got you here, and thank goodness you're all right now!" she said. No more was said about the phone call, then. We said our goodbyes and Verline left.

On the day I was being released from the hospital, Ruth came into my room. Gene was there and we were gathering my things in preparation to leave.

"Hi Pat. How are you?" Ruth's cheery voice rang out as she walked in. "I see you're doing much better," she said, walking over towards me and giving me a hug.

"Much better. Thanks." I replied. "I apologize Ruth, if I wasn't very coherent the last time I saw you." I laughed.

"Totally understandable, and no apologies necessary." she smiled. "I am just so glad I was here, and I made that trip down to the ER again at the time you were brought in."

"Yeah, me too. I think." I laughed. "I really don't remember much."

"Funny, how some things are just *meant to be*," she said. "I had already been to the ER about half an hour before. My friend was working the desk that night and I had gone down to visit with her. I left, went back up to my patient on the third floor and started to read a book. *But there was this persistent, loud thought in my head to go back down to the ER. So I did.* I saw you on the gurney, and I inquired as to what was going on with you. My friend said that the emergency room doctor felt you were having an anxiety attack and ordered some Demerol for you and was going to send you home. I probably could have been fired on the spot, but I had to open my mouth. I told him you had a history of blood clots, which I knew about from your brother, John. He kind of shot me a look, but I went over and asked my friend to call Dr. Rousseau to look at you, anyway. And well, you know the rest," she ended.

"How can I ever thank you? If it wasn't for *you* and Doctor Rousseau, I probably wouldn't be here now," I said, putting my arms around her and hugging her. After Ruth left, again no more was said. It was a good *coincidence*, we thought.

I never did share my *visit* with dad and Jim with my husband; I guess I didn't want him to think I was crazy. He had been through enough emotionally with my near death experience and I didn't want to add another burden to him thinking I was now losing what little I had left of my mind.

Life continued and we thought things were finally back to normal when I discovered a little pimple on my left arm, about two inches below my shoulder. I didn't do anything about it right away it didn't bother me or cause me any pain, I figured it was just that; a pimple. After a couple of months or so it started to enlarge some and my friend, Jan, suggested I see a doctor. I just didn't want to go through any more doctors or put my husband through anymore-medical bills. Gene insisted. I called Dr. Colletti and made an appointment. Gene went with me, and the pimple turned out to be a tumor. Dr. Colletti removed it in his office under local anesthesia. I was a nervous wreck. It's a wonder he could even cut it out the way I was shaking. Gene was talking to me, trying to calm me down, but my body just continued to shake uncontrollably. The Doctor had to make a rather large incision a little over an inch long to remove the tumor, which was probably a little bigger than a half dollar and had membrane type cells attached to it. It reminded me of a jellyfish. The good news was, it was benign. Dr. Colletti explained to us that my body could very possibly manufacture these kinds of tumors. Well, we certainly didn't like the sounds of that. How right he was! Within a year I was back in his office, now with a tumor in my left breast. He had made arrangements for me to have the tumor removed; another trip to the hospital! Was this ever going to end? Unfortunately, I was not a very good patient. I was very scared. I didn't return smiles, or talk to too anyone. When I woke up from the surgery there was a bandage wrapped completely around my chest and back. The bandage was so thick I could not tell if my breast was there or not!

I began to push the call button rapidly and when the nurse came into my room, I demanded to see Dr. C. right away! I guess I made an impression because within a few minutes he was there.

"Take this bandage off!" I demanded. "I want to see!"

"Patti," he began to say softly, "just take a deep breath and calm down. I only removed the tumor. Everything else is ok."

I didn't believe him. I wanted to see for myself and again I demanded that he remove the bandage. I wasn't going to calm down until I took a look myself. He called the nurse into the room and removed the bandage so I could see, and then wrapped me back up again.

"See. I only took out the tumor," he smiled.

I started crying, and with a very shaky voice, I pleaded, "Wh-h-a-at kind of tumor was it? Do I have cancer?"

He took my left hand in his, turned my hand over and with a black pen from his pocket he wrote on my hand; Fibro adenoma.

"No. It was also benign," he said, looking over at Gene smiling. With a little laugh in his voice, he continued, "She's a real hot pepper!"

"You're telling me!" Gene laughed.

"Patti. You will be able to go home tomorrow. I will send you home with some instructions. Follow them, okay?" he stated, patting my hand. Then he turned and walked out the door.

I started to cry pretty heavily now, all my fears flooding in tears of relief. Gene held my hand and whispered, "I wish I could hug you, but I don't want to hurt you and anyway you couldn't feel it through all this bandage." Then he laughed, making me laugh too.

The crisis passed. Life was good again for a little while. We bought a house and we were so delighted! We were refurbishing the kitchen, dining and living rooms. We had the backyard leveled and we were putting in a swimming pool. David was thrilled! Life was wonderful and then some strange things began to happen. When we were redoing the living room it seemed as though *someone* or *something* was watching us. Neither Gene nor I mentioned anything to each other at first. Then one night we just had to!

Simultaneously we exclaimed, "Did you see it?"

"What the hell is that?" Gene asked, with a curious frown on his face.

"I have no idea," I muttered, walking over the stone flooring we had laid in leading to the outside door. "I've seen it before, Gene. Have you?" I asked, turning around to look at him.

"Yes." he said, a very matter of fact tone in his voice.

It was a very dark shadow of a tall man, wearing a cape and a brimmed hat. We kept it to ourselves for the longest time, not telling anyone.

Then other things started to happen in the house. Lights were being turned off after we had left the house, mostly the porch light. We would turn it on before we left and when we returned it would be off. I had a small TV in the kitchen on the counter. I would turn it off when I left the house and when I came back home, it would be on. These events continued the entire time we lived in that house. Then one night when I had invited my cousin, Ron, and his wife Edie over for dinner, and we retired into the living room to watch TV, the shadow appeared again and they *saw* it too. Ron didn't want to discuss it. All he said was, "What was *that?*" All that was mentioned was that we all had seen it. The relevance comes later.

We were living in this house for approximately two years when I began to develop very bad headaches. Light, especially bright light seemed to cause intensity to the aching. I had x-rays taken and we weren't given any conclusive findings. The headaches continued and then I began to experience severe pain in my abdomen and reproductive organs. I had unusual bleeding and other related problems. It meant another appointment with the doctor, this time, the gynecology group, Drs. Bingham and Watson. After an examination I was scheduled to go into the hospital for a laparoscopy.

This was a procedure that could determine what was going on inside of my body. Dr. Watson explained that an instrument with a camera-like scope would be inserted through my navel and see what was happening internally. I had to sign a document giving the doctor the okay, if in the event he found it necessary, to perform a hysterectomy at the same time. I was very frightened and confused about this. I was only 29 years old!

The prospects of never having a child with Gene and major surgery were very overwhelming.

I just wanted to have a normal life! Was it ever going to happen? My frustrations and fears were now just directed at God.

"What have I done to *You*? I don't know why *You* hate me so much! Every one that I have ever loved *You* took away from me or caused them so much pain and suffering! Wasn't I taught in Catechism and in Mass that *You* were a Merciful and Loving God? Why are *You* putting Gene, David and me through this?" I cried each night, thinking if there *was a God*, a miracle would happen, and there would be no need to go into the hospital for the procedure.

The day finally arrived. It was May 1978. My anxieties and fears were totally out of control. I was an emotional wreck. I couldn't talk to anyone and I kept my terror, and confusion locked up inside of me. After all the preliminary blood work and other tests, I was admitted to my room. Gene stayed as long as he could and then he left to go home. I remember lying in that hospital bed and having a very serious and long conversation with God. I was really ticked off at Him and I made no bones about it. I told Him, I *knew* he didn't exist!

We were allowed to smoke in the hospital then and I was chain-smoking like crazy. I would smoke in my room and then get up and go down to the "Dad's waiting Room" lobby. I sat next to this young blonde girl who was sort of bragging to another patient about this being her third abortion and how simple the new vacuum surgery was. It made me sick to my stomach. Here I was facing the possibility of a total hysterectomy and this was her *third* abortion! I wanted to yell out, "*practice some birth control.*" I left the lobby and headed back to my room. On my walk back, I was muttering under my breath, "Yeah, You exist all right! How come she doesn't need a hysterectomy?" I was convinced. He didn't exist. Period.

I didn't sleep a wink all night. Gene was in my room bright and early the next morning.

"I will be right here, hon. I will be waiting for you when you come out of recovery," he said smiling, hugging me and giving me a kiss.

Within a few minutes the nurses came into my room with a gurney. One of them gave me an injection, and then they rolled me onto the gurney and wheeled me to the operating room.

The next thing I remember were nurses clamoring all around me. One nurse was trying to get an oxygen mask over my face and another one was checking my vital signs, while yet another was putting some medication into the IV. After that, according to my husband, I was *out* for two days.

That first night I was awakened, so I thought, by the sound of a man's voice, an unfamiliar voice and tone, calling my name. I opened my eyes and tried to adjust my sight to the dimly lit room. I looked at the clock on the wall. It read; 3:10. As I looked toward the foot of the bed and to the left of the room near the window, I *saw* a man there. He was between the chair and the window. I closed my eyes tight and then opened them up again. I looked in that direction again and he was still there. It appeared as though he was suspended or something. Funny thing though, I was not frightened at all. The top of his head was completely bald and he had graying hair on both sides, sort of long and combed back. His features were that of an older man in his seventies. His eyes were small and piercing, set very deep in his head. His nose was rather large and he had small thin lips. Even though there were no more words spoken, I sensed a kindness about him and a caring from him towards me. I closed my eyes again and when I opened them he was gone.

In the morning, which I thought was the next day after my surgery, Gene and his brother, Frank entered my room.

"Ahh, so you're awake, huh?" Gene asked walking over to my bed and giving me a gentle hug.

"It's about time," he said with a big smile on his face.

"What did they do to me, Gene?" I asked.

"Not again, Pat" Gene smirked winking at his brother. "I have told you three times already, but you were out cold so I guess you don't remember."

I looked at him totally perplexed. "I don't remember you telling me anything," I sighed. "Did you tell me yesterday when I got back to the room?"

"Yesterday?" Gene exclaimed. "Pat. You had your surgery three days ago!"

"Three days ago!" I exclaimed. "What day is this?"

"It's Thursday," he said and continued, "You gave the staff quite a scare again. Your lungs filled up with fluid, you ran quite a temp and we thought you were going to buy the farm again. You've got to stop doing this to me. You're gonna make an old man out of me before my time!" He started laughing again and gave me another gentle hug. Usually his jokes and teasing were for my benefit, so I would laugh too. This time I just wanted to know what happened to me and I wanted to tell him about my visitor.

"What did Dr. Watson have to do to me? Be serious Gene." I stated, pointing to the other chair across the room for Frank to sit in. Gene sat down in the chair in front of my bed. Then he began, "Well you had quite a mess inside of you. The doctor said you had a very severe case of endometriosis and some kind of tumor growths. The lining of your uterus was infected. Some tubes of some kind. I don't remember what he said. And both your ovaries were bad. Oh yeah, and some part of your colon was affected too. He said you were going to be okay. It is just going to be a while for you to recuperate, six to eight weeks or more. You had a total hysterectomy plus the colon thing," he ended.

No wonder my stomach was so sore. It hurt like crazy when I coughed or moved. "I want to tell you about this man that came to visit me," I said, not absorbing what he had just told me.

"What man?" Gene asked with a bewildered look on his face.

"I don't know who he was. But he was right there," I said pointing my finger to the left of where he was sitting. Gene shot a look at Frank as I continued. "He was sort of floating. Like suspended in the air."

"You were on some heavy medication. Morphine I think. You were probably dreaming."

I was frustrated with his remark. I *wasn't* dreaming! The man was *real* and I *knew* it. I didn't have the energy or the strength to have a debate. So I just clammed up and didn't say another word about it.

I didn't have to. I had no idea then, that we would cross *Paths* again.

3 ►►

The Path

===

It started off like a routine day, although exceptionally warm for September. The sun was shining brightly and the air had a summer hint about it. I had just finished my run and headed home. I parked the school bus next to the sidewalk in front of the house and headed up the walk to the porch. "R-r-r-ring!" the phone sounded, making me hurry into the house.

"Hello," I answered, my mind still wandering back to outside and how lovely the day was.

"Hi. What's up, kid?" my sister-in-law's cheery voice replied.

"Oh, hi Chris. Nothing much going on around here."

"Is Gene home yet? There is something going on and I want to let him in on it. You too, if you're interested," she added with that cat-that-ate the-canary voice.

"No. He's not here yet," I said, my curiosity rising. "What's going on?"

"There are some classes that are going to start in two weeks; something to do with psychic phenomena. Should I go on?" she asked smugly.

"Nope, that's quite all right," I answered snidely, knowing darn well she knew how I felt about that stuff. "I'll tell him to call you when he gets in."

"Okay," she said. "Bye."

"Bye." I said and hung up the phone. "It's not bad enough that all those two talk about is psychic crap," I thought to myself, "now she is talking of taking classes!"

Gene came in about four o'clock. We chatted about the events of his workday and I made dinner. I cleared off the dinner table and put on the coffee.

"Oh, by the way, hon.," I stated nonchalantly, "your sister called earlier. She wants you to call her."

I heard Gene dialing the phone and I went down to the basement and gathered my laundry. When I returned upstairs Gene told me about his conversation with Chris.

"I told Chris we would talk about it before I decided on whether or not to sign up," my husband said with his boyish grin and an all to familiar manipulating tone when he wanted to get his way. "Think about it, Pat. You know, you might enjoy going to these classes and learning something about it."

"Okay, I promise to think about it." I said, rolling my eyes.

Gene always did his best to provide. He made certain that we always had the necessities, along with a few luxuries. Since he worked a rotating shift and could not attend all of the classes, I reluctantly agreed to go, but I let him know that by no means was I happy about this! And I would only be acting as his *secretary* and take notes on the nights he would not be there.

The weather was beginning to turn colder now and the foliage was just about at its peak. I was feeling the best I have ever felt physically. I had healed up very well from the hysterectomy and I was truly enjoying my life! It was our first beautiful fall in a long time. I didn't realize then, just how fruitful things were going to be-and not only with the weather!

> *　　　　　*　　　　　*

"Hurry up, Pat!" Gene yelled. "We're going to be late!"

"I'm coming!" I yelled back at him. "I'm combing out my hair!"

He was so excited about attending these classes. Tonight's was the first of a total of eight. "I'll just have to make the best of it," I sighed, "*for his sake.*"

The classes were held at a local junior high school. We were the first ones there, naturally and we waited for his sister. "You know, Gene, you are going to be in for a big surprise," I said, tugging at his arm as we were walking toward the classroom. "I am going to turn out psychic! What do you think of that?" The words shocked even me, "why the heck did *I* say that?" I wondered.

The classroom was not set up with desks and chairs the way I had expected. Instead there were several long tables and regular folding chairs arranged in a circular fashion. We chose the front table and sat down. Shortly thereafter the room began filling up with people. I searched about to see if there was anyone I knew. Just as the class was about to begin, three girls walked in. "I know one of those girls," I said to myself. "What is her name? Sue. Sue Reardon, that's it." I decided to say hello when the class took a break.

"So you're into this too, huh?" I asked, walking to her table.

"Hi Pat!" she replied. "How have you been?"

We chitchatted back and forth for a while and I was really glad that I had bumped into her. "Maybe I have been a stick in the mud about this psychic phenomena," I thought to myself. "Sue's a school teacher and she's into it…maybe I will really pay attention and see what it's all about."

About halfway through the last hour of the class something very strange happened to me. The instructor was talking about some of her life's experiences that were not very pleasant. I found myself feeling very sorry for the agony she had gone through. Suddenly I realized I was very much aware of a purple substance shooting from her fingertips! It looked like purple lightning bolts! I rubbed my eyes. "I must be tired," I thought to myself. When I looked up at her again, the same thing happened.

On our way to the car, I stopped Sue. We lit a cigarette and I asked her if she had *seen* anything strange. "Like what?" she asked, taking a long drag on her cigarette. "Well anything different. Like maybe some colors or something," I stammered, not wanting her to think I was nuts. "Colors?" she asked a bewildered tone in her voice. "Well I saw colors shooting out of her fingertips. Purple colors." She began to laugh rather hysterically and then looked at me and said, "Right. And I saw little green men too!" I knew she was only teasing me, but I didn't want to carry the conversation any further.

In the car and on the way home I wondered just how I was going to say this to Gene. After all I always scoffed at him and Chris whenever they talked about ghosts and other paranormal phenomena. I decided to brave it out and I mentioned it to him anyway. "How do you explain that?" I asked, bewildered. "I don't know. Why don't you ask the instructor? She should know. "I was probably just overtired. She might think I am nuts or something." I told him what Sue said to me and we both laughed.

                    *   *   *

The week passed by quickly. I didn't want to admit the fact to myself, but I was anxious to attend class again. I would ask her about the event I had witnessed, but it would be in private.

As it turned out, I wasn't the only one who had seen it! Several people mentioned seeing something glowing around her. However, only three of us saw the color purple.

"Why is there such a glow around you?" a young lady asked, a very curious look on her face. "I am a healer and I possess a lot of energy," came the reply from the instructor. "Those of you who can see the color are probably gifted in certain areas yourselves. There are people who possess the ability of reading into the auras of others," she continued. "What this means is quite simply this; each of us has an aura, or as it is sometimes referred to an energy force field around us. If a person can see the color of this aura he can usually tell a person's character. He can also tell if the person is talented and in what areas. You see, different colors represent different meanings. There are, of course, hues and tones that must be considered also in a character reading of the aura." She continued on with the explanation, but my mind was reeling. "What did she mean 'gifted' in certain areas?" I kept thinking, "I don't believe in this kind of stuff." I tried convincing myself. "But then why did I see that?"

"Well, that's all for tonight class; and remember, try to pick up the Book, *Huna*, it will help you to understand," she said, collecting the items on her desk in preparation to leave.

"This is the time to approach her. Go up and ask her about seeing the color," I told myself.

"Mary, can I take a minute of your time, please?" I asked, feeling awkward and a little uncomfortable.

"Sure. Your name is Pat, isn't it?" she asked, gathering her things and placing them in her briefcase.

"Yes. That's right. You know, last week I saw the color purple too. It seemed to me it was shooting out of your fingertips. Maybe I had better start at the beginning and explain something to you, before I continue." I said, rather sheepishly and looking toward the floor.

"What do you want to explain?" she asked with a grin. "The fact that you don't believe in psychic phenomena?"

"I—uh, well, something like that," I stammered, sort of surprised by her question. "How do you know?"

"By deduction, that's how. Many people who sign up for these courses are curiosity seekers or non-believers," she smiled warmly, apparently not one bit upset.

"I honestly joined this course to please my husband, but last week I saw that color! Now, I am very confused, I am a skeptic, hard-core! After hearing you remark about being gifted, I felt I should inquire a little more." I smiled.

"Naturally I can only theorize, Pat, but if I were you, I would pick up some reading material. You might surprise yourself with your own possibilities! If my assumption is correct, you are a *sensitive*; a person who has very strong psychic abilities, which could be brought out with training. Next week, I am going to introduce a method-meditation. Meanwhile, good night, and think about my suggestion," she said, picking up her briefcase and then walked toward the door.

"Good night and thank you," I answered, somewhat befuddled. "A *sensitive*, me? Ridiculous!" I thought, walking to meet Gene. "Hmmm. I will take her advice and pick up a book on the subject," I smiled, and left the room.

A few days had passed since the night of class. Edie telephoned and asked me to meet her for lunch. The restaurant we chose was in our local mall. The mall had a huge bookstore and I decided to investigate its selection on psychic phenomena.

I found the book the instructor had mentioned. Opening it, I perused its contents. It appeared to be interesting. I took the book and walked over to the counter. There were a few people in line, so I walked around glancing at the paraphernalia on the shelves. My eye fell upon a book, entitled Tarot…and next to it, was a small very picturesque cardboard box. Written on the box were the words, Tarot Cards. "Hmmm," I murmured, picking up both items. As I read the words, "cards for fun and fortune-telling," on the cover of the book, a strong compulsion to buy them came over me. "***Buy me! Take me home!***" they seemed to shout at me. "What for?" I argued with myself. "You don't know anything about card reading. Plus you can't afford to buy these!"

"What are you looking at?" asked Edie, peeking over my shoulder. "You must be really engrossed in it. I called you three times and you didn't even hear me!"

"I happened to see these things on the shelf, so I picked them up," I said, showing her the book and the box of cards.

"Tarot!" she laughed. "Boy, for someone who use to think everyone else was a nut that talked about psychics and readers! You!" she continued, laughing really loud now. "The biggest skeptic ever! You're certainly doing an about face!"

"Yeah. I know!" I laughed. "I think I'm going to buy them. Just for general purposes. You never know. Maybe I'll get good at it!" I chuckled again, giving her a hug and walking over to the counter.

I dropped Edie off at her home and drove straight to my house. I couldn't wait to sit down and read the book.

The book's index explained the different *spreads* of the cards. There were sketches that displayed the proper way to setup each spread. With each display there was an explanation on how to *read* the past, present and future. The cards themselves were very picturesque. They were also divided into two categories, the Major Arcana cards, which consisted of twenty-two cards, and the Lesser Arcana, consisting of fifty-six. Each card had a specific meaning.

"Who can I experiment with?" I asked myself, shuffling the cards. "It's got to be someone I don't know very well." After a few moments of thought, I came up with the very person. "Sue Reardon! I wonder if she would be game." I hadn't seen her for years before that first night of class. I decided to give her a call.

"Sure! Why not? You always were a little eccentric!" she laughed in response to my invitation. "Anyway, it will be great just getting together. We can catch up and talk about old times. When would you like me to come over?"

"How about tonight?" I replied. "Gene will be working, and I'll have the house to myself."

"Okay. See ya around seven."

The events of that night are still very vivid in my mind, and Sue's. It is a night we will both remember forever.

The evening was planned for fun. However, it did not turn out that way at all. There was so much more in store. I just thought that *I had planned it.*

I handed the deck of cards to Sue and said, "Ok. Now according to the instructions, close your eyes, shuffle the cards and then hand them to me."

I spread the cards according to the directions, but when I looked up the description attached to a particular card...a very startling event occurred. I looked up the revelatory meaning from the book, and closed my eyes for a moment when suddenly I was actually "seeing" my own meanings! Also,

I started to perceive images of people! Then I saw places! I was also beginning to *sense* impressions and information about the people and places I was *seeing!*

"I don't believe this!" I blurted out, opening up my eyes. "What's going on here?" I gasped, totally bewildered, and looking at Susan who was now staring at me very curiously. "I can see things in my head! People! Places...a school. I can describe it and everything!" I remarked, totally shaken by the experience.

I described the woman, the school and the area that I had *visualized.* I was also able to depict the woman's character. Her mannerisms and what I felt about her personality!

"Oh my God! Whatever it is, you got it kiddo!" Sue exclaimed, looking equally mystified. "You described the college I attended in Vermont to a tee! Not only did you describe the drama teacher, you pinpointed her character and mimicked her mannerisms perfectly! That was amazing!"

"Sue, you don't understand. I'm not getting this information from the cards," I said, a look of amazement on my face, "it's simply popping into my mind! When I picked up the first card, I felt a funny sensation, a strange feeling, going through my body. I closed my eyes for a minute and the kaleidoscope of colors were very bright and then they disappeared and I saw that school!"

"No kidding!" Sue exclaimed. "Colors? What do you mean colors?" she asked, with intrigue in her voice. Then she added with a note of enthusiasm, "You must be psychic! Why have you kept it a secret? I think it's great!"

"I always see colors when I close my eyes, don't you?" I asked a bit perplexed.

"No." she said, bluntly. "I see black. So explain it to me."

"Well, I just thought everyone did. I have always seen colors. Ever since I can remember. I just thought it was normal. I-uh mean, it's not something you discuss when you're a child. Or an adult for that matter," I said, getting up to make a pot of coffee.

"Well, you're going to discuss it now!" she laughed, getting up to get the coffee cups.

As we sipped our coffee I tried to explain the *colors* as best as I could so Sue would understand.

"You remember those kaleidoscope toys when you were a kid, don't you?" I asked.

"Yes. The cylindrical ones that were made out of cardboard and cylindrical and you twisted the part at the front." She said, reaching for a cigarette.

"Yes. Remember there were odd shapes and pretty colors?" I asked. "Well that's what I see when I close my eyes. Not as many shapes as in a kaleidoscope, but odd shapes and really pretty colors. Most of the colors are blues, yellows, greens, and many different shades of lavender." I remarked, lighting a cigarette too.

"Pat." Sue said, smiling. "You need to find out about this."

"I am. I am going to talk to the instructor. She said something to me the other night about a sensitive. I need to know more. Especially after this! I still can't believe what just happened! I want to know *why*!"

The next couple of days were a blur to me. My concentration and actions were totally blocked...blocked by the episode of that night with Sue. I wasn't able to think of anything else. There was no *logical* explanation for what had transpired. It kept me in constant turmoil; I knew I would not be able to wait for answers...I picked up the telephone and dialed Mary's number.

"Hello," her soft voice answered.

"Hi. This is Pat Gagliardo," I said, some timidness in my voice. "Forgive me for disturbing you at home, but I really need to talk to you."

"You aren't disturbing me. What's the matter?" she asked, a note of curiosity in her voice.

I told her of the entire experience I had had with Sue. I explained in the best way I could, my mixed feelings.

"I don't believe in the unexplained phenomena," I rambled on. "We touched on that, that night at class. I guess you can say I'm kind of a Doubting Thomas. I haven't been very religious either over the past several years."

"I see," she said, a note of empathy in her voice. "It sounds to me that what you are really questioning is not the fact that you have a gift, or why, but where it comes from. Is that correct?"

"I suppose. I really don't know. So many things are going through my head at this point."

"Well," she interrupted, "maybe you had better do some soul searching. I'll see you in class; maybe the meditation exercises will help you."

"Thank you," I said, still confused. "I hope you are right."

We said our goodbyes and I placed the phone in its cradle.

*　　　　　*　　　　　*

The night was here. I remember the anxiety I felt as Gene and I walked into the classroom. My heart began pounding, and I felt uptight and tense. After the first half hour, however, a feeling of tranquility had replaced the tension. As Mary was instructing the class on deep breathing exercises, her eyes seemed to be talking directly to me. She would walk over to other individuals, to assure them that they were doing it right. I could see her looking over at me. I was getting the feeling she was quite curious about the outcome of my meditation in particular.

"Class, before we begin to meditate, there is a prayer I would like to recite. Those of you who do not believe in the Supreme Being," she continued, looking right *through* me, "do not have to bow your heads. For those that are interested, I have some copies up here that you can get after class."

I closed my eyes and bowed my head and I listened to her recite the words of the prayer. Silently, and not knowing why, I found myself muttering, "Please protect me, God, and forgive me..." I became more relaxed and felt at ease with myself.

The meditation exercise was about to begin. She had a recorder set up on her desk and she explained that we would be listening to a man that would be counting us down into a passively aware state of mind. This man would then take us on a mental visualization journey. She told us the entire experience would be approximately twenty-five minutes long.

The meditation experience had very rewarding results for me. It was sort of a hypnotic kind of induction. We were counted down from the number twenty-eight to the number one. He then took us on a mental *journey*. The experience had given me a very soothing, wonderfully relaxing and fantastic journey. What I didn't realize was that the trip *I* took had absolutely no *connection* with the one on tape! I had passed the level intended, and 'tuned' into my higher self and my psychic awareness!

Everyone that wanted to was given the opportunity to share his or her experiences. Many of the class participated. But when my turn came, I hesitated to reveal my occurrence.

"How about you, Pat?" the instructor asked, her eyes as big as saucers. "Would you like to tell us about your journey?"

"I-uh don't know if I heard the same tape as everyone else," I began, stammering. "I don't recall hearing anything about a waterfall or a raft." The class burst out laughing.

"Class! Class! Shhhhh. Quiet please!" she remarked, putting her finger to her lips, and then looked right at me and said, "Please continue, Pat."

All eyes were on me. I felt really awkward, embarrassed and uncomfortable. Turning and looking at Sue, I muttered under my breath, "They're going to think I'm crazy." Sue shrugging her shoulders, smiled, and said, "Go for it."

Taking a deep breath, I turned and looked at the instructor and began again, "Well, I heard the countdown, but after that I had the *sensation* of spinning, like my arms and legs were extended away from my body and I was rotating, like a wheel and all around me were beautiful soft *colors* and I felt very relaxed. Then the next thing; I was walking barefoot on a sandy beach, I could *feel* the cool sand between my toes." I stopped talking then and glanced around the room. Everyone was staring at me with looks of genuine interest. "Then I saw a cave," I continued, feeling that the rest of the class really did want to hear more. "In the cave were *rocks*, large and *small* in size. I had no choice but to climb over them as they were all along the *path* of the cave. Then I saw the light at the end of the cave and when I approached it the opening led me to a beautiful field of flowers.

I felt so happy and there was such a feeling of peace there. I continued to walk through the meadow and came to a very busy street. Above me was a very large sign that read: ONE WAY. I kept walking in the direction I was heading and then I found myself at a very busy intersection. There were one-way signs pointing to the left and to the right. For a moment I didn't know which way to turn. Funny thing though," I said, closing my eyes, trying to fight the emotion that was causing tears to form as I reminisced this part of the experience. "After what seemed like just a brief instant...I *knew*," I continued, opening my eyes to find Mary's eyes staring right back into mine. "If I had turned left, I would have wound up in a very busy circle. There were people everywhere running around like crazy, going in circles. On the road to my right, there was no activity going on. I could only see structures. Buildings and I think, houses. The road was at an incline and I couldn't see over the top of the hill, yet I *knew* that was the road I had to take."

"Pat, you said you knew what all this meant," Mary interrupted. "Do you mind explaining it to us?" she asked.

"Actually, it was a *feeling, an impression* I was perceiving, seeing all of those things." I answered.

"Go ahead. Describe them to us," she said, smiling, with a note of encouragement in her voice.

"Sure. Okay." I said, and sat down in my chair.

"When I was spinning in that tunnel I felt like something was saying to me, "This was you. You in the past, never being settled down. Always feeling like your life was out of control and leaving you insecure and scared. You *are* secure now. Be at peace." Next thing I know I am in that cave walking over those rocks. I felt that this meant I had made it over my problems big and small and no matter what continued to come my way I would get through it or over it, thus walking over the rocks. When I was in that field of flowers, I was extremely happy. I felt such love and joy. I felt like I had finally won. I found my happiness. I have a wonderful husband and family and we are happy. The one-way street made me think of the psychic phenomena. Should I continue, or turn back? I got this feeling to go forward. That's why that one-way sign was so huge. I kept going forward. When I came to the intersection, it was like a big decision for me. I looked to the left and saw all of those people going around in a circle. I felt that if I went that way, I would continue with my old way of life, just existing, going round and round in a circle of confusion, with no direction and no purpose in life. When I looked up the road to the right, a very peaceful feeling came over me. There were buildings and houses, large and small and separated quite far from each other. It made me feel as though I would have to take things as they come, one at a time, and that when it was meant for me to know what was over the crest of the hill…I would find out—when I reached the top. I guess, what I am saying is…I have been given a *path*…it is now up to Me." I ended, a tear rolling from my eye.

The room was silent. Many people there had wet eyes. Mary was speechless for a moment, and then she said, "Pat, that was beautiful. You have already mastered your first step toward developing your own latent abilities. Would you mind if I divulge some personal information to the class? I won't mention any specific details, just a few that might hit home with some of the other members." She smiled warmly at my silent assent and continued looking at the class.

"When Pat walked into this class, on the first evening, I felt she had very strong psychic tendencies. Of course I did not know in what area. She, like so many others, was not herself aware of the possibilities. I am going to ask her if she would try something tonight," she said, making a gesture with her hand for me to come to the front of the class. "Let me clarify something right now. I don't want anyone to misconstrue; you don't become psychic overnight. Evidently, Pat has always had latent psychic abilities. I believe because of her skepticism and lack of acceptance of it as such, she has probably kept it pushed back in her mind. Through meditation, her subconscious was brought to the fore," she stated, making a motion with her hand going to the back of her head and bringing it up to her forehead. "She was faced with it in a relaxed state, so she had no choice but to deal with it".

"Pat," she said, handing me her watch, "I want you to take a deep breath, close your eyes and tell me what you see or feel."

"I don't understand," I said, taking the watch and shrugging my shoulders. "I don't know what to do..." Suddenly, as soon as I had closed my eyes, I saw another kaleidoscope of *colors*...they disappeared and a picture of a blue house began to form...it was on a hill...then I could *see* inside the house! I described the kitchen, dining and living rooms and what was even hanging on the walls, in perfect detail!!

"That's enough," she said calmly, taking her watch from me. "Now, you have described my home perfectly, inside and out..." She turned to the class again and remarked, "Pat has never been to my home, and I have never laid eyes on her before these classes!"

"How is it I can do that?" I asked, totally shaken by the display. "What do you call that ability?"

"It's called psychometry. People that possess this particular ability can be very helpful in finding lost items, jewelry, letters, money, and most importantly, people! A good psychometrist can also discern the character of individuals, which simply means, that not only can a sensitive handling an item belonging to an individual make physical descriptions, but perceive impressions about that person's personality, as well."

Everyone in the class gathered around us. People were asking a hundred questions. Some of them I had asked myself a dozen times since the card episode with Sue. One lady said something, though, that struck a nerve in me. As it turned out, it would be the first *Pebble On My Path*...a stepping-stone to shattering old beliefs and an opening awareness of the intended purpose of my life…

"God brought you here," she said, in a very flat tone of voice, walking over to me. "He's got things in store for you. Take my word for it. Its no *coincidence* that you're here…It's by HIS Hand." She smiled then, and turned away and left the room without further comment.

Having an analytical mind, I simply could not accept the events of the evening. There must be answers somewhere! And I was going to venture down every avenue possible until I found them! Little did I know that the following day would bring even more startling developments my way!

In the morning I contemplated visiting my sister-in-law, Chris. She would certainly know about some reading material about the phenomena. "This is certainly a switch!" I laughed out loud. "Me…asking her about psychic books!" I decided to invite myself over to her house.

"Hey! Anybody home?" I shouted, walking in the front door.

"Sure is. Come on in, Pat," Chris replied.

"What's all that racket coming from upstairs?" I asked, entering into the kitchen.

"Oh, that's Ray. We're remodeling the bathroom," she said, while putting on a pot of coffee. "I'm glad you came over. I was going to call you today and ask you to stop by. We found something in the walls and I wanted you to *feel* it," she grinned. "It's an old dish cover, made out of some kind of pottery. Maybe if you hold it, you can find out where it came from and who owned it," she added, her back to me as she took the coffee cups out of the cupboard.

"Gee, that's funny, I came over here to ask you to let me borrow some of your books. After last night, I am really curious to know more." I said, pouring the coffee into the cups.

"Boy!" she laughed. "Talk about your turncoats! When Gene and I use to talk about this stuff, you thought we were nuts! You even use to leave the room! Shoe's on the other foot now, huh?"

"Yeah, I know. I was thinking about that while driving over here. I still don't understand what's going on. But, I have to find out, or it will drive me crazy!"

"I don't have any books on psychometry. I just read a lot of stories involving peoples' experiences. I've read about Sybil Leek, Hans Holzer, and Edgar Cayce…folks like that. You'll probably have to go to the library for what you want." She said.

"Yeah. I guess you're right. I don't know myself what to look into first. Maybe some books on testing your ESP, areas like that, will give me a start anyway. I'll go to Otis, maybe someone there can give me a list of categories." I said.

"Good idea. Now what about that dish cover? Want to try it?" she asked, her face bright with excitement and anticipation.

"Why not?" I smiled, "Where is it?"

"Pour yourself some more coffee. It's upstairs— I'll go get it." Chris said, getting up from the table.

Within a few minutes, Chris returned. In her hand was a lovely cover. It looked hand painted and was a solid piece of cream-colored material. On it was a pretty floral print. The floral design was one color. It looked like a wine tint. There were no markings, seams or trademarks, nothing to indicate its age or its origin.

"That's lovely Chris. Where did Ray find it?" I asked, taking the cover from her.

"We had to put new sheetrock up. When he tore out the old stuff, he found this in the partition. This house is over a hundred years old. For all we know, it could have been up there since way back then!"

"Maybe it's worth something. It might be worth your while to have a professional look at it," I said, beginning to feel warmth in my hands, especially my fingers, holding the cover.

"I doubt it," Chris remarked, "but maybe I will. Let's see what you get from it first."

"Okay. I'll give it a try," I said, taking a deep breath.

I placed the cover on the table and took one more deep breath and placed my hands on top of the cover. I began to see the kaleidoscope of colors. When they dispersed, I perceived these snapshot type images. The first image was of an old four-poster bed. Around the top of it was a beautiful canopy. It was solid white. Then suddenly, in the next image, there was an elderly woman lying in the bed. I *sensed* she was an invalid. The images faded away, followed by the appearance of more colors. Another vision immediately followed. It was an elderly man. He appeared to be dressed in minister's clothing. That was my impression from the clothing he was wearing. The coat was dark and had tails. The pants seemed to be quite baggy. The clothing was unfamiliar to me, but reminded me of the type of clothing seen in the movies, like Charles Dickens's, Scrooge. The man was tall, with thinning hair, and he appeared slender in build.

"Are you seeing anything?" Come on! What's happening?" Chris's voice rang out.

"Yes. I am seeing a couple of people. An old woman, an invalid, I think, and a man, who may be a minister," I replied, and opened my eyes. "This is really strange, Chris. I don't understand what and why this is happening!"

"What's to understand?" You're psychic! It's as simple as that! I think it's fantastic! Stay with it!" she commented, nudging me to continue, "Maybe there's more."

I took another deep breath and closed my eyes again. This time I saw a room. There seemed to be some type of braided rug on a wooden floor. I *felt* the rug was made up of some kind of cloth, though, not like the braided rugs found today. A wooden chair was in the corner of this room and then what I saw was very difficult for me to explain...

"I'm seeing something," I began, "I'll do uh, the best I can to describe it, Chris, but I-umm, don't know what it is," I said, somewhat confused by the image.

"Well, what is it? Maybe I can help." Chris said.

"It's some kind of furniture, I think. It's dark wood; there are small doors to the left and right on top; the legs are similar to the legs on a piano; the doors are real pretty-they have a real pretty print design in each one! I just can't tell what it is!" I said, opening my eyes.

"Wow! This is so amazing, Pat!" Chris remarked, her voice shrill with excitement. "Maybe it is a piano."

"I don't think so. If it is, I've never seen one like it."

"Keep going...what else is there?"

What happened next, neither one of us was prepared for, especially me.

"There's a medium sized black dog...and a child! He's wearing what looks like knickers! He has blonde curly hair, but his skin looks so white. I mean sickly, pale white. And his clothes are hanging on him, they look too big for him or something." Then something truly shocking happened...another pebble on my path...

"Chris! My God! His name is Jonathan!" I bellowed, my eyes flying open. I stared at her in disbelief over what had just transpired. I was visibly shaken by the episode.

"What's wrong?" Chris asked, her eyes wide open, and staring at me. "How do you know that?" she continued, "You're shaking like a leaf!"

"He-e-e-e *told* me," I stammered. "I know it sounds crazy. I don't know myself what just happened. I don't know how to explain it..."

"He talked to you!" Chris shrieked.

"Well, sort of. I could hear the voice in my head I–uh...got this funny sensation, and then I just sort of *heard* the name Jonathan! And that's not all. Those two people I told you about, well, they aren't his parents, but sort of took care of him. And uh, I know what that piece of furniture is too...It's called an orchestrion.... and..."

"What!! Wow! A what?" Chris remarked, interrupting me, a look of complete bewilderment on her face. "I've never heard of it..."

"An orchestrion." I repeated. "There's more. He's not living. He is, or I should say, was, English. He was going to be a musician, but he became ill and died when he was twelve," I stated, suddenly feeling very calm and confident.

"You sound very sure of yourself. You're not kidding, I can see it in your face!" Chris commented.

"No. I am not kidding. It's really a strong feeling. I simply can't explain it properly. It's too difficult to put into words. I believe I was right about the elderly man too. He is…was…a minister and Jonathan's tutor!"

"How are you going to find out if you are right?" Chris asked, with a strong note of anticipation and curiosity in her voice.

"It's just a *hunch*, I guess. I believe I'm going to get some pertinent information from this cover that I'll be able to validate. The first thing I am going to do is find out what this orchestrion thing is."

"If there is such a thing, I'll be surprised," smiled Chris, "Do you want to do some more psychometry, now?"

"No, I don't think so." I said, handing the cover to her. "I am a little tired. And I am still trying to absorb everything that has already happened. When I did the psychometry last night with the instructor, I felt a little tired too. I wonder if it depletes my energy?"

"According to some of the material I've read, it does. It makes sense. You are doing all this mentally, so it has to take its toll somewhere, right?"

"Sounds logical to me," I grinned. "I hope I can find some good reading material at the library. As a matter of fact, I'm going there right now. I want to look up this orchestrion."

"Good luck. If you find out anything, call me as soon as you can!" Chris beamed, walking me to the door.

I parked my car on Main St., directly in front of the Otis Library. I felt the anticipation rising in me as I opened the front door and walked in. Seated behind the information desk was a pretty dark haired woman.

"Good morning," I smiled. "I'm looking for some books on psychic phenomena and also on musical instruments. Can you tell me where to find these categories, please?"

"Sure," she replied, returning the smile. "Go to the rear of the building. If you know the author's name, you'll find it in the files on the left. If not, go to the files on the right and check the subject index files."

"Thank you very much." I said.

I began searching the subject index files. I found the category musical instruments and searched alphabetically to the letter O. My heart was pounding so fiercely in my chest, I thought it was going to explode. And then I *saw* it!

Orchestrions and Nickelodeons... Upon seeing the word orchestrion, I exclaimed, "There is such a thing! And it has to be an instrument!" I looked around, making sure no one had heard my outburst then took a piece of paper and a pen from my purse and wrote the information down. Isle 900 F. I found the racks of the 900 series. I began searching for the book, and then I saw it! On the cover was a picture of two instruments, the nickelodeon and the orchestrion. The instrument on the cover was not like the one I had envisioned, however, it was somewhat similar. At the far end of the rack were a table and two chairs. I walked over and sat down and began flipping through the pages. About half way through...my eyes became glued to the picture on the page. "Here it is! The same one!" I sighed, my heart now pounding again with excitement. I read the caption under the picture; it told of its origin and the year it was built...1845! "That's nearly a hundred and fifty years ago!" I muttered under my breath, the words echoing through my mind as I closed the book and tucked it under my arm. I decided to go back to the subject files and look under 'Pottery,' hoping I might find something out about the dish cover.

I found a book on the subject. The particular design of the cover was not in it. However, I did find a similar pattern. It was called earthenware, and that design was a hundred years old! The entire episode was becoming very intriguing! I was so enthralled with the discovery of the orchestrion; I didn't look for any books on psychic phenomena. I walked back to the counter, checked out the two books, and drove home.

Once in the house, I decided to call Sue. I wanted to tell her about the days' events.

"Hello," she answered.

I was so excited trying to explain to her, I just kept rambling. "Do you believe it? I've never heard of an orchestrion! I've got a book here from the library, tells about them, with pictures. I'm going to read more about it. The one I saw at Chris' was built in 1845. Maybe that boy was born some time in the 1800s!"

"Gee, Pat, it is really fascinating," Sue said. "Are you going to do any more psychometry with that cover?"

"I sure am. I've got this feeling that there is a lot more to find out!" I commented.

"Keep me posted, Madame Lazonga!" Sue giggled. "Cause when you hit the big time-the Johnny Carson Show-I want to be there!"

"Johnny Carson!" I laughed. "Boy, have you got big dreams for me!"

We said our good-byes and hung up. Once I was off the phone, I picked up the book again and sat at the dining room table. My mind was reeling as I stared at the cover of the book. I had already *proven* one fact from the "reading." The orchestrion was real!

I tossed and turned all night. I couldn't wait for tomorrow. As soon as I finished my morning school bus run, I would head straight to Chris'.

"I'm back again!" I yelled, as I entered through the front door of Chris's house. "I've got a book I want you to see Chris!"

"In the kitchen, Pat. Come on in." Chris replied.

We sat at her kitchen table and I handed her the book.

"It says here that the harpsichord was derived from this orchestrion instrument," remarked Chris, after examining the page.

"Yeah, I know. I read about it last night. While you're looking at the book, can I hold that cover again?" I asked.

"It's in the living room, on the shelf under the end table. If you want to, you can stay right in there where it's quiet," Chris offered.

I took the cover off the shelf and sat on the couch. I took a deep breath, closed my eyes, and placed my hands on the cover, which was resting on my lap. The same thing occurred. First, the colors formed, and when they dispersed, the *image* of Jonathan appeared immediately. The information *he gave to me* was absolutely phenomenal!

The impressions were very strong. I was "told" to check the name, Burgess. I would find out that a family with this name had lived in Chris's home many years before. The Burgess family was related to a family called, Lucas. The Lucas' operated a mill on the river, behind the house. Large boats and ships traveled up and down the river to the mill carrying wool. I would investigate and validate this information! I also perceived *impressions* that, at that time, the area was referred to as, Poquetanuck.

I placed the cover back, and headed into the kitchen.

"Chris, I've got more information!" I blurted out, as I pulled a chair out from the table and sat down. "Do you know if this area was ever called, Poquetanuck?" I asked.

"Yes it was, years ago. This wasn't called Hedge Avenue, either. I think it was called Elm Street, and it was part of Preston, not Norwich. Hmmm, I think, if I'm not mistaken, the river is the Poquetanuck," she said, making a frown. "What information did you get?"

"Chris, have you got all the deeds to this house?" I asked, with the very evident excitement now noticeable in my voice.

"They must be around here some place. I don't know if I have all of them, but I'll check. Why?" she asked, with the tone in her voice filled with curiosity.

"We have to check and see if the name, Burgess, is on those deeds." I said. "Did you know there was a woolen mill on the river at one time?" I asked, staring into her eyes.

"A wool mill? Not that I know of." She said, giving me that, "*you had better tell me exactly what happened look*" as her curiosity was getting the better of her.

"Well, that's what I have got to find out." I smiled.

As Chris made coffee, I told her of my entire experience. "Chris, if you have time, can you please look for the deeds. I'll help you if you want me to."

"Of course I'm going to look!" Chris grinned, and continued, "You don't have to help me look. Do you want a piece of paper and pen to write down the information, before you forget it!" She laughed, opening the "junk" drawer and taking out a pad and pen.

She placed the items on the table next to me, and then she headed upstairs.

I wrote down all the information and waited anxiously for Chris to return.

"I found some," she said, walking into the kitchen. "Okay, let's make our coffee, and see what's in them."

We started to look through them and then, there it was! BURGESS! "My God, Chris!" I shrieked. "It's here! There was a family by that name!"

"Not only that! Look at this deed!" Chris exclaimed, placing the deed in front of me. "Samuel and Betty *Lucas* sold this house to Emeline Brown in 1882. Edwin L. Burgess and Martha A. Burgess sold it in 1899! So Brown must have sold it to the Burgess family. They had to live here for seventeen years!"

We both just sat there for a few minutes staring at the deeds, not saying a word. We were both dumbfounded.

"Pat. I have never looked at these deeds. Even when we bought the house." Chris said, breaking the silence. "I am completely amazed."

"So am I!" I said, with a bewildered tone in my voice. "Chris let me write down all this information. I am going to go to the town hall and see what else I can find out."

The "Jonathan" thing was becoming an obsession. I felt *compelled* to learn as much from the dish cover as possible. The information I had learned thus far was only the beginning...More Pebbles were yet to come...

That afternoon, at the town hall, I corroborated more of the information. I found out that the two families were indeed related. The Lucas's were from Hampden County, in which the city of Springfield, Massachusetts is located.

The big search was about to begin. I went through the local phone book, and wrote down the telephone number of every Burgess listed. I told every person that I spoke to that I was doing a genealogy of my sister-in-law's home. I wanted to find out if any of the Burgesses' were related to the Burgess that had lived in Chris's house. Finally, after five or six phone calls, a very nice elderly lady, from Lebanon, CT, invited me to visit with her. She informed me that she had an entire genealogy of the Burgess Family. What *luck*! I accepted her invitation and we set a date for the next evening.

Before going to her home, however, I *had to read* the cover again. Maybe I would perceive more information that I could validate while visiting the elderly Burgess woman. As it turned out, there was a lot more in store for me…

Chris was always willing to comply. She was just as anxious and as intrigued as I was, as well as our husbands, and of course my wonderful and supportive friend, Susan.

Once at Chris's, I went into the living room right away. When I reached for the cover from it's resting place, I found that Chris had placed the pad and pen next to it.

The same thing happened again. This time, after Jonathan appeared, and I perceived the name, Lillibridge, I mentally asked *him* a question…

"Is this Your Name, Jonathan?" I asked, with my eyes still closed, waiting for a response. The *voice* and the vibration that I felt told me that it was, indeed, his last name. More impressions revealed that his ancestors were from Berkshire, England, Yorkshire, and London. I had high hopes of confirming these facts with Mrs. Burgess.

I was filled with so many questions and different emotions as I drove on route 87, heading to Lebanon. I was amazed by my connection with Jonathan, yet, surprisingly, it felt *natural*, and I was totally comfortable with it.

I found the address and pulled the car into the driveway. The house was quite old and not well kept. It was small and set back from the road. The grass was in need of mowing, and the house, white in color, could have used some paint.

I got out of the car and walked to the front door.

"R-r-r-ing," I head the doorbell sound inside. "I wonder if I should tell her how I came about this information," I pondered, waiting for her to answer the door. "I think I will just wait and see how it goes first."

The door opened and a short, white haired woman stood before me. In her right hand was a cane, and she was slightly bent over.

"Mrs. Gagliardo, I assume?" she asked, with a warm smile on her face.

"Yes. That's right." I said, smiling back at her.

"Please, come in," she said, as she turned and walked away from the door.

"Thank you," I replied, following her into a living room.

The furnishings were very old, but everything was neat and in place. "She must live alone," I reflected.

"You'll have to excuse the appearance of this old place," she said, smiling. "I live alone and must depend on others to help care for this place. If I don't ask for help, as you can see, no one offers a whole lot."

"She's such a sweet woman," I sighed to myself. "There's no need to apologize, Mrs. Burgess. I am just really glad that you are giving me this time to talk to me," I smiled.

"Oh, it's my pleasure. I rarely have company and I'm glad you're interested in seeing the Burgess Family Tree. I took it down from the shelf right after you called. I haven't gone over it myself for years! Now, what Burgess do you have in mind? I'll need the name of the man." She said, flipping the book open.

I gave her the information and waited anxiously for the results. She began to rattle off a few names.

"Now, let's see here…ah, here's something…Edwin L. Burgess, son of Edwin and Mary Fanning Burgess. Born 1824. What did you say this Edwin's wife's name was?" she asked, looking up at me, her eyes peering above her glasses.

"Mary," I replied, my heart racing with anticipation.

She looked back at the book, flipping a page and scrolling down the list with her finger. "Yes. Here it is," she said, and continued, "Says here her name was Cobbs, and they had thirteen children. Want me to name them?" she asked, keeping her eyes focused on the page.

"If you don't mind please." I answered. "I'm trying to find out if there is a connection with the name, Lillibridge. And if so," I added, "Were there any from England."

"We'll have to work backwards for that," she grinned, "I'll start with Edwin's father again, Edwin, Senior."

She continued to quote the names. The name Lucas came up several times. And then the name I had waited for...Lillibridge!

"Can you tell me some of the locations of that family?" I asked. "Only the ones from England, if there are any."

"Sure. I'll be glad to." She said. "This particular family of Lillibridge is, or was, I should say, from London." She flipped through a few more pages and then said.

"This family was from Yorkshire." She smiled, looking up at me again.

"Thank you so much. That's fine. I don't think I *need* anymore." I said, getting up. "You have no idea how gratifying this visit has been. You have been so kind and very helpful." I said, walking toward the door.

"Must you go so soon, dear?" she asked, a note of sorrow in her voice. "Won't you please stay for a cup of tea?"

I felt she enjoyed the visit as much as I did. "She's so lonely and has been so kind," I thought. "Sure, I would love to. Thank you." I answered aloud.

Later on that evening, I knew I had to do some more checking. I didn't have any encyclopedias or an atlas of my own, so I decided to contact Sue and ask her if she would help me locate the towns in England. I would ask her to circle them on a map. All the information I had received so far was *correct,* but I still had to find out about the mill. I knew it was late, but I just *had* to phone Sue.

I walked over to the small table that stood between the two windows in my dining room, picked up the handset from the telephone that rested on top of the table, and telephoned Sue.

"Hello," she answered, a note of tiredness in her voice.

"Hi Sue. It's me. I've got more information on the Jonathan Saga. I know it's late. I'm sorry for calling…but. I-uh, really need your help with something." I quickly added, with an apologetic sound in my voice.

"It's okay, Pat. What've you got?"

"Do you have a map of England anywhere?" I asked.

"I do at school, A World Atlas. I don't have any here at home," she replied.

"Great. Would you please, when you have time, mind circling in pencil, or maybe make notes on where, Yorkshire, Berkshire and London are located?" I asked.

"I'll look it up and call you and let you know. Okay?"

"Thanks so much, Sue. That will be just great. Before you hang up, can you please tell me how I can find out about that mill?"

"I'm sure you can find out at the library. Ask someone at the circulation desk in the back. They must have all the historical info about Norwich," she answered.

"Thanks a lot, Sue. And Sue, I really appreciate your help." I said, warmly. "Don't mention it. What are friends for? I'll call you tomorrow. Good night," she said and hung up.

I placed the handset back into the cradle of the telephone and prepared myself for bed. The puzzle was nearing completion. Tomorrow I would visit the library again.

Most of the night I tossed and turned with questions running through my mind of, "Why is this happening to me? What does all this mean?"

Morning came. I couldn't wait to get to the library. I finished my bus run and then drove straight to the Otis Library.

I walked to the rear of the library and to the circulation desk. The woman behind the counter was extremely helpful. After about an hour of searching through the historical records, we found it…there was a Lucas Woolen Mill! It was in operation on the Poquetanuck River in the late 1800's!

All the information about the events, I logged and kept a record of.

A few days have now passed after my visit to the library. I tried to put the episode out of my mind. I kept telling myself it wasn't necessary to do any more "readings" with the cover. Yet something inside of me was nagging at me to do it once more.

It had been nearly a week and still the nagging persisted. I had to go there once more! This would be the final time. I didn't know it then...I had no idea of what was coming!

I telephoned Chris and told her that Gene and I wanted to visit. She invited us to come over. I told her about the compelling need I had to handle the cover again.

When we arrived at Chris's house, I went directly to the living room, and Gene and Chris stayed in the kitchen. The information I received that night was the best and most concrete of all. I *knew* by the end of the evening why I had to perform the psychometry this one last time...

Jonathan was from a town in England called, Scarborough. He was also buried there, in a cemetery called, Westwood. I wasn't given the dates, but it wasn't necessary...I did the inevitable...

"Chris, I'm going to use the telephone, alright?" I asked, entering into the kitchen and walking past them toward the phone on the wall.

"Sure. Go ahead," she answered.

"Who are you going to call, Hon?" asked my husband.

"Just a *friend*," I smiled, "I'll tell you when I hang up."

I picked up the phone, and dialed the operator. "Please give me an overseas operator," I said, softly.

In a moment, a woman said, "Overseas operator. May I help you?"

"Yes, please," I replied, "I want to place a call to Scarborough, England."

"One moment, please. I'll connect you." She said.

A man's voice came on the line. His accent was very pleasant.

"Call, please?" he asked.

"Sir. Would you please give me the number of the caretaker of the Westwood Cemetery in Scarborough?" I asked.

"One moment, ma'am," came the reply, and after just a few seconds, he said, "I must inform you, it is no longer known as Scarborough…it is Scarborough Corporated, and the caretaker's number for the Westwood Cemetery is…"

I didn't even hear the exchange that he gave me. My throat was dry and my heart was nearly jumping out of my chest. There *was a Westwood cemetery* in Scarborough…a place I had never been to, and one from which I knew no one…

I said thank you, hung up the phone and walked over to the kitchen table, pulled out a chair and sat down.

"Your face is as white as a ghost! What's the matter?" exclaimed Chris.

"There *is* a Westwood Cemetery in England…Everything fits. I don't understand, how is it possible for me to know and do all this?" I asked, with a befuddled voice.

"What are you talking about? What do you mean there's that cemetery in England?" Gene asked, joining in.

"I just telephoned England; Scarborough, and the cemetery is there. I *knew* it would be!" I commented.

"You just did what? Are you crazy or something? Do you know what that bill is going to be?" Gene shrieked.

"There won't be any charge," I laughed, looking at Chris, whose eyes were as big as saucers. "I didn't complete the call. I only spoke to the operator." I said, solemnly. "Everything has been proven. Every detail. I just have to find out why. What is happening to me?"

News of the Jonathan experience spread quickly among friends, family and co-workers. Soon, everyone wanted me to perform "readings" with their items. I agreed, as I was just as amazed, if not more so, than they were by the results. It appeared as though the more I practiced the gift, the more powerful in details it became. What became most evident to me was how beneficial a reading could be to the recipient. Naturally, they would have to pay heed. In this particular reading, a friend, Carole (Sullivan) McCarthy, did not…

It was a lovely spring day. I had finished my household chores early and decided to ask the girls over for a visit.

Within the hour, all three arrived. Carole, her sister Joanne, and Sue. We had been chitchatting about various matters when Carole asked me to give her a reading.

"Patty, you've given Sue and Jo readings, how about doing one for me?" she asked, with her eyes bright with excitement.

"Okay." I answered. "What do you want me to hold, your ring or your watch?"

"Use my watch," she said, removing it from her wrist. "I don't wear this ring very often."

I took the watch from her, took a deep breath, and held her watch in my right hand. The colors appeared immediately, followed by a very disturbing vision. I saw Carole in a car, crossing over the Groton Bridge and then an accident! At first it upset me. I didn't want to *know* if anything serious or harmful was going to happen to her. In the next couple of seconds, the entire detail came to me. I saw a small white car, and a blue station wagon. Both vehicles were involved in the accident. I saw Carole's car with the bumper on the driver's side, smashed. I also knew it was raining lightly— a drizzle kind of rain.

I also felt it would be happening soon. Something was telling me to tell her. *"If you warn her…it can be prevented"*…If she avoided the bridge in the rain within the next couple of weeks, I felt she would avoid the accident.

"Carole," I began, "Do you have to go over the Groton Bridge to get to work?"

"Yes I do. Why, what do you see Patty?" she asked, her voice a little shaky.

"Within the next two weeks, on any day it's raining, or drizzling, please avoid the bridge. Go the long way around. I am trying to help you avoid an accident. Please don't get scared, Carole. I didn't feel it was a tragic accident, more like a fender bender. I *see* your bumper and fender on the right side of your car damaged. A small white car and a blue station wagon are also involved." I said.

"Really? Oh my goodness. I'll certainly remember that!" she remarked, now laughing, and with a hint of doubt in her voice.

"I'm serious, Carole," I said, opening my eyes to look at her. "I know you aren't going to be hurt. You'll be shaken up, though."

"You better take her seriously, Carole!" Joanne piped in. "Remember the reading she did for Bob? Everything she said came to pass."

"Oh yeah, that's right," Sue said, "And he still hasn't gotten over it."

We sat and reminisced over the events of the reading I had done with Bob, Carole and Joanne's brother.

It had only been a few weeks earlier that Bob had given me a black bic lighter to handle. Some personal information was very accurate and he was really amazed. I had also told him that I saw him in a bar/restaurant and gave him the description inside of the establishment. I described a tall, slender, brunette that he would have a conversation with and start up a relationship with her. She would have one child and drive a red sports car. Within one and a half weeks of the reading; he met her. She had a red sports car and one child and worked at the Picadelli Restaurant Bar.

"He and Ginger are still together! I guess I'll have to keep my eyes peeled for those two cars!" Carole remarked, grinning.

The girls left. Life continued normally for a week or so and then Carole called. She informed me that she had witnessed a car accident on her way to work that morning.

"Is it possible you saw that accident, Patty?" she asked. "The vehicles didn't match the description, but is it possible it was that accident?"

"I don't think so, Carole," I replied. "I would still take the longer route."

"I've been a nervous wreck since you told me that last week." She retorted.

"I am sorry Carole. I didn't mean to scare you. I was trying to help. Well, a week has passed already, if nothing happens this week, then you can forget about it," I laughed, trying to cheer her up. I felt badly at having frightened her, but my mind was saying, "You did the right thing!"

"I'll be glad when this week is over," she said. "I have to go and start dinner. See you later." We said our goodbyes and hung up.

Three days later, Carole telephoned me again. She was upset, but not distraught.

"Hello."

"Hi, Pat. I am not disturbing you am I?" asked Carole, her voice calm, but with a note of sadness.

"No, of course not. What's the matter?" I asked.

"You know it was raining this morning…and I was running late and I didn't listen to your advice. I had to go over the bridge to save time, and I had that accident! And the white and blue cars were in it! I saw it coming and I immediately saw your face! I wasn't hurt, but I sure was shook up! And my fender is crumpled up!"

"I-I'm really sorry to hear that. I am so glad you're okay, though. You know, Carole, I felt terrible when you called the other day. I didn't mean to upset you. I just felt I did the right thing in telling you, in the hopes of avoiding the situation." I replied.

"Oh, don't blame yourself, Pat! It's my own fault. Maybe it was meant to happen. I-uh don't know if I really believed it," she added.

"That's what I figured, or maybe it was just meant to be. As long as you're all right, that's the main thing. And look at it this way, you don't have to worry about it anymore!" I laughed, trying to ease the situation.

The Jonathan experience and Carole's reading had increased my curiosity more than ever, but I *wanted answers* to why this was happening to me, it was all I thought about!

The *proof* was there. The major issue, which I faced daily, was why? I simply could not accept that I could perform these feats without knowing how or why.

I decided on another trip to the library. It was Thursday and the library would be open late.

The selection was very limited. I could find nothing at all on psychometry. I did pick up some literature on different areas, however-clairvoyance, ESP, and dreams. Upon examining several chapters, I realized I would not get any knowledge on *how* it happens; the material only explained the results of *what* happens when having the abilities.

Just as I was about to give up all hopes of finding out anything about the phenomena, a yard sale came to my rescue.

Driving home Friday morning after my run, *something* compelled me to take the longer route than normal to my home. I found myself driving up Dunham St., which is two miles from my own street, in the opposite direction.

About half way up the street, I saw a sign that read, Yard Sale. Impulsively I pulled my car over. An older man was walking out of the garage with a cardboard box, filled with books.

I got out of my car and walked over to him.

"Good morning." I said, smiling at the man.

"Hi there." He replied. "Yard Sale doesn't start until tomorrow, though."

"Oh. I'm sorry," I said, my eyes glued to the title of this large book that was resting on top of the other books in the box. It read; "Nandor Fodor of Psychic Sciences"

"Excuse me, sir," I said, with a pleading voice, wanting to have that book. "Since, I am already here, and I am interested in books only, can you please tell me what you're asking for that book?" I asked, pointing to it.

"Well, I want to sell all the books in this box together," he smiled. "All the books in here are on the same subject. Twenty bucks, you can have the whole box."

"Can I buy them now?" I asked, reaching in my purse for my wallet.

"Sure. Okay." He answered.

He placed the box on the front seat of my car and I drove straight home.

Once inside the house, I made a pot of coffee, and put the box on the dining room table. The Nandor Fodor book was an encyclopedia of all phases of the parapsychology field. The explanations of such abilities as astral travel, telekinesis, automatic writing, psychometry and clairvoyance, intrigued me, but *one particular chapter* written by a Dr. Maxell on *Mediums*, captivated me...

Dr. Maxell explained that *all* persons he had interviewed that claimed to have mediumistic abilities had unusual markings in one of their eyes. Some of these markings resembled parts of a cat, a paw, ears, etc.

Upon reading this information, I immediately rose from my chair and went into the bathroom. I placed my face as close to the mirror on the wall as possible and began to examine my eyes. To my amazement, looking into my left eye, was tiny tiger-eye colored dots with a glow around them forming a shape that looked like a kitten's face! This discovery catapulted me into another search, an extraordinary pebble on my path, one that led me to spirit guide intervention and spiritual enlightenments...

4 ▶▶

Spirit Guides Introduction

The winter passed by very quickly. Already summer was upon us. So many wonderful things had happened in my life over the prior months. The word spread quickly of my psychic ability. My friends were calling me to perform 'readings' for their friends. They would be fascinated by the results. I, too, was eager to comply with their demands. Each reading supplied more and more fascinating results. It appeared as though the more I practiced the 'gift', the more intense and detailed the experiences became. Yet, inside me, was a persistent *need to know why* I possessed this capability.

It was toward the end of July that *I* decided I needed to do some investigating from a scientific approach into the phenomena. A scientific explanation! Maybe that was the *answer!* After checking nearly every resource in the state of Connecticut and coming up empty, I made a telephone call and spoke with a New York operator.

The operator was very helpful. She gave me several names and phone numbers of different organizations. One place stood out from the rest, 'The American Society of Psychical Research.' "Hmmm, I'll call and find out what this society is all about," I decided.

The receptionist I spoke with at the 'ASPR,' suggested that I make a trip to New York and speak with the scientist there, Dr. Karlis Osis.

I called Karen, Edie and Joanne. Joanne was a friend of Karen's that I had met a couple of months earlier. I asked the girls if they would like to make a trip to the 'city' with me and I explained my reasons for going. All of them said yes. The plans were made. We would be going to New York by train.

We must have chosen the hottest day of the summer to go to New York. Nearly everyone we saw looked miserable and spent. The four of us shared in their misery.

"At least they all seem to know where they are going," Karen laughed, as we were walking on a street in Manhattan looking for the subway station.

Finally we saw a policeman and he helped us out of our dilemma. He gave us directions and what connections to make.

At last, there it was. The sign on the front door of the building read: A.S.P.R. I felt some anxiety begin to build inside of me as we walked up to the door and I rang the bell. A buzzer sounded and we walked in. I walked up to the desk, while the girls sat down in the lobby chairs.

A woman that looked about middle age was seated behind an information desk. The girls sat down in the chairs in the lobby and I walked over to the woman.

"May I help you?" she pleasantly asked.

"Yes, please. I called a couple of weeks ago and would like to see Dr. Osis." I answered, smiling.

"Do you have an appointment?" she asked.

"No. Not a definite scheduled time. I just told the receptionist that I spoke with that I would be here sometime today." I answered, feeling some disappointment.

"Just a minute," she replied, picking up the handset to her telephone, "I'll see if he can speak to you now."

I walked away from her desk and over to the center of the hall and looked at the posters that were displayed on the tables. The posters had details about the different types of testing that was done there. One poster had a picture of a woman with wires attached to her head; another had a picture of a man staring at some geometric shapes on a screen. Below each picture were captions explaining the tests.

"Miss. Miss." The receptionist called to me. "Dr. Osis will be down in a moment."

"Thank you." I replied, and continued to examine the posters.

Only a few moments had passed when a tall, elderly gentleman entered into the lobby and walked toward me.

"Dr. Osis. Can I help you?" he asked warmly, in a strong German accent, stretching out his arm to shake my hand.

We shared introductions and I told him of my purpose for the visit, and then I introduced him to the girls.

"Would you like to see the laboratory?" he asked. "Or perhaps we should get a little better acquainted. Follow me, please, we'll go into my office."

I smiled at the girls, raised my eyebrows, and with an *I'll be back in a while* look, turned and followed him to his office.

His office was very simply decorated, a couple of chairs, a desk, and several large filing cabinets. The walls were painted an eggshell color and decorated with many plaques and frames with certificates inside of them.

I liked him immediately. He made me feel comfortable and at ease with myself. I told him everything about my situation. I explained to him how I felt, my skepticism, and how I had discovered my psychometric ability.

"It was like opening Pandora's box," I said. "I know what I do is real. I just need to know why and how I do it." I said, smiling.

"I see," he replied, returning a smile. "So you thought that by coming here you would find the answers, hmm?"

"Well, I was hoping to." I answered.

"It's not that simple, my dear," he said, as he rose from his chair and walked over to one of the file cabinets. "You see these?" he asked, opening a file drawer. "These are all cases we have tested. We can only theorize about the results and assume that what happens has a cause. We don't have all the answers yet."

He went on to explain some of the cases. It was interesting and all, but I still didn't get the answers *I needed*. At this point, I felt I had made a mistake by going there, I didn't want to wind up as another one of those people depicted on the posters. I thanked him for his time and walked out of his office.

When I returned to the lobby, and looked at the girls, all I noticed were three sets of eyes, as big as saucers, staring at me. I just smiled at them, shrugged my shoulders and shook my head from side to side.

We were all pretty exhausted by the time we reached the train station. The heat was really unbearable. We got on the train and took our seats. They all had this great anticipation and expectation that I was going to have all the answers. I explained what had taken place in the office to them, and then I said I wanted to take a nap on the train ride home. They all wanted to rest too.

I settled into my seat and laid my head back. I closed my eyes, but my mind was reeling. "Was I ever going to know what was going on?" I wondered. "I knew that I didn't want to have wires placed on my head and be tested like a guinea pig." I sighed.

"*Why don't you try meditating?*" a voice inside my head said. "*You won't get answers anywhere else. Through meditation you can solve the big mystery!*"

That was the last thing I remembered. I woke up at the New London terminal.

We all piled into my car and I drove the 22 miles back to Norwich. None of us mentioned anything about New York. I drove into the driveway and said goodbye to the girls, each one of them getting into their own car. I walked with Karen to her car. "Don't be discouraged, Pat," she said, giving me a hug. "When the time is right, you'll get your answers."

"I hope so." I said smiling and then watched her drive away.

"How was the trip, Pat?" asked Gene, greeting me at the door. "Did you find out anything?"

"Not really. We discussed a lot of interesting things. He showed me some of the cases, people he had tested in the lab; but even scientists don't know why some phenomena occur." I said, walking over to the coffee pot.

"Well, some things just are not meant to be known," Gene said, getting the cups.

"I was starting to feel that way too, but you know what?" I asked, pouring the coffee. "I want to start meditating on a regular basis."

"That sounds like a good idea. Remember that night in class? You got some answers then. Maybe you should have been doing it all along!" Gene declared.

I walked over to the hutch in the dining room, opened the top drawer and pulled out an order form that had the address of the foundation for the audiotapes we had used in class. I ordered the entire series, consisting of 12 cassettes, enclosed a check, and placed the envelope in our mailbox.

A little over a week had passed when I heard the mail truck pull up out in front of the house. It was the mail truck. I greeted the driver at the front door. He handed me a small cardboard box. I thanked him and quickly made my way back through the hallway, into the living and on into the dining room. I placed the box on the dining room table and opened it.

I took each tape out, one at a time and read the label. One title seemed to *jump* out at me. It read: 'Your Higher Self.' I became very intrigued. I *had to experience this mental journey* as soon as possible.

When Gene came home from work an hour or so later, I showed him the cassettes. We decided to call Karen, Joanne and Chris and see if they would like to come over and meditate with us. Over the summer we had also become friends with Karen's husband, Fred and Joanne's husband, Mark. I made the phone calls and everything was all set. Karen, Fred, Joanne and Mark were coming. Chris could not make it.

It would be a night to remember and cherish for the rest of my life! A new beginning that would ultimately shatter my skepticism, cynicism, doubts and old beliefs!

Everyone arrived at our house at approximately 7 pm. Then Gene and I prepared the dining room to become the *meditation room*. Gene pulled all the shades down on the windows. I went into the living room and picked up the small Panasonic recorder, which was on a shelf under the end table and I brought it into the dining room. I placed it on top of a small cabinet in the dining room, across from the dining room table, and plugged it in. I took the cassette out of the box marked "Your Higher Self" and put it inside the recorder. All of us sat down in a circular fashion around the dining room table.

I instructed everyone on how to perform the diaphragmatically deep breathing exercises that we had learned in the classes. When everyone was sitting comfortably and had their eyes closed, I pushed the play button on the recorder.

The man's deep but soothing voice rang out from the recorder into the room. He began by saying that he would be counting down from 50 to 1 and at any time that we wanted to end this exercise all we had to do was simply open our eyes.

By the time I heard the number 25, I was totally relaxed and my eyelids felt like they weighed 10 pounds apiece. That was all I remembered from the audiocassette.

The first thing I had experienced was seeing myself, like watching a movie, when I was a child, approximately 8 or 9 years old. Then I witnessed different *scenes*, like video clips, of my childhood. I remember feeling so happy and content. My father and my brother, Jim was in several of the clips. Two of the scenes had a powerful impact on me in the meditation. In one of them, I was looking at a photograph of my brother Jim, when he was a young teenager, and he was dressed in a dark suit. In the photograph he was standing with my Dad on a sidewalk next to the church. Dad had his arm around Jim, and my Dad was beaming. In the other scene, I was walking with Dad down the sidewalk at Sts Peter and Paul Church. I was wearing my white First Communion dress, and Dad was dressed in a dark blue suit. Dad was smiling and looking at me so lovingly. I remember the emotion that stirred inside of me when I recounted those moments in my life. And then suddenly the scenes faded away and I became surrounded in a beautiful soothing mist. Out of the mist I saw what looked like a silhouette of a man. As it drew closer to me, I was able to define a long dark brown robe with a gold braided rope around the waist and long gold tassels that hung down from the waist to the bottom of the robe. There was a hood pulled forward over the face of the man, preventing me from seeing any features, yet I *sensed* a familiarity about him. As the figure came closer, the left arm extended out from the sleeve and I could see long fingers on the hand and I *felt a* touch that was so powerful, so filled with love, and safety and security that I had never known! "Who are you?" I questioned.

No audible words were spoken from the man, yet I *heard his voice in my mind clear and precise, with tone, diction, articulation and a slight accent.*

"My beloved," the voice began, *"So shall you know at the appointed hour the identity of my physical existence. I have been sent from the Lord, to help guide you. I cannot interfere with your free will. I can only watch over you, and offer direction. You must make your own choices. Life consists of learning and trial and tribulation. He, who has faith in Our Lord, will overcome hardship. When the spirit leaves the terrestrial life and returns to Spirit Consciousness there are still realms of learning and knowledge that must be experienced."* With those words, the image faded away and the mist began to clear. As I started to come out of the meditation and become more aware of my surroundings, the thoughts "read the Bible, Acts 1 and 2" were prominent in my mind.

When I opened my eyes, I realized that my lashes were wet and the skin on my face was tight from dried tears.

Everyone was gazing at me, especially Gene. He was staring at me with a look of total shock and bewilderment.

"What happened to you?" he shrieked. "Where did you go?" he asked, in a bellowing tone. "You shook the table and broke me right out of my meditation! I looked over at you and your face was a funny color, grayish. You were sitting there like a stone! Then you were crying. I wanted to shake you, but when I looked over at Karen, who was also awake, she shook her head, saying no, and motioned to me with her hand to wait."

I recounted the meditation to them, and then I remarked, "We need to get a Bible, I want to read a couple chapters in it, Acts 1 and 2."

Gene was flabbergasted. "A Bible! Guardian Angel!" He snickered, staring at me and shaking his head from side to side. "You! I would never have believed in a million years, that I would ever hear anything like this out of **you!**"

All of them knew how I felt, and they equally shared Gene's comments.

"I know," I sighed, in a low voice. "He was *real*, Gene. I can't put into words what I felt. I just *know* that there is more to come, and I have to read those chapters."

"I know one thing," Karen, chimed in. "I would like to do this on a regular basis. I was feeling really good and so relaxed. How about you guys?" she asked, glancing around the table.

Everyone agreed. It would become a regular Saturday night ritual in our home that lasted over two years. We said our goodbyes and everyone left. I got up from the dining room table, walked over to the hutch and took out a pad and a pen, returned to the table, sat down and wrote down my meditation.

That night while in bed I tossed and turned. The meditation experience was still very vivid in my mind. There were no words or emotions that could adequately describe my experience. I only knew that I now had a determination to seek unceasingly the *truth*.

The next day, Gene was a little late coming home from work. He had to remain for a union meeting. When he walked through the kitchen door, I noticed a wooden box tucked under his left arm.

"What's that?" I asked, greeting him by the door.

"You're not going to believe it, Pat." He said smiling, as he walked over toward the dishwasher and placed his lunchbox on top of it.

"You know I had the union meeting today, and the union official handed these out to us." He said, handing the box to me.

I looked at the symbol of a white cross-imprinted in the center of the box.

"There is a Bible inside of the box." Gene said. "It's white. They used to give these out to the families of someone who died. *Now*, they have decided to give them out to the employees anyway." He smiled, shrugging his shoulders. *Coincidence?*

After we had dinner and I cleared the table and did the dishes. Gene and I sat down, and over coffee, I read the Chapters of Acts 1 and 2. As I read the accounts of the 'Acts' of the Apostles out loud, excitement began to rise in my voice.

The first chapter was explaining a letter that was written to someone called, Theophilus. It went on to explain that Jesus had *chosen* Apostles and gave them instructions through a Holy Spirit, and how a *cloud* had enveloped Him and taken Him from their midst. It spoke of two men who *appeared* to the people, dressed in white and spoke about the day Jesus would return. "Men of Galilee, why do you stand here gazing up toward heaven? This very Jesus who has been taken away before your eyes will return to you in the same manner that you have seen Him ascend to heaven."

The first chapter went on to explain how one of the Apostles, Peter, stood before a crowd that numbered about a hundred and twenty and said, "Brothers, the words of the Scriptures spoken by a Holy Spirit through the mouth of David must be fulfilled." It went on to say that another man from the crowd would be *chosen* and be counted as one of the Apostles.

The second chapter, sent shivers through both of us, as I continued to read aloud:

"Then Peter stood up and addressed them in a loud voice and said, 'Men of Judea, and all you who live in Jerusalem, make no mistake about this, but listen carefully to what I say...

"In the days to come-it is the Lord that speaks-
I will pour out my spirit on all mankind.
Their sons and daughters shall *prophesy,*
The young shall have *visions,*
The old shall dream dreams."
Even on my slaves, men and women,
In those days I will pour out my spirit.
I will display portents in heaven above

And signs on earth below.
The sun will be turned into darkness
And the moon into blood
Before the great Day of the Lord dawns.
All who call on the name of the Lord will be saved."

Gene and I just sat there in silence, trying to absorb the *message* in the words. I picked up the book again and read these words. "My dear brothers, I suppose I may speak freely to you. The patriarch David was a prophet of God." I scrolled my finger a bit further and read these final words:

"*Change your inner attitudes*," said Peter, "and let every one of you be baptized as the outward sign of his faith in the Lord Jesus, the Messiah, for the remission of your sins of apostasy. Then **you** too will receive the gift of the *Holy Spirit* world."

5 ▶▶

Spiritual Revelations & Enlightenments

I spent a very restless night. So many questions were running around in my mind. "What was happening to me? Why did I *see* that figure? Who was he? Was it my imagination? Was I just simply losing my mind?"

The morning light peering through the bedroom window woke me up. I got out of bed and walked through the house into the kitchen. Gene was already up and had the coffee on.

"Didn't sleep real well last night, huh, hon?" he asked, pouring me a cup of coffee.

"No." I said flatly. "Do you think I'm crazy Gene?" I asked sheepishly, staring at him.

Gene walked over and put the cup of coffee on the table in front of me, and giving me a very warm hug, he said, "No. Of course I don't."

"What do you think it all means then? I'm really confused. I mean, if there really *is a* Spirit World and if there were a God, why would He send a spirit to *me?* He *has to know* that I don't believe in..." Suddenly my sentence was cut short by a booming thought that entered into my mind. "*A change of inner attitude.*"

"Pat, I can't say that I understand either," Gene smiled. "We all know that something is happening to you. I mean, look at the readings you do. Where is that information coming from? I've thought about it all, too," he continued, "The classes, the dish cover and last night. Trish, I was watching you, I know that *something unusual was going on!*" Gene remarked, calling me by my nickname. "I've got to leave for work, try not to worry about it."

"I'll try." I said smiling, walking with him to the door. "Have a good day." I said, closing the door. 'I'll just stay busy, and put it out of my mind,' I pondered.

*   *   *

It was the middle of August and it was a sunny, hot day. I stayed busy and got my chores done fairly early. I decided to call Edie and Sue and invite them to come over and lie in the pool and get some sun. They both agreed and in no time we were all on our rafts and floating in the pool.

As we were floating, I told them about the *visitor* in my meditation.

"He must be a Guardian Angel!" Sue remarked. "Pat, this is really incredible, if I hadn't been involved with this since the beginning, I would have a hard time believing all of this!" she commented, and then continued, "I have been, and I am still in awe of it all!"

"If you think *you're in awe*," I laughed, "You should be in my shoes!"

"Hey! Let's meditate here on the water!" Edie said. "I'll bet it will be great!"

"Sounds good to me. You Sue?" I asked, as I maneuvered my raft toward the stairs in the pool.

"Sure." She said.

"I'll go in the house and get the recorder and a tape. I can plug it in out here." I said, getting off of my raft and walking up the pool ladder.

I grabbed the towel off of the railing, wrapped it around me and hastened toward the house. I went into the living room and picked up the recorder and the box of cassettes. I took a tape out labeled, "Advisors" and placed it in the recorder, then walked out of the house and back to the pool.

I set the recorder up on the picnic table on the deck, and plugged it in to the receptacle that was attached to the pool pump. I pushed the play button and went into the pool and climbed onto my raft.

We followed the deep breathing exercises and began the meditation induction.

The experience of my meditation was so powerful and the information that I perceived was so detailed, that *it led* to another very important pebble on the path. It would be the beginning of future recordings of approximately two hundred plus audiotape cassettes. The tapes would be filled with remarkable details of clairvoyance and other spiritual gifts. The tapes included taped telephone conversations with police and private persons nationwide seeking my aide with missing persons and various criminal cases, as well as spiritual revelations and enlightenments.

When my mental *journey* had ended and I slowly opened my eyes, becoming more aware of my surroundings, I saw Edie and Sue sitting at the picnic table up on the deck. They were both anxious to hear what happened to me.

"I don't know where to begin," I said, paddling over to the stairs. "I saw and *heard* so much. It's just so hard, I-I, uh, don't understand," I stammered, feeling the emotions stirring and knowing I was going to cry.

"Are you all right, Pat?" Edie asked, with a concerned look on her face, as she got up from the bench and walked over towards me.

"It-t-t-s just so overwhelming," I cried taking Edie's hand and walking to the bench. "And there is so much to tell you, but first I need to get a pad and pen and start writing it all down, I don't want to miss, or lose any part of this."

"You'll be better off to tape it," Sue said, handing me a cigarette, so I would calm down. "Do you have any blank tapes?"

"Good idea, Sue. I think so, I am going to run up into the house and find one. I'll be right back."

Once inside the house I made a beeline into the living room and searched feverishly through the stereo cabinet and I found one brand new blank tape, still sealed in the plastic case!

I went to the door, opened it and yelled for the girls to come up to the house and to bring the recorder with them. They walked in through the kitchen door. Sue placed the recorder on the dining room table and Edie made a pot of coffee in the kitchen.

"Don't start without me," Edie yelled, "I'll be right in."

I plugged the recorder into the wall receptacle, which was located beneath the air conditioner, in the dining room. I put the air control knob to low, and called Edie to come into the room. Edie walked into the dining room carrying a tray filled with cups of coffee, cigarettes and an ashtray.

We all took seats close to each other around the oblong dining room table. I sat closest to the recorder, and I placed the blank tape inside of it. I pushed the record button, closed my eyes and allowed my mind to recall the events of my meditation experience…

"I remember a very heavy feeling," I started, "and then I couldn't feel my body anymore. I felt like I was floating or suspended or something, and then I saw that mist again." The meditation had such a profound effect on me that while I was sitting there with my eyes closed and recounting the events, it was as though I was experiencing it all over again.

"This time," I continued, "I was in a room that was like glass, sort of transparent like, that had a couch and a coffee table with a beautiful flower arrangement on top of it. The colors in that arrangement seemed to be glowing, and there were shelves and shelves of books, from the floor to the ceiling and all along the width of the walls. It's hard for me to try and explain this, I mean the transparency part of it."

"Don't try, Pat," Sue said, "Just talk about what happened. We can discuss it later."

"Okay," I agreed and continued, "Then the next thing I saw were two figures. One was the *man* I had already seen and the other figure, which seemed to be, standing a bit of a distance away, was shorter and appeared heavier. He was wearing the same kind of robe, same color, gold belt and tassels. Then, the taller figure spoke to me. His face was still shrouded under the hood, but I *heard* every word he said, and I just can't tell you what happens to me *the emotion that I feel in his presence.*

"My beloved, I am from the realm of Our Lord and Saviour, Jesus Christ. Greetings." Mentally again I was asking who he was and who the other figure was.

"I have been sent to guide you. As long as you choose to remain on my learning plane, so shall I enlighten and guide you. Be not concerned of identities. Be comforted in the knowledge that when this phase of learning is needed no more, so shall you know me. My spiritual brother is the "gatekeeper", so shall he guard against evil influence. Seek trust in the Lord, ask, and so shall it be given to you."

I opened my eyes and looked at the girls and said, "After those final words, they both faded away and so did the mist.

Sue and Edie were looking at me so intently, both of them quiet. Then Sue said, "Pat, I believe in Guardian Angels. You should just keep meditating and find out what's in store. I am so amazed."

"I agree." Edie said. "Maybe you'll *see* Jimmy and your dad someday."

Edie's statement brought back to my mind the *visit* I had had with Dad and Jim when I was in the intensive care unit in the hospital. I decided not to say anything at that time to them about it, but the memory of that visit and this meditation convinced me to meditate on a daily basis.

We finished our coffee, and then the girls were getting up to leave.

"If I were you," Sue said, walking toward the door, "I would get some blank tapes and keep them on hand."

"Yes. I will. I am going to go to Benny's and buy some." I smiled, said goodbye to them and closed the door.

I couldn't wait for Gene to come home from work and tell him about the meditation. I looked at the kitchen clock on the wall; it would be at least an hour and a half before he was to arrive. I had enough time to change and get to Benny's.

I changed my clothes, grabbed my purse and walked out of the house. On the drive to the store, thoughts of the meditation were still very vivid in my mind. "What did he mean, "As long as you stay on my learning plane," I wondered. As it turned out, I wouldn't have to *wonder* about it long.

As I was preparing dinner, I heard Gene's truck driving into the driveway. I couldn't wait to tell him about the experience. As soon as he walked in through the kitchen door I greeted him and started rambling, "Hi hon., I almost called you at work today. I can't wait to tell you what happened."

"Oh yeah," he smiled, giving me a kiss. "So what happened?" he asked, walking over to the kitchen table and taking a piece of cucumber out of the bowl of salad.

"I invited Edie and Sue over for a swim and we meditated in the pool!" I exclaimed. "Gene I saw that man again and this time he had someone else with him."

"Let's sit down," he said, "tell me all about it." His eyes held a look of curiosity and excitement.

"I taped it." I said, walking over to the hutch and picking up the recorder. "I want you to listen to it."

We sat down at the dining room table and I rewound the tape and then I pushed the play button. Both of us just sat there listening in total silence. When the tape ended, I looked at Gene and asked, "What do you think it all means? Could *they really be* Guardian Angels or Spiritual Guides?"

"Pat, didn't he say you could ask?" Gene commented with a very serious tone to his voice. "Next time maybe you should ask questions."

"I am going to try and meditate every day. I think you and I should together on the nights that you are home." I said, and then I added, "And of course on Saturday nights too with Fred and Karen, Mark and Joanne and anybody else that would like to join us."

"It's fine with me," he replied, getting up from the table and walking into the kitchen. "Let's have dinner. They are coming over tonight, remember?" he asked, grinning.

We ate our supper and I cleaned up the kitchen and the dishes while Gene prepared the dining room for the group meditation.

At approximately 7 pm the four of them arrived at our home. Fred, Karen, Jo and Mark. A few minutes after I saw another car driving into the driveway. It was Chris. When Chris came into the house all of us stood in the kitchen for a few minutes chitchatting and then we went into the dining room and took our seats around the table. I was just about to look through the box of tapes, when the phone rang.

"Hello." I answered.

"Hi. You didn't start yet, did you?" Sue's cheery voice, asked.

"We were just about to," I answered. "Why are coming up?"

"Yes. I would like to." She said.

"Okay. We'll wait for you." I replied, and hung up the handset. Sue lived just a little over a mile away from us.

"That was Sue. She is coming over too," I said, and walked over to the box of cassettes. "Hmmm, which one should we use tonight?" I thought, while I flipped through the tapes and read the labels. "This one *sounds* good," I said, reading the title aloud, "Smashing limitations".

I had just finished putting the cassette into the recorder and plugged it in, when Sue arrived. Gene walked over and let her in and they both walked into the dining room.

"We're going to have to put one of the extensions into this table, honey." Gene said, picking up the last dining room chair from it's resting place near the window. "As it is now there isn't much elbow room."

"Not yet," I said. "It's nice this way, kind of cozy, I think, unless anyone is uncomfortable."

Everyone just nodded his or her heads in agreement. "If anyone else joins us next time, we'll put the leaf in then." I said, smiling at Gene. He gave me a wink and smiled.

We all did the deep breathing exercises and I was just about to push the play button when Sue said, "I know most of that protection prayer by heart, if anyone cares to say it."

"Yes. I think we should." I answered, smiling, "It would be a good idea to start each meditation session with it." As Sue began to recite the words, "Heavenly Lord wrap us in Your White Light and Protect us from all that is unholy..." and as we repeated them, I felt a soothing calmness and a comfort come over me that I can't describe. An *inner attitude change* was beginning to take place inside of me...

On this particular mental journey, the countdown started from the number 28 to 1. We were then to be taken on a visual journey into our minds and find our own limitations, such as low self-esteem, lack of self-confidence, etc. and break free of them.

Just as before, I didn't take the author of the tapes journey. I was taken on another spiritual journey, one that would free me completely from my *limitations of skepticism* and the discovery of *shining* pebbles on the path...

As this meditation began I felt like I was floating upward in a slow spiraling fashion. All around me were brilliant, but soft colors; there was such a presence of peace and love that I felt as though I were enveloped in them. Next, I saw myself sitting in a field of pretty flowers, much like the field I had visualized before. There was a gentle mist over the field and I *sensed* that I had to get up and walk into it. When I did, the mist faded away and then I saw a long rectangular table. Seated at the very end of the table, to my left, were three figures, at the far right end of the table there was one figure sitting. As I drew closer to the figures on my left, I could *clearly* see who they were, Dad, brother Jim and my cousin Joe. Joe had died at the age of 21 from an aneurysm while he was driving his car. Two months earlier than my father. I wanted to run up to them, but *something* stopped me. I looked toward the center of the table on the opposite side of where I was standing, and there stood the slender man in the robe. Not far behind him, the shorter and heavier figure was also standing. I walked closer to the center of the table and looked to my right. The figure that was sitting alone at that end was now also clearly visible. It was my grandmother, my father's mother, who had died a month before my dad and also in the same year! They had all died within three months of each other. I looked at the slender man who was across from me, his face still masked by his hood. So many questions were going through my mind, "Why was I here? Why was 'nana' alone? Why couldn't I speak to *my family*?"

*"Greetings My Beloved. I come to you from the Realm of Our Lord and Saviour, Jesus Christ. You must first learn in order to obtain and gain knowledge. Do you not learn to crawl before you walk? You must learn patience and recognize reaction to action. Seek in earnest and so shall you be given the **truth**."*

The next experience sent such a tremendous electrical current through me; everyone at the table felt it!

After he said those words, he walked away from the table and although he didn't tell me to follow him, I *knew* that I should. We entered into what looked like a glass sphere and then suddenly in the middle of it, I saw ***Jesus on the cross!*** It was such an emotional and powerful vision! I could actually *smell* the scent of blood! The slender man was standing to the left of Jesus and he said…

*"Make no mistake that His Death did not happen. Let no man convince you that this is not real. Our Lord died and was borne again for the redemption of sin and for the salvation of souls. So shall you read in Matthew when Jesus ascended on the Mount. Then shall you be given of the **Truth**."*

I was very visibly shaken when I 'woke up' from my meditation. Everyone was waiting anxiously to hear my experience. I couldn't talk. I just sat there and cried. Gene came over to me and put his arms around me and said, "It's okay. We'll hear it when you're ready. How about a cup of coffee?" he asked, wanting to see a smile on my face.

"That would be nice," I answered glancing around the room. "I just need a few minutes everyone", I said, getting up and reaching for the pad and pen in the cabinet. "I need to write this down first, and I can't promise that I will be able to tell all of you what happened without crying."

Gene and the guys went into the kitchen to make the coffee, while the girls stayed in the dining room with me. They were quietly chitchatting among themselves about various matters, but I knew they really wanted to share in my experience. I just didn't know how I was going to put into words the occurrence that took place. There were no words to describe it. I finished writing, telling myself that later I would record it all on tape.

When we were all drinking our coffee and I felt that I had calmed down enough emotionally to verbalize, I began to explain the vision. About half way through I became emotionally overwhelmed again. I decided to hand the pad to Karen and asked her to read it to everyone, which she did. Everyone remained speechless afterwards. Gene got up and went into the living room and brought out the Bible.

Since none of us were very familiar with the Bible, it took us some time to find the correct passage that was mentioned. 'Matthew' was one of the gospels written in the Bible and the ascension on the 'Mount' was located in Chapter 5.

As I began to read the words of Matthew, a *compelling* force came over me and this was the *interpretation* I perceived for the written words:

'Jesus seeing the crowds went up the hill. There he sat down and was joined by his disciples. Then He began to speak. This is what He taught them.'

'How happy are the poor in spirit; theirs is the Kingdom of God'
"God's spirit world will communicate with them"
'Happy are the gentle'
"They will have happiness in their earthly existence"
'Happy are those who mourn'
"Those who grieve over their estrangement from God will know comfort"
'Happy are those who hunger and thirst for what is right'
"Those who please God will be fulfilled"
'Happy are the merciful'
"God will be merciful unto them"
'Happy the pure in heart'
"God knows each and every pure heart and they shall be closer to Him"
'Happy are the peacemakers'
"Those that keep faith close in their hearts in time of temptation and trial will be counted among the faithful"
'Happy are those who are persecuted in the cause of right'
"So shall you communicate with the Holy Spirit Kingdom"

'Happy are you when people abuse you and persecute you and speak all kinds of calumny against you on my account'

"All of God's instruments before you were reviled and persecuted. Rejoice for you shall know the Kingdom of God and your soul's salvation"
I continued to read one more paragraph.

'You are the light of the world. A town built on a mountaintop cannot be hidden. When men make a light they do not put it under a cover but on a stand, so that it may give light to all in the household. So shall your light *Shine* before men, that they may see your good deeds and thereby be led to honor and praise your heavenly Father.'

I had no idea what was happening to me at that time. The words of interpretation came out of my mouth, but they were not my own thoughts. I would find out later it was another gift; it would be called 'Direct-voice'.

There was a lot to absorb that night. As we said our goodbyes we shared the same feelings, how was this happening to us? How and why was it happening to *me?*

*   *   *

Summer was just about over. There was only a week left before school started again. Over the past two and a half weeks I had meditated daily. Gene joined when he could, as well as Sue and Edie and of course our Saturday night group. The *spirit guides visited* nearly every meditation and encouraged me to read certain quotes and chapters in the Bible and then *I would be given the right interpretation in preparation of what was to come.*

*   *   *

It was the first week of September 1979, Saturday night. The number of people in our meditation group had grown. Besides our regular group several additional people had decided to join another friend, Carol M., my brother-in-law Frank, my cousin, Ron and us.

I chose the cassette labeled, "Visualization" for our meditation. The group always enjoyed the benefits they received from the exercises, the peace and relaxation the *journey* provided for them. As for me, it was just the *countdown* that I needed, which all of the tapes began with. The countdown put me in a very deep hypnotic trance, which enabled me to *attune to* a higher vibration of consciousness.

This meditation was *different* than any I had experienced previously. I began to *see future events.* I always saw the colors in one form or another or in a combination. In this day the colors began like a kaleidoscope, in the same manner as when I was doing a 'reading'. When the colors dispersed, images like snapshots and short video clips began to appear. The first thing I witnessed was a mountain exploding. Then I saw Ted Kennedy standing on a podium, accompanied by a strong impression that he was talking about a presidential candidacy. Then I saw a large boat collide into a bridge and another strong impression of people screaming and death. I saw a man in uniform, a light blue car and an eagle and another strong impression of death. And I kept seeing the numbers 3 and 4. They would just pop in bold and black.

When the meditation had ended and I slowly opened my eyes, I reached for the pad and pen that was now kept right next to me. All of us had adopted a new routine over the past couple of weeks. Gene and the men would go into the kitchen, while Gene made the coffee, Karen and the girls would get the cups, plates for the dessert someone brought and I would be writing down my meditation that would be shared while we were enjoying the snacks.

There was a lot of discussion after I read the events of my meditation.

"It sounds to me like you are having visions of things that are going to happen," Sue said. "I don't recall reading anything like that in the paper."

"I haven't heard anything on the radio either." Edie said.

"What did you say about that man in uniform again?" Sue asked with a curious look on her face.

I read the description again. Sue looked thoughtful and then she said, "I remember reading something in the paper in April about a missing Coast Guard guy. Do you remember that?" she asked.

"No. Gene and I along with Carol and her gang took our kids to Disney world in Florida for two weeks in April, remember?"

Everyone laughed. Carol just nodded and then she added, "We were going through a tornado at that time! I remember that!"

"Me too!" Gene joined. "I was trying to get us to safety driving through that blinding wind and huge hailstone storm!"

"That's right. I remember" Sue said, and then she continued, "Well I am pretty sure it was in April that this man disappeared in New London. I keep my newspapers so I am going to check it out."

Edie was sitting quietly, but she had an, *'I've got something to say'* look on her face and then she burst out with, "I think you need to go on the Potpourri radio show! I think Norwich needs to know there is a psychic that's real!" she proclaimed.

"Potpourri!" I retorted, "What are you talking about? I haven't done anything spectacular! What on earth would I talk about?" I asked.

"You could talk about what's happening to you, and the readings that you have done. Maybe you'll get some listeners who will want to talk to you and come and see you! There are people out there that you can *help!*" Edie remarked.

"Edie, what makes you think I can talk to hundreds of listeners?" I laughed. "I can't even discuss the meditations here without crying. I don't want to make a fool of myself."

"Well *my thoughts* were pretty powerful that you should do it! I know you can. I am going to call my sister, Donna. She knows Stu Breyer." Edie stated.

Stu Breyer was a local disc jockey on the Norwich AM station, WICH. Every morning at 10:05, Mondays through Fridays he was the host of a morning talk show, 'Potpourri'. The show was broadcast live and there were usually guests that spoke on various topics. I told Edie that I really didn't think that I had anything great to talk about and I left it at that.

It was getting late and everyone was preparing to leave. Gene and I walked everyone to the door and we said our goodbyes and we shared hugs.

"Pat. You should do a Potpourri show, it just feels right for me to call Donna." Edie said, as she hugged me. "If Stu's not interested, then we'll forget about it."

"I don't know, Edie," I said. "I don't have that kind of confidence, and I wouldn't know what to talk about."

The next day was Sunday. Edie called me around 2 in the afternoon to tell me it was all set. I was going to appear on Potpourri, Monday, the next day!

I was very nervous about the whole ordeal. How would I present myself? What did I know about being a radio guest?

Since it was Edie's idea, I asked her to accompany me to the studio. We arrived at the radio station around 9:45 am.

The AM studio was located on the second floor of the building. When we reached the landing and walked around the corner, we were greeted by the receptionist. I told her who I was and that I was there to see Stu Breyer. We waited only a few minutes, when a tall man with thinning brown hair and glasses entered into the hallway.

"Hi. Stu Breyer," he said, stretching his arm out to shake our hands.

"Hello. I'm Pat Gagliardo," I said, shaking his hand, "and this is Edie. You spoke with her sister, Donna."

"Nice to meet you both," he smiled, looking at her and then back at me.

"You can have a seat right out here, Edie. Pat, please follow me and I will show you where you're going to be," he said, as he started to walk away.

I followed him around the corner to a small booth. He opened the door to the booth and inside the narrow room was a plain stack-type chair, and a Plexiglas wall. Along the width of the wall was a narrow shelf. There was a microphone sticking out of the shelf and a pair of headphones next to it.

"I'll be sitting right across from you," he said, pointing to the glass wall. I could see into a large room that had a lot of electronic equipment, reel-to-reel recorders, and a panel with a lot of buttons. There was an armchair and a large microphone right in front of the wall.

"Have a seat, Pat. I want to check your mic and the headphones." He smiled, "And don't be nervous. We'll have fun. Before we go on the air, I'll ask you some questions, okay?" he asked, giving me a wink and closing the door.

I sat in the chair, closed my eyes and took a slow deep breath, "Please help me," I whispered.

I saw Stu walk into the studio. He sat in the chair and motioned for me to put on the headphones. He placed a set of headphones on his head and speaking into his microphone, he asked, "Can you hear me, Pat?"

"Yes, very clearly," I replied, speaking into the microphone.

In between his announcements and playing songs he would ask me questions. He was very pleasant and kind and seemed like a very sincere man. I felt very comfortable and relaxed.

"Stay tuned for Potpourri right after the news at 10:05. My guest this morning is a young local woman with a fascinating story on psychic phenomena! The number to call is…Stay tuned", he said, speaking into his microphone and smiling at me.

During the five minute news broadcast, Stu asked me questions like how I became aware of my psychic abilities, what kind of information I perceived in a 'reading', how did it happen, etc.

I looked at the panel of buttons on the phone. There were five red buttons and all of them were blinking.

"Good morning everyone and welcome to Potpourri. My guest this morning is Pat Gagliardo. Good morning, Pat," Stu said, motioning for me to reply.

"Good morning Stu. Good morning everyone," I said calmly.

"The lines are already lit up and I'll get to them in a moment, but first, Pat, tell us about yourself, and when did you realize you were a psychic?" Stu asked.

I was listening very intently to Stu's *voice*. In the same manner as the night I interpreted the Bible passages, the *answers* came through in my voice, but the *thoughts* behind the answers seemed to be *someone* else's.

"Actually, I have come to understand that I was born with these abilities, but my skepticism kept them suppressed until such a time that I learned the art of meditation that they were brought to the surface." *I answered.*

"Meditation? Is that like hypnosis?" he asked.

"Similar. Yes. It is self-induced and allows me to enter into a passively aware state of mind. Science refers to it as the Alpha state of consciousness. It was in this 'state' that I became aware of my latent abilities." *I* replied, and added, "It wasn't my first experience, however. Last year I attended some local classes pertaining to psychic phenomena and *on a whim* I purchased some tarot cards. That was my first introduction to my latent abilities." I said.

"Fascinating. Let's get to the lines." Stu said, pushing the first red blinking button.

"Hi. Pat, do you give tarot readings?" a woman's voice asked.

"Tarot was just an introduction for me. I didn't 'read' from the cards, they just provided a focal point, a concentration tool, if you will. I have done readings for friends and their friends using what science terms as 'psychometry,' which means I hold an object belonging to them, usually a piece of jewelry." I said.

"Are you going to offer these readings to the public?" she asked.

"I haven't thought about it. I don't know what the future holds for me right now." I replied, *sensing very strongly that she needed help, insight about a daughter.*

Stu placed a piece of paper up against the glass, it read; "Do you want me to give out your phone number after the program?"

Without any hesitation at all, I nodded my head, yes.

Other calls came in from people asking about the different aspects of psychic phenomena. One caller asked about the electro-magnetic force associated with the solar plexus area of the body.

"What do you know about the electro-magnetic force field?" he asked.

"Theoretically speaking," I began, "This force field is located in the solar plexus region and enables a *sensitive* to attune to this energy source, tapping into a higher vibration of consciousness. This vibration, electrical impulses, can be perceived by the sensitive much like an antenna; thus providing snap shot images, impressions and other sources of information."

The time passed by very quickly. It was time for the program to end. Stu seem well pleased, he thanked me and asked me if I would return again.

As I walked to the area where Edie was waiting, another gentleman approached me. He was of average height, a little heavy set with very curly dark brown hair.

"Hi, I'm Dennis MacCarthy," he said, smiling and shaking my hand. "WICH newsman."

"Hi. Nice to meet you." I said.

"I'm Edie." Edie said, smiling.

"Would you consider letting me interview you for a story?" he asked.

"A story? What kind of story?" I asked.

"This psychic business-you might say is 'in' these days. I would like to do a special assignment." He explained, "A human interest aspect."

"Sure, if you would like to." I said.

"Come on into my office. We will set up a meeting. You can come to, Edie," he smiled.

We decided on the last day of the week, Friday. I invited him to come over to my house.

As we were preparing to leave, Stu met us and said, "The general manager is here and he would like to see you. Could you come back into the studio?"

"Fine, I would like to meet him also, and thank him for allowing me to do the show." At that moment I didn't know what I was up against. I never once considered the possibility of running into another skeptic. I guess it didn't enter my mind because of my own change of heart.

This man was not only skeptical, but he was crude as well. He introduced himself very arrogantly and his questions were sharp and extremely critical. I experienced another aspect of my abilities; one that I did not know *existed* until that day!

"Why don't you give me a reading?" he asked with a sneer.

"Something inside me was saying, "No. Don't do it!"

"Come on," he said in a sarcastic tone. "Come into my office."

Reluctantly I followed him, my old fears and insecurities rising up and taking over. I was *afraid* to say 'no'.

He handed me his watch. I closed my eyes, took a deep breath and the familiar routine started, the colors and then images. The information was pretty specific, but when I asked him about the information that I had perceived, he denied the validity of everything.

"I guess it doesn't work with us," I said, handing him back his watch.

"Just what I expected. Most people I've met that thought they were psychic usually turned out wrong!" he laughed, a mean laugh.

Well, that wasn't the end of it. As it turned out, he simply had been untruthful about his answers. Stu, Edie and I went into another room in the building. It was a small recording studio. There were several employees there that he introduced us to, Pearl Miller, being one of them. The manager walked in shortly after we did. He made me so uncomfortable; he had such an awful attitude.

"How did your reading go, John?" Pearl asked, as he entered the room.

He shot me a look and then said, "I didn't get anything out of it. She batted zero with me!" he snickered.

"What were some of the things she said?" she asked.

He didn't answer her; instead he stuffed his hands in his pockets and walked out of the room. She looked at me, but I didn't say a word. In a few minutes he returned. I looked at Edie with that, 'let's go look'.

"What's the matter? Are you afraid to tell us?" One of the disc jockeys teased.

"The details were general. The house she described could have fit a number of houses!" he muttered, with noted sarcasm in his voice.

"Oh really? Give us a for instance! What were some of the details?" Pearl asked, a note of sarcasm now evident in *her* voice.

"I told him the description of the house, that he was remodeling in one of the rooms and that he was looking to buy another house." I interjected.

"General? I don't think so! That's true enough!" Pearl snickered. "You know you've been looking at houses for the past week! And you're remodeling, too!"

I looked him square in the eyes. "He lied to me!" I thought, furious with his attitude. "Why couldn't he just have been truthful?"

"I'll tell you what; give me a number of the dog that will win at the racetrack tonight and I'll believe in you!" he commented facetiously.

"Even if I could, I wouldn't," I retorted. "God didn't give me this ability to offer persons material gain!"

He shot me a nasty look and stormed out of the room. Everyone there became absolutely silent.

"I'm awfully sorry," I said, feeling the tears coming to my eyes. "I owe all of you an apology for my outburst."

"Don't apologize, Pat," Pearl asserted, a note of sincere concern in her voice, on how she felt his behavior had affected me. "He deserved it."

"I suppose I'll have to get use to that if I plan to continue in this field. Its just I-uh didn't expect it. You know, I was very much like him myself, skeptical, that is. Maybe that's the reason I let him upset me."

Suddenly he was back in the room. He rushed towards me, making ugly gestures with his hands. He was throwing them up in the air, calling himself Satan! I couldn't take it anymore, and I fled the room in tears. I was so upset by the time Edie and I reached the bottom landing, I was shaking.

I stood there next to the inside entrance of the FM studio and did an exercise that we had been taught in the classes for releasing tension. I did not know, however, that it might cause complete chaos at the station! It is a simple exercise; take several deep breaths and entertain the thought, 'I am releasing my tensions and my anxieties' and on the last exhale, you shake off the tension and anxieties by shaking your hands at your sides, and visualize the negative energy coming out of your fingertips. I didn't realize that by releasing all of his negative energy from me and into the atmosphere of WICH, the effects it could have!

The occurrences that happened from the power *surges of energy and the effects it caused* would become commonplace for me; the explanation comes later...

At approximately two o'clock that afternoon I received a telephone call from Dennis MacCarthy.

"I don't know what *you* did up here today, but this place is in a shambles!" he said, a very serious tone in his voice.

"What are you talking about, Dennis?" I asked.

"Right after you left, all of the electrical equipment began to malfunction! We had our engineers up here and they have checked out all the possibilities! Their conclusion is a *super surge of energy* was the cause of the problems. This isn't a laughing matter-I hope you're taking me seriously!" he exclaimed.

"I don't understand what's going on!" I stated, totally bewildered by what that had to do with me.

"I'll tell you," he said very matter of fact. "The first mishap was with the electric typewriters. As soon as you walked out the door, they stopped working, all of them. Then the intercom buzzers kept going off! We couldn't get them to stop. Thirdly, the clock on the FM computer system went haywire."

"Wait a minute!" I shrieked. "Do you think I'm responsible for this?"

"I listened to your broadcast this morning. You stated that people with your ability have an inexhaustible source of energy, correct?" he asked.

"Well yes, that's true; at least that's what it says in the books I have read. That was part of the theory I was talking about, that energy can also be used for telekinesis, mentally moving objects."

"Let me continue please. That's not all that's happened up here!" he remarked.

"You mean there's more?" I asked, my mind racing over what he had already said.

"The three year old transmitter overloaded and shut down! The FM towers are out! The FM station that is automated was receiving wrong signals and spitting out information over the air it wasn't supposed to! The only explanation the engineers are coming up with is the possibility of an unknown power surge coming from an *outside source*. It must have been **you**! They have never experienced any difficulties up here before today!"

I thought of the 'release' I did before I walked out the door.

"I-uh, don't know what to say, Dennis. I'll look into it and see if I can find some answers," I said.

"Well, they are hoping the problem will correct itself. The head engineer says that once the power source is depleted, everything should return to normal", he said, and added, "I'll let you know. Bye."

His phone call shook me up. "Could I really be responsible?" I wondered. I decided to look through the dictionary of psychic sciences, Nandor Fodor. It would give me some understanding, and my spirit guides would enlighten me later...

It was true according to the information in the book. There was a list of the types of abilities that were forms of this energy and also how it could be localized. Psychometrist was among those listed. The definition explained that some psychics that possessed this much energy have learned to localize it in one area, thus causing PK, (psychokenesis) which means the moving of objects with unseen force. Others who have not been able to localize, have been known to *cause electrical malfunctions of numerous variety*. "Could it be true?" I wondered.

When Gene came home from work that afternoon he was anxious to hear how the program went. I told him all the details, everything that happened at the station, Dennis' request for an interview and Dennis's phone call.

"Dennis is coming over here to do the interview Friday at 4:30." I said. "You will be home then, and I want you to meet him too. Okay?" I asked.

"Sure. As for the stuff that happened there, sounds to me like the manager was being a jerk! He's lucky I wasn't there with you. He had no business treating you like that." Gene retorted.

"It really upset me. I can't believe I made such a fool of myself, crying and feeling like I had to defend myself ", I said.

"He was the fool. Not you, hon.", Gene said and gave me a hug. "We are meditating tonight, right?" he asked.

"Yes. I am going to ask questions, if I can." I smiled.

As we were preparing for our meditation, the phone rang. It was the woman that had called at the station. She asked me to *please* consider giving her a reading.

"I want to know what you charge," she said, a pleading in her voice.

"I have never charged my friends or their friends. As I said, I haven't considered a service to the public at this point," I answered with a compassionate tone in my voice. The impressions I had felt earlier when I spoke to her over the air returned to me. A *thought* inside my head said, "You can help her, she needs your insight." I asked her to hold on a minute and I covered the mouthpiece and asked Gene what he thought I should do.

"It's really up to you, Pat. You have a lot of free time during the day in between your runs. You could make appointments," he answered.

"I wouldn't know what to charge. I-uh don't know what to do," I sighed.

"Ask her if she has had another reading somewhere, and what the fee was." He said, shrugging his shoulders.

"Hello, thanks for holding on," I said, uncovering the mouthpiece. "Have you had a reading before?"

"Yes." She said, and told me the person's name.

"Do you mind if I ask what the fee was?" I asked.

She told me and I decided I would use that amount as a basic charge. If I *felt I wanted to charge less, it would be my prerogative.*

I made an appointment with her for the next morning at ten a.m. The reading lasted forty-five minutes. Upon handling her watch, I was overwhelmed by sadness. She and her young daughter of 14 years were having major difficulties in communicating. The girl's father had left a year before and she was acting out rebelliously. I was given the insight to tell her how and what to do to improve the situation. To this day, she remains, as hundreds of others, a regular client.

Her phone call was the first of many that began on a daily basis. Some that called had heard the broadcast, and most from 'word of mouth.'

Gene and I meditated together each night. In the meditations I would always see the man in uniform, the blue car, the eagle, the bold numbers 3 and 4 and one new image added each night. On Monday, I sensed water, like a body of water. I didn't see the spiritual guides that week, but I *sensed their presence.* Patience, and faith were being taught to me, and I would *come to know this,* in the next couple of weeks.

Tuesday night, those same images were accompanied by the visualization of two large equipment cranes. Wednesday night, the same images, accompanied by some items that were wrapped and lying on the floor in the blue car. Thursday night was different. All the same images, but this time, I saw what looked like a brick sidewalk, and buildings very close together and written in red letters, the word 'fire,' and a quick image of my cousin, Sam.

*   *   *

Finally it was Friday afternoon. The jitters began to set in as we waited for Dennis's arrival. I hoped everything was normal again at the station. The face of the clock read 4:30.

"He should be here any minute," I said to Gene. No sooner had I spoke the words, when we saw him walking up the sidewalk.

"Anybody home?" he asked cheerily, as he knocked on the kitchen door.

"Come on in, Dennis" I replied, opening the door.

Gene and Dennis shared introductions and then we sat at the dining room table. Dennis didn't hesitate to fill us in on all the details that happened at the station.

"The F.A.A. was called in. They wanted those towers operating immediately!" He said. "Things are back to normal, now."

"I don't know what to say. Maybe it's just a *coincidence!*" I blurted out. "I did read in my psychic dictionary that these things could happen. How do you feel about it?" I asked Dennis.

"I witnessed those things happening-I'm willing to bet there is a connection!" he laughed. "You radiate energy. I can feel it when I am around you."

We got off the subject and began the interview. During the interview he had mentioned that a friend of his was connected with the Otis Library, and I should consider giving a lecture there.

Then out of the blue he asked, "Do you believe in UFO's?"

"If you want a logical answer, I'll tell you how logic dictates to me. We are only one planet out of many; it doesn't seem feasible to me that we would be the only life form. So, I guess you could say I believe something is out there." I smiled. Gene nodded in agreement.

"Did you ever hear of Betty Hill?" he asked, looking back and forth to Gene and me.

"Yes. She was allegedly abducted wasn't she?" I asked.

"That's right. I interviewed her by phone. Would you like to meet her?" he asked enthusiastically.

"Sure. I think it would be fascinating to hear her story." I said.

"Great. I'll arrange it, and get back to you on it."

"Why did you ask about UFO's anyway?" I asked curiously.

"I don't know. It just popped into my mind," he replied.

"That's funny. But I'm glad you did. I'll be expecting to meet her now." I said, giving him a look of excitement.

As he was getting up to leave, he let out a yelp. "My watch stopped working! Look at this! This is a self-winding watch! I've had it for five years and it has never stopped!"

Gene and I both looked at the watch. He was right. The watched had stopped for twenty minutes; a self-winding watch that he had had no previous trouble with. Another coincidence?

Meeting Dennis was going to enhance my life and be a benefit to others. I didn't know then just how much. *It was meant to be!*

Dennis telephoned and informed us that he had made arrangements for the last Saturday of the month for us to go to New Hampshire and meet with Betty Hill. He had also arranged a date and time for me to give a lecture at the Otis Library the next week!

The lecture was held in a medium sized room located in the downstairs portion of the library. Approximately 100 people gathered in the room. After I introduced myself to the crowd, I began to tell my story, how everything had started for me. About half way into the lecture, I felt it necessary to tell the audience of my new religious outlook. I told them of an experience I'd had while in a meditative state.

"It's not an easy thing to face about yourself-your vices and shortcomings," I began, feeling the tears well up in my eyes. "Whether it's gossiping about someone, or saying something hurtful to someone, whatever the case may be! But let me tell you," I continued, the tears rolling down my cheeks now, "those of you who want to open your own psyche-be prepared, you may not like what you find out about yourself!" I turned and walked to the desk, wiping the tears from my face. I regained my composure and made one more statement. "You will have to make changes," I said. "It won't happen overnight; but with practice you can become a better person, a Christian, a God fearing person, if you will." The entire room became so silent, you could have heard a pin drop. Then I asked if anyone had questions, and selected by raised hands.

One woman asked, "Have you worked with missing persons?"

"No, not yet, but I do believe there is a purpose for these gifts, to help mankind and to enlighten persons about the *here and the beyond*." I heard myself reply.

Everything in my life was being carefully planned. Each pebble on the path was perfectly placed like pieces of a puzzle. My routine style of living was rapidly changing. Lectures and radio programs were becoming a large part of it. It gave me great personal reward to stress to others how psychic awareness had not only changed me, and my way of life, but could change them too.

*   *   *

Saturday was a gorgeous fall day for the trip to New Hampshire. We had made arrangements to meet Dennis in Massachusetts at a restaurant parking lot. When we arrived, Gene pulled the truck up alongside his car. He asked us if we had heard the news that morning. The vision that I had had of the boat accident in my meditation happened! He told us 52 people were killed. He also said that Mt. Fuji had exploded! The time frame from the night that I had had those images was *3-4* weeks!!

It took us a little over three hours to reach Betty Hill's home. It was in a very picturesque town, called Portsmouth. We arrived at her house and walked up to the front door. A woman with short brown hair and petite build greeted us at the door.

"Come on in," she greeted us with a pleasant smile.

She seemed so happy to have us visit. She was warm, charming and appeared to be a very sincere person. Listening to her tell her story to Dennis was very intriguing. Gene and I just sat in the living room with them drinking coffee that she had made.

We had been there visiting about an hour and a half, when we heard her doorbell ring.

Betty excused herself and went to the door. Two gentlemen and two women walked into the living room. Introductions were exchanged. We met Larry Fawcett, a policeman from Coventry, CT, who was also a UFO investigator, and his wife Lois, Robert Bletchman, an attorney from Manchester, CT and his wife, Adrienne. After half an hour or so of conversation, Dennis pipes out with, "Pat, is a psychic!"

"Oh really," Larry said. "Well I would like to talk to you, Pat."

"Sure." I said, getting up off of the couch and walking over to him."

"If I give you something, can you tell me about it?" he asked.

"I can try." I smiled, watching him take a small piece of cloth tied up in a ball out of his jacket pocket.

Larry handed the item to me. I took a deep breath, closed my eyes, the colors appeared in kaleidoscope form as usual, then dispersed, and I saw a middle-aged woman and an older white house with black shutters, set back off of the road. I sensed that the woman was distraught about something on her property.

"Okay, Pat." Larry said, smiling a huge smile, he was quite pleased with what I had told him, but didn't say anything to me *then*.

"Give her something, Bob," Larry encouraged.

Bob, was skeptical, I sensed it very strongly. He urged his wife to give me something, which she did, her ring.

I began to describe a brown house, sort of L shaped. I also told her some personal information about herself. I gave her the name of a woman in her life and some details of their relationship. She was quite pleased, and thanked me. I was about to give her back the ring, when Bob said, "Wait a minute. There is something in my neighbor's yard. Can you tell me what it is?"

I took another deep breath, and mentally asked, "Please help". In just a few seconds an image of a wooden fence appeared to me and then this strange vision appeared. I thought to myself, "He will think I am crazy if I try to explain this."

I must have had a funny look on my face, as I heard Bob ask, "What is it? Are you seeing something?"

"Well yes-s-s," I stammered. "There is this huge pole or pipe jutting way up out of the ground, and on top of it is a dog house!" I exclaimed.

"Interesting. Very interesting; there is *no way* you could have known that, unless you've been there!" Bob remarked. "Not too many people have soaring doghouses in their yards! He built that thing as a conversation piece!" he laughed.

"Pat, have you ever considered working with the police?" Larry asked.

"I haven't yet, no. I have performed readings for friends, that's how I basically started and I do offer a service to the public. I'm sure something else is in store for me. I just don't know what or when though!" I grinned.

"I would like your phone number. Is that all right?" Larry asked. "You could probably be very helpful with missing persons or crimes."

"If I can help, sure, I'll give you my number," I said, looking at Dennis who had already written my number on a piece of paper and handed it to Larry.

"You can also help me with UFO cases, if you want to!" Larry said, "That house you described is perfect and the woman too, she called me and told me that she woke up one morning and found all this web-like substance hanging off of her trees. The ball of material belongs to her," he smiled.

"That sounds very intriguing," I grinned. "I'll do what I can."

It was getting late and we all had a long drive ahead of us. We thanked Betty for her hospitality and the wonderful visit. She hugged me and said, "I do hope we see each other again." I smiled at her and said, "Perhaps we will."

On the drive home, Gene and I chatted about the visit and what a *coincidence* it was to meet Larry, Bob and their wives.

"Seems to me there has been an awful lot of *coincidences* since all of this started to happen with you," Gene commented. "I'm not psychic, but when I think of everything that's happened, I get a feeling *something big* is about to happen," he stated, making a frown and shaking his head from sided to side.

Little did we know then what *Spiritual Enlightenments* were in store for us. That the Grand Architect would again send His Spiritual Guides with images and in depth explanations of death, suicide, life between life, reincarnation, spirits, karma, the spirit world, how mediums are prepared and of the gifts... *The Pebbles On My Path...*

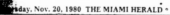

...rday, Nov. 20, 1980 THE MIAMI HERALD

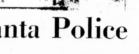

Psychic Led Atlanta Police To Bloody Jacket and Shirt

ATLANTA — (UPI) — The bloody windbreaker and T-shirt police uncovered last week near a graveyard was located by a Connecticut psychic who said something at the site could be linked to one of the 15 cases of slain and missing children, it was revealed Wednesday.

City Councilman Arthur Langford said psychic Pat Gagliardo of Norwich, Conn., took him and a number of tracking dogs to Lincoln Cemetery in northwest Atlanta last Friday and pinpointed the location where she thought something related to the cases may be buried.

Langford, who organized five massive volunteer searches for clues in the cases, said the dogs sniffed the area and within minutes located the windbreaker and T-shirt, both of which were bloodstained.

Atlanta Public Safety Commis-

> City Councilman Arthur Langford said psychic Pat Gagliardo of Norwich, Conn., took him and a number of tracking dogs ... and pinpointed the location where she thought something related to the cases may be buried.

sioner Lee Brown said Wednesday he has received a preliminary oral report of laboratory tests on the clothing, but refused to disclose those findings until after he receives a written report.

Langford declined to comment on the lead except to say that the dogs were sent out Wednesday "to follow up on some information she has

given to us."

Langford said Gagliardo was in Atlanta on a three-hour layover on a flight from Connecticut to Columbus, Ga., where she was going to help a south Georgia family find its son.

Gagliardo, 31, is the second psychic to participate in the case. Last month, psychic Dorothy Allison of Nutley, N.J., spent a week in Atlanta assisting the 35-man task force investigating the slayings of 11 children and the disappearance of four others. But police have refused to discuss whether the leads provided by Allison have panned out.

Langford said Gagliardo told him "there was something" near the Lincoln Cemetery related to the disappearance of 11-year-old Jeffrey Lamar Mathis, who disappeared from his southwest Atlanta home March 11.

Atlanta
Continued from Page 5.

sensitivity of the investigation, she is not able to say more about it.

A practising psychic for only two years, Pat Gagliardo is credited with having assisted New London police in locating the body of missing Coast Guard warrant officer, Richard Eastman, who had been missing for several months, when he was found in a car pulled out from a spot in the Thames River which she had indicated. "By using psychomatry on Eastman's credit card, I was able to locate him," she said.

In addition, she claims to have located, "two missing girls in Reno, Nevada, two from Ledyard, Conn., a man from Coventry, two people from Stonington and one from Maine."

Prior to September 1978, when Pat Gagliardo discovered her "gift," she claims she had never had a vision in her life. "I'm a very hard-nosed skeptic," she said, "I suppose I had a normal amount of ESP. My husband and his sister were fascinated by that stuff, but I

thought they were crazy."

In the course of taking a course on the art of meditation, she learned she had some latent psychic abilities which her skepticism had been supressing. When the instructor had talked about the ability to see colors or "auras," Mrs. Gagliardo discovered she was seeing purple coming from the instructor's fingertips. "And I don't even believe in this stuff," she told the instructor.

The instructor then handed her a watch and asked her to close her eyes and tell what she saw. "I began to describe the instructor's house, inside and out in every detail and I had never seen it," she reports.

She began reading extensively on psychic phenomena and by October 5th, she began to see visions. The first one was of a man in uniform.

That man turned out to be missing Coast Guard warrant officer Richard Eastman. Mrs. Gagliardo was called back to Atlanta following her initial 30-minute visit and stayed for several days working on the case. On her return to Connecticut she said, "I cannot disclose at this time what is happening there."

12-C... THE ATLANTA CONSTITUTION, Thurs., Nov. 20, 1980 ....

Probe

Continued From Page 1-C

But Mrs. Ritter reportedly said that she still has complete confidence in Mrs. Gagliardo's abilities.

Langford said the psychic "asked me if there was a Lincoln Park in Atlanta."

"I said, 'No, there's a Lincoln Cemetery.' "

Langford and Mrs. Gagliardo then took a Philadelphia man and his trained dogs to sniff out her vision at the cemetery.

Though the psychic told Langford they would find a body of one of the missing children, Langford said he was impressed that they found even the clothing.

In another development in the children's cases Wednesday, the Grant Park Community Club announced it will sponsor a volunteer search of the community this Saturday.

Though none of the children has disappeared in the immediate Grant Park area, the search sponsors said the purpose would be to clear vacant lots in case any evidence has been dumped in them. Searchers will gather at the corner of Atlanta Avenue and Boulevard at 9 a.m.

A simultaneous search, sponsored by the DeKalb Community Relations Council, will take place along a section of Memorial Drive near the home of 11-year-old Christopher Richardson.

The youngster disappeared on June 9 on the way from his home at 1495 Conway Road to a nearby swimming pool.

Between 400 and 600 DeKalb police and fire officers and volunteers are expected for that search, the sponsors said Wednesday.

On Wednesday, the Atlanta Branch of the National Association for the Advancement of Colored People announced the beginning of a prayer observance each day at 12:30 p.m. in connection with the series of slayings and disappearances.

The Rev. Frazier Todd and the Rev. Barbara King, who co-chair the NAACP's Religious Committee, said their organization "is calling on every man, woman and child to stop whatever they may be doing at 12:30 p.m. each day and say a prayer for the missing and murdered children, for their families, for the apprehension or surrender of the guilty party and for unity among all our citizens.

The Rev. Todd said the committee had developed a "Prayer of Affirmation" which would be shared with the entire city and contains "a positive statement about what we, as human beings and children of God, mean to each other."

The NAACP committee also is spearheading a drive to have each church in Atlanta join the effort by ringing its church bells or chimes, or having its organ or piano played, at 12:30 p.m. every day.

Schools and other public institutions will be asked to cooperate by distributing copies of the prayer and keeping the daily observance.

SECTION C
.... Thursday, November 20, 1980 .

City/State

THE ATLANTA CONSTITUTION

Metro/State 2

Business 13

Psychic Led Way To Bloody Clothes, Councilman Claims

By Ken Willis
Constitution Staff Writer

A psychic led tracking dogs to a child's bloody windbreaker and T-shirt found last Friday in an Atlanta cemetery, City Councilman Arthur Langford said Wednesday.

The clothing items were turned over to the Atlanta police Special Task Force that is investigating the cases of 11 slain children and the disappearances of four others. Langford said police have not told him whether the clothing is related to the cases.

The councilman added, however, that Public Safety Commissioner Lee Brown has notified him that some weapons discovered during a series of volunteer searches over the past few weeks apparently have no relation to the children's cases.

In discussing the psychic's role in last Friday's find, Langford said, "I'm a skeptic on these psychics, but you can't rule anything out," and then he told how the psychic had been on target Friday.

The psychic, Pat Gagliardo, was brought to Langford's attention by Nancy Ritter of Peachtree City. Mrs. Ritter said she hired the Norwich, Conn., psychic to help her find her husband, who disappeared last year while flying in the Caribbean. Her husband has never been found; the terrain pinpointed by the psychic was too rough to search.

See PROBE, Page 12-C

Channel 8 News, New Haven, CT Tony Pagnoti,
Covering Story of Richard Eastman

Channel 6, News, Providence, RI Interview

ids Police to Missing Man's Body — 15 Feet Underwater

THE EXACT SPOT: Patricia Gagliardo points to water where she told police they'd find body of man who had been missing for six months.

National Enquirer February 1980

Mark Wile, PM Magazine at WICH

Otis Library Lecture, Norwich, CT PM Magazine with Mark Wile

Otis Library Lecture, PM Magazine with Mark Wile

Otis Library, Mike Caisseri Cameraman, PM Magazine

Police admit success of Norwich psychic

By Steven Slosberg
Day Staff Writer

NEW LONDON — Pat Gagliardo established her exotic presence among the computers and gadgetry of modern crime detection in October 1979.

She did it by walking into the state's attorney's office in New London and telling investigators she could help locate the body of Coast Guard Warrant Officer Richard Eastman, who had been missing since April of that year.

She dispelled the skepticism she knew she would encounter, eventually was accompanied by the investigators to City Pier and, after experiencing what she calls uncontrollable vibrations, said Eastman would be found in the waters beneath the pier.

She was right.

In the methodical and sober world of police procedure, Pat Galiardo, a psychic, had proven herself.

And, as she told a group of 25 people attending a workshop Saturday morning at Mitchell College, she has volunteered her services in more than 30 investigations since, including the search for whoever is responsible for the child murders in Atlanta.

Among those participating in Saturday's workshop were Sgt. Thomas O'Connor of the State Police sex crime analysis unit, Trooper Donald Barry of State Police Troop E in Montville, who demonstrated the use of composite sketches and Lt. Robert O'Shaughnessy of the State Police emergency services unit in Colchester, who talked about detection methods ranging from bomb squads and scuba teams to trained dogs.

Mrs. Gagliardo, who is 32 and lives in Norwich, said she was skeptical herself about psychic abilities until she started taking a class in Norwich three years ago called "Getting to Know Your Psyche."

About three weeks into the course, at the encouragement of the teacher, Mrs. Gagliardo participated in an experiment in psychometry.

The teacher took off her watch, gave it to Mrs. Gagliardo to hold, and as Mrs. Gagliardo stood with her eyes closed, she proceeded to describe the teacher's home in uncanny detail.

She began to understand the extent of her abilities.

"I don't think it comes from Satan," she told the group Saturday. "Today, I am a much more religious person than I was three years ago. I

Pat Gagliardo

bring happiness to people. The devil doesn't want that."

Mrs. Gagliardo said the experience in the Eastman case has allowed her to work with police again without meeting a wall of skepticism.

She is called frequently to assist in missing person cases, and state troopers participating in Saturday's workshop with her attested to her abilities.

Mrs. Gagliardo has been to Atlanta three times since the bodies of black children were found, and she said she blames the media for making the case more difficult to solve.

"I really think the media should stay out," she told the group. "I have a feeling that some type of small cult was involved in the first three or four murders. But now, with so much attention, I feel there may be more than eight, nine or 10 involved."

She also said she encountered much competition among police and detectives there, each trying to horde information in order to gain national attention for breaking the case. A vision she had about a man was ignored by police, she said, but a man fitting the description was later identified as being seen with some of the children who disappeared.

"I'm still a skeptic," said one of the state troopers who works with Mrs. Gagliardo. "It's tough when you deal in facts to have someone tell you these things. It's almost scary. She'll describe places in very, very vivid detail. And you know she hasn't been there."

Psychic

(Continued from Page One)
told O'Connor the body was on a sandy area, near rocks.

"He told me he knew right where I meant," she said.

Thursday's search was concentrated between the Mystic River and the southwest end of Masons Island where Whittemore was last seen.

When divers resumed the search at 8 a.m. yesterday, the area was widened.

Three hours later, Navy petty officers John Ramos and Gregory Day, both of the USS Fulton, located the body. It was near a small rocky island — the "something round" sensed by Gagliardo — off the southwestern end of Masons Island. It was only 20 feet to the left of where divers searched Thursday.

Whittemore was visiting his grandparents, Mr. and Mrs. Charles L. Auger Jr. of Skiff Lane, Masons Island.

GAGLIARDO

He was described by friends as being an excellent swimmer and an accomplished wind surfer. He was found wearing only a bathing suit. No life preserver was found.

Interview after the missing windsurfer was located, Norwich Bulletin

Bulletin photo by John Shishmanian

Pat Gagliardo, left, is congratulated by New London Police Captain Richard West during an open house for her Center for Psychical Consulting and Development in Norwich Sunday. West gave Gagliardo a commendation from New London Police Chief Donald Sloan for using her "psychic powers" in helping find Richard Eastman's body in 1979.

Psychic opens Norwich office

NORWICH — A psychic noted for helping police find missing persons opened a Center for Psychical Consulting & Development at 18 Oneco St.

Pat Gagliardo of Norwich offers psychic consultations and hypnosis to help with smoking, dieting, stress control and other problems.

Workshops will cover tension release and relaxation exercises,

meditation techniques to improve self-awareness and instruction in positive thinking. The workshops will be held once a week for six weeks.

Registration for the workshops began yesterday. Center hours will be from 9 a.m. to 4:30 p.m., Monday through Friday. Appointments also may be made Saturdays and some weeknights.

Norwich psychic to open business

NORWICH — Pat Gagliardo, a psychic who has helped police in missing person cases for several years, has opened a Center for Psychical Consulting & Development at 18 Oneco St.

Mrs. Gagliardo, a Norwich resident, will offer psychic consultations (readings), hypnosis to help with smoking, dieting and stress control and regressive hypnosis.

She will conduct workshops covering tension release and relaxation exercises; meditation techniques for opening the psyche to improve self-awareness and instruction in positive thinking. Workshop classes will be one night a week for six weeks.

Registration for the workshops began today.

Center hours are from 9 a.m. to 4:30 p.m. Monday through Friday. Additionally, Mrs. Gagliardo will take appointments Saturday and one or two evenings a week.

Mrs. Gagliardo is recognized in

southeastern Connecticut for her role in helping police find the body of a Coast Guard warrant officer who had been missing for seven months in 1979.

Seeing mental pictures of a uniformed man's body slumped in a car underwater near a pier, Mrs. Gagliardo went to police with the information. Soon after, police retrieved the body of 49-year-old Richard Eastman from a submerged car off City Pier in New London. Since then, she has assisted in missing person cases locally and outside the state.

Last summer she helped authorities find the body of a missing windsurfer who had last been seen in the waters off Masons Island in Stonington.

Living

Pat Gagliardo, standing, demonstrates device with aid of Chris Morgan

"Dry" Floatation Device for Meditation, Installed in Office of CPCD

Lobby of American Society of Psychical Research, NY

Patricia and Betty Hill, Portsmouth, New Hampshire

Wili, Willimantic, CT with Mark Roy, Interview and Call-ins

Wili, Willimantic, CT, Mark Roy

Pat Gagliardo

Sight unseen

Thomas Hinds Sr.

Families of the
to psychic for c

By Gail A. Poulton
Staff Writer

Thomas Hinds Sr. gently presented a worn leather flight jacket — and his hopes — to the psychic waiting in room 107 of the Howard Johnson's Motor Lodge Monday afternoon.

He said he will try anything to find the jacket's owner, his missing son.

"It's a hard thing being in the dark, not knowing whether he's alive or dead. I think of it when I'm alone. When you go to bed you think about these things. I still feel that he's alive and yet I'm teetering," said Hinds, of 641 Alabama Ave., west of Fort Lauderdale.

Fort Lauderdale News

Metro

Tuesday, Dec. 15, 1981
Section B

e missing turn
:omfort, clues

Hinds, 82, was one of 19 people who consulted psychic Pat Gagliardo, who was brought to the area Saturday for a four-day visit by Operation Retriever, a committee formed as a clearinghouse for information about individuals reported missing in the Caribbean.

Hinds' son, Tom Jr., 42, ran a charter air service based in Sebring. He disappeared Feb. 1, 1980, when a plane he was flying either ran out of fuel or was forced down by a Cuban plane, according to the Coast Guard.

"I can't give up hope," said Hinds. "I have a gut feeling that he's still alive and one of these days he's

Please turn to page 5B, column 1

Pat Gagliardo, who practices psychometry, listens intently.
Staff photo by DEBORAH MEEKS

Ft. Lauderdale, Fla. Operation Retriever for Missing Pilots

6 ▶▶

The Pebbles

•Communication with the Spirit World:

Many changes had taken place in our lives over the past year. Aside from what had happened to me, Gene and I also sold our house and purchased my family home from my mother. We had also established a new routine with our group and personal meditations. We would play a 'journey' cassette in the stereo tape deck in the living room, while a blank tape was placed in the small Panasonic recorder in the dining room. We would have the blank tape on record during the entire session, as it was easier to verbalize the meditations, rather than writing them down and having to record them afterward.

I was home about half an hour from my meeting with the detectives, Mr. Pickett and Mr. Rainville and search for Mr. Eastman, in New London, when the phone rang.

"Hello," I answered.

"Hi, Pat. It's Edie. How did everything go today?"

"Hi Edie," I said, "Gene should be here in about 30 to 40 minutes. Why don't you come over and you can hear the whole story when I tell him about it."

"Okay. Do you need anything?" she asked.

"No. I am all set. Thanks. Coffee is on all ready." I said. "Bye."

We had only confided in a few people about my meeting with the detectives. Our group, naturally, as they were a part of everything from the beginning, and Gene's sister, Chris.

Edie arrived about 10 minutes before Gene did. She helped me finish with the preparation for dinner. Over dinner, at the dining room table I told them about the events of the day. I especially spoke of Mr. Rainville's attitude and criticism, and how kind Mr. Pickett was.

"I know that Mr. Rainville didn't want to admit to the details of his reading, but I was so happy that he did. It made me feel so much better after the incident at the City Pier." I said.

"Well, hon.," Gene began, "Just remember you were like him once, and not only that, they are policemen, they deal with hard facts."

"I know, but was I crude or mean about my skepticism?" I asked frowning.

"No, but you made no bones about laughing and scoffing at Chris and me a lot!" he laughed.

"Well you're family!" I laughed.

"So I guess that explains why you used to needle me too, huh?" Edie teased. "Because I am married to your cousin, Ron!"

We all laughed. "Well, anyway, I believe that Mr. Pickett will do exactly what he said he would. He is going to check everything out. He was so kind to me, and he was really amazed by the reading. Thank you, God." I said.

"Pat, I have to go back to work for four hours tonight," Gene said, getting up and bringing his plate into the kitchen.

"Okay. Edie, do you want to stay and we'll meditate together?" I asked.

"Sure. I would love too."

We prepared the dining room in the usual manner. I put a blank tape in the Panasonic recorder and chose the 'visualization' cassette for our meditation.

Tonight would bring more revelations and enlightenments concerning the 'beyond' and would answer the question '*is there life after death?*'

We were meditating about 10 minutes after the countdown; I was in a very deep trance-like state, when the room became very cold, colder than usual. Since the metabolism slows down, it is not uncommon to feel coolness, but this was a 'cold' that was external, not internal.

In my meditation, I saw my brother, Jim. His image was so clear that I felt I could touch him and behind him a little distance away, were the two 'spiritual guides'.

A strong odor of smoke permeated the air and Edie began to speak, breaking me of my connection.

"Pat. P-a-at," she said, her voice breaking because she was crying. "There is something in the room. I saw a shadow next to you and then it walked behind you." She said, her eyes as big as saucers and tears running down her cheeks. "I s-m-ell smoke, too." She stammered.

I opened my eyes, as the 'connection' was lost. "Shhhhh." I whispered, placing a finger to my lips. "Yes. I smell the smoke too." I said, looking at her and then around the dimly lit room. The room now was ice cold, there was a knocking or rapping sound on the table, and the top of it was so cold, we took our hands off of it.

The smoke odor had cleared and then instantly we could smell a familiar scent. It was Jim's favorite cologne, Canoe.

Edie was not able to contain herself; she coughed and then said, "Jim. Jim I know you're here."

We sat there in silence for a few minutes after she called out. Mentally I was asking Jim to talk to me. I 'knew' he was there and I wanted to 'hear' his voice so badly.

What we didn't realize then, his *voice* was being *recorded* on tape!

We waited a few more minutes, and we thought things were slowly returning to normal. The room was still cold, but the shadow had gone as well as the scent of his cologne.

We sat there and started to discuss what had transpired. It was late, but I wanted to call Sue and tell her what happened. The tape in the recorder was still on and recording. In the excitement of what was going on, I had forgotten about it and had not shut it off.

"Sue. Can you come up here?" I asked excitedly, when she answered the phone.

"Pat. What's going on? I really can't right now," she replied.

"Edie and I were meditating and I think my brother Jim was here!" I exclaimed. "The room became really cold, and then we could smell smoke and his shaving cologne. There was a shadow here too!" I remarked.

"Pat. I wish I could come up, but I can't," Sue repeated. "You're all right aren't you?" she asked.

"Yes. I know it is Jimmy!" I said, "I'll talk to you tomorrow." I said and hung up the phone.

Edie and I sat there talking about my brother. She and Jimmy had met many years back, even before she knew Ron.

We were still talking, when Gene arrived back home. It was now midnight.

"Still here, Edie?" he asked walking into the dining room to join us.

"Gene a lot happened here tonight." I said, "We've never experienced anything like this before." We told him everything that had transpired.

"Pat, there always seem to be something 'new' to learn about. You need to start asking questions to the guides. I believe they will tell you." Gene smiled.

I was about to answer him, when he noticed the recorder, and asked; "You taped the session tonight, didn't you?"

"Yes. I didn't even hear it shut off. Edie and I were just so consumed by what happened, we forgot about it." I answered.

"I am going to take the tape and play it in the stereo in the living room," he said, taking the tape out of the recorder and into the living room.

Edie and I continued with our conversation while Gene was listening to the tape. Then we heard him yell out, "Come in here, both of you!"

As we entered into the living room, Gene was rewinding the tape. "Listen to this and listen carefully!" he demanded.

On the tape you can hear Edie cough and then hear her say, "Jim. Jim I know you're here." Then there is a moment of silence and then in a very low dragging voice that sounded like it was in a tunnel, we heard, "*Tri—sha. Tri—-ssha. I've got to tell you something…*" I began to cry. Trisha was the nickname that Jimmy had always called me. Edie started crying too. I was about to say something, when Gene interrupted, "There's more. Hold on!" he said. He pushed the fast forward button, quickly and kept stopping until we heard on the tape, "Sue. Can you come up here?"

The same voice and in the same manner says. "*Nooo. Noooo. Nooo.*"

Gene stopped the tape and took it out of the stereo. "Pat, put this somewhere safe," he said, handing it to me. I took the tape from him, shaking, and really crying. "He was here, Gene. My God, he *really was here*! He said he had to tell me something!" I cried.

That night's experience was the first of many to come. Spirit intervention and communication would come on a regular and consistent basis. It is the only 'voice' of Jim on tape, but there would be *another voice*, one that *spoke through me* by utilizing me as a channel and by direct voice! To try and explain how these *visits* have impacted our lives is impossible. I can only share with you the measures we have *all* taken and continue to this day.

*   *   *

On Saturday, I still had not heard from the detectives. I had thought about it several times over the past couple of days, but not as much as I had thought of my brother Jim and the experience of that night. I wanted to know what he had to tell me. I wanted to speak to him so desperately.

Everyone had arrived, plus Susan and Chris. The first half hour before we began our meditation, I talked about the meeting with the detectives, and then took out the tape of 'Jim' and played it for them.

Everyone was emotional. Karen made a comment that touched us all so deeply.

"I can't tell all of you what this has meant to me, hearing that tape." Karen began, her voice cracking. "I have had that question in my mind for so many years, since my mother's death. I would talk to her, never really knowing if she could 'hear' me, or where she really was, if the body just died, everything," she cried. "I am so relieved. She isn't really 'gone', just her body."

"Me too, Karen," I said, getting up to give her a hug. "I know exactly how you feel. I can't tell you the peace it has given to me and finally a 'truth' that removes any doubt."

"I have written down some questions for tonight," I said, pointing to the yellow pad next to me. "Gene reminded me the other night that 'I was told' I could ask questions. Mentally I am going to go over them in my mind and if I 'see' the guides tonight I am going to ask."

"Let's try to keep things as quiet as possible tonight," Gene interjected. "I think more could have happened if Pat didn't lose the 'connection'."

Everything was set. We did our deep breathing exercises, the blank tape was in the recorder and the journey tape was in the stereo. We held hands around the table and said the protection prayer and began our meditation.

It seemed like only a couple of moments had passed, when I detached from my physical surroundings and went into that wonderful place of peace and the mist. I was there for what seemed like only a few seconds, when the taller slender guide appeared. The 'gatekeeper' was there too, but he always remained a bit in the distance. I remembered 'seeing them' and that was all I could remember. I felt like I had gone to sleep! What I hadn't realized, *I was sleeping*, in a manner of speaking, as my body was being utilized and occupied by the spirit guide! On this night there would be a wonderful new experience in store for us, especially for me! One that changed our meditations and *me* forever!

"Greetings, my beloved children of the earth plane. Be not afraid. I come to you from the Realm of Our Lord and Saviour, Jesus Christ. And so tonight, shall be a night of learning. So shall I enlighten you of the truth of which you seek. If you so decide to continue on this journey, so shall you question from where you receive this knowledge. I tell you that I am of the realm of Our Lord, Jesus Christ, Master of all that is holy. In time of ere, you have questioned the existence of evil, and I tell you, make no mistake that evil does

exist. Unholy influence abounds of your physical world and so too it exists in the spiritual realms as well. So shall I reveal these truths in time to come. So shall I now speak of which you question. In the physical life the dead is referred to as the physical body dying and interment. So shall I tell you, there are physical death and the spiritually dead. Those who are spiritually dead are separated from God-consciousness. The spirit is removed from His Realm of holiness. Those who have physically died and their spirits have remained faithful to God continue in the spiritual realms with tasks and other duties that are performed which I shall also reveal in time to come. The spiritual realms are parallel to the physical world. They are not, as the general conception construes, millions of earth miles away. The existence in the spiritual world is quite similar as that of your physical world. The spiritual world is transparent, nonetheless similar, as I have stated. Those who have been given the gifts of clairvoyance, clairaudience and mediumship are able to attune to the vibration of the spiritual world as you have witnessed. These attunements are intended solely for the purpose to benefit mankind to enlighten him as to God's existence and His Plan of Salvation. So shall you be given the understanding this night of the attunement that the channel has made with the spirit of the one you have known as her physical brother. Spirits learn and grow on the spiritual realms, just as they do while inhabiting the physical body. So shall you come to know the power in prayer, not only for the sake of your physical existence, but also for those who have left the physical realm and are now here in the spirit world. There is much to do here. Faith in prayer helps to escalate the spirit, physically and spiritually. Negative emotions are useless and prevent the spirit from escalating. So shall you speak to the channels physical brother, and learn that he harbors much guilt. It is this guilt that causes him to mourn needlessly over the loss of his brother. So I say offer prayers to the Lord thy God, so that his burden may be lifted, and the spirit that now resides in this realm may continue on its journey. So shall I reveal to you in time to come all that is necessary for your spiritual growth. May God continue to grant you His Love, His Peace and His Guidance."

When I opened my eyes, again they were wet and heavy. Everyone was staring at me in sheer disbelief! Especially Gene! No one was talking. Not even a whisper! It is extremely difficult for me to try and convey to you that wonderful and enlightening channeled experience, and the effects it had on me and to all in the group! The next day revealed the 'truth' in *his* message that was given through me. It would be the beginning to our 'prayer and meditation group'.

*   *   *

Santo and I never discussed any part of the spiritual experiences I had in the past. And only briefly did I talk to him about anything pertaining to the 'psychic awareness' that was unfolding in me. We were just on different wavelengths and I had accepted it. He was nearly eleven years older than me and we had never been close. We had never discussed Jimmy either. I would talk to him about everything else, but not those subjects, until that day. I had to fulfill the request made by the spirit world.

I invited Santo over for coffee. Gene had already placed the tape in the stereo and we were planning to play it for my brother. Shortly after he arrived, he started to tell us something that happened to him a couple of nights earlier. Gene and I were amazed as he told us the episode.

"It was very late Thursday night," he began, "I had fallen asleep, I was so tired. I had done a lot of paperwork Thursday. I must have fallen asleep around 9. Then about 10 o'clock, I woke up. Jimmy was on my mind so strong. I got up and walked out into the garage. I don't know why," he said frowning and with a very serious look on his face, "but I found myself going through all of his things, which I had packed in the boat. You know how much he loved that boat, Sis. I was looking at his yearbook from college and the newspaper clipping for when he took that trip out West on his motorcycle. I just couldn't get him off of my mind."

"Sant," I started, calling him by the family nickname, "I know from a long time ago, you had some issues about your relationship with Jimmy.

You 'know' that he loved you, and you know that you loved him. I hope you don't feel guilty about anything. If you do, you need to let it go."

He looked at me peculiarly, his expression asking, 'how did you know?' "I do feel guilty about some things," he said.

"Sant, I want you to hear something," I said, interrupting him. "You don't have to explain. I want you to know that Jim is all right and happy. Come into the living room a minute." Gene walked over to the stereo. "This happened Thursday night, right around 10 o'clock," I told him. The words on the tape seemed to ring out louder than they did the first time we had heard them. Santo listened, began to cry and turned and walked away and out the door, not saying a word.

It was never mentioned again between my brother and me. Jim's spirit's plea was heard. The message was passed on and Jim could now continue his growth in the spiritual realms.

It didn't end there for *me* though. Even though I believed everything that happened and was part of the experience that night with Edie, *I* still needed an explanation! I called Stu a couple of days later at the radio station and told him about the tape I had, and that I wanted to have 'the voice' analyzed. Stu invited me to the station and said he would see what could be done. The equipment at WICH was not sophisticated enough, so it was suggested that the tape be sent to TM Productions in Dallas, TX. I didn't want to let the original tape out of my sight, so Pearl, Stu and I used her recording studio to re-record that part of the tape on a reel-to-reel tape. The strangest thing happened! After the recording was finished, *none* of Pearl's equipment operated for nearly a half hour! Again there was a super surge of power and everything was shut down! The report that came back said, "The voice on this tape is of unknown origin, but the *source of energy* connected with it is so powerful that it removed the entirety of the emulsion coating, which can only happen when there are hours upon hours of constant play." Soon, I would learn about this source of energy *and* my curiosity would be completely satisfied! I would never have to question it again!

*   *   *

• Development of Mediums: Clairvoyance, Clairaudience & Channeling:

After my brother left, Gene and I sat in the living room for quite a while talking. We were discussing the 'visit' from Jim, and how it *precisely* coincided with the same time Sant was awakened from sleep with 'strong thoughts' of Jimmy. We began to reminisce. One 'thought' would prompt another and the conversation turned to the day Gene and I met. The conversation led to some questions, which needed answers, which we hoped could be provided by the spirit guides.

"Oh my God!" I shrieked, "Gene, that visitor I had in the hospital, the 'man' I told you about that was in my room! I saw *his face*! I'll bet he is the same spirit that I have seen in meditation and the one that spoke through me!"

That memory prompted a series of 'thoughts'. "Didn't Ruth the nurse tell us she had a *persistent thought* to have to go back to the ER while she was reading?" I exclaimed.

"How about Dennis? Meeting Larry? Working with police?" Gene retorted. "How often have we said, 'There's an awful lot of *coincidences!*'"

"Honey, let's meditate. Maybe he will come through again and you can ask for an explanation for all of this," I insisted. "And tonight, if I just 'see' him I am going to ask if I may know who he is now."

The information that came through was also very powerful and the 'proof' and validity would be given to us again. A trust would begin to build and a faith so deep that it would become unshakeable.

Everything was set. Gene and I held hands, did our deep breathing exercise, said the meditation prayer and started the 'journey' tape.

It was becoming easier and easier for me to detach from my physical surroundings. In no time at all, I entered into, what I now called, 'the room of knowledge' as it was the 'library' room. Both of the guides appeared immediately. Again I entered into a peaceful sleep. When I 'awoke' Gene played the tape for me.

"*Greetings, my beloved brother of the earth plane. I come to you from the realm of Our Lord and Saviour, Jesus Christ. And so shall this be a night of learning. So shall I enlighten you of that which you seek. Of this terrestrial life, so shall you learn of patience. I shall reveal to you that which is necessary, at certain stages, in order to provide a proper foundation for your spiritual growth. So shall I provide the truth on preparations of mediums employed by the spirit world of God. Mediums are instruments that are utilized solely for the purpose of communication with the spirit world. Mediums are the source of energy that is necessary for the spirit to derive its power from. In simpler terms, you cannot operate an electrical appliance without having first a power source. The physical body of the medium is this power source. The body is made up of solid substance. Substance is matter, and matter is energy. Since the spirit is devoid of solid substance, it must utilize the energy from the medium. There is much preparation from the spiritual world that is involved with the development of a physical medium. So shall I speak of this in time to come, as well as the gifts of clairvoyance and clairaudience. And so before my departure, I shall reveal my first name of my past life and from where I had lived. My name was Vincent and I had resided in the Pallotine Hills. So shall the channel recognize me, as I shall reveal myself before releasing my spirit, but you shall **know** me when you are given the information from your physical friend and your research is complete. May God continue to grant you His Love, Peace and Spiritual Guidance.*"

Before 'I woke up', I was permitted to see the spirit guides' face! It **was** the same man that 'visited' me in the hospital room! Gene and I sat for over an hour discussing 'Vincent's' visit. I was rambling about the 'visit' from the man I had seen in the hospital, how he was dressed, what he looked like and I remembered that he had one arm across his chest pointing up toward his shoulder. I also remembered that his pinky and ring fingers were bent under his hand and his index and middle fingers were shaped in sort of a V position and his thumb was extended outward.

"Pat. That is the position your body was in when you channeled Vincent!" Gene remarked.

"You thought I was hallucinating when I told you about that visit," I said, smiling at Gene. "It is the same person, spirit!"

"It is all so incredible, Pat," Gene, said, "I wonder if the 'shadow' in our old house has anything to do with him too!"

We sat and reminisced about all the *coincidences* we had experienced. How everything seemed to be so perfectly planned.

"What do you think he meant when he said, 'you will know me when your physical friend gives you the information and your research is complete'?" I asked, looking into Gene's eyes.

"I don't know. Maybe you have to check with Susan. Remember he said the same thing about your brother, and when we asked your brother, we found out it was the truth."

"That really was amazing, the fact that Sant was probably experiencing 'Jimmy's presence', at exactly the same time Edie and I were, and he just didn't realize it." I said.

"You know what else is amazing? I didn't 'ask' any questions. I didn't have too! 'Vincent' already *knew*, and we need to work on 'patience', too." Gene smiled.

Over a week had passed by now, since my meeting with the detectives, and still I had heard absolutely nothing. In that time, I had telephoned, Susan, and asked her about 'Vincent'. Susan had absolutely no idea who he might have been, or about the Pallotine Hills.

$$*\qquad\qquad*\qquad\qquad*$$

Saturday, October 13th. Gene had to work on the day shift. I busied myself around the house and finished all of the chores. I had also baked a cake to offer as dessert following our meditation.

I was putting the plates out on the dining room table, when I saw Gene driving the truck, a bit too fast, down the driveway. He got out of the truck and was running up the sidewalk.

"What's the 'fire' all about?" I laughed, as I greeted him at the door.

"You're not going to believe it, honey!" He said beaming from ear to ear and almost throwing his lunchbox up on the dishwasher.

"What?" I asked, excitedly.

"Do you remember my friend, Clarence?" he asked, his face bright like a child's.

"Clarence?" I asked.

"Yes. Clarence Lacasse. You met his wife, Eleanor, and him, when we attended one of the union's picnics last summer," he answered.

"Hmmm. That's the older man, short, slender and wears glasses? His wife had her hair pulled back in a French twist?" I asked.

'Yes. That's the one," Gene smiled. "He came over to me today and you won't believe what happened!"

"What? What?" I exclaimed.

As he walked over to the coffee pot and poured coffees for both of us he said, "You know that Clarence and his wife both are very religious. Well, why he decided to come over and talk to me about this, I am still wondering!" he said smiling and sitting down at the kitchen table. I sat down next to him.

"What Gene? Talk to you about what?" I asked, my curiosity now going crazy.

"I was in the office, talking with a few of my mates, when Clarence walked in the door and asked if he could speak to me outside for a minute", he smiled. "So I walked with him over by the bails, where it is quiet. Then he starts to tell me about this man who is handicapped and works at one of the hospitals and in his spare time makes rosary beads and just gives them to people. Clarence then shows me a small cardboard box that is filled with really pretty rosary beads. They are all different colors. As a matter of fact, I left some in the truck, I have to go get them", he said.

"Wait, don't go this minute! Then what happened?"

"Well, he asked me if I would like a pair and if I knew anyone else that wanted or needed some rosaries. He said the man didn't charge for them, it was something that he just got a lot of pleasure in doing for people. Pat, it just 'popped' into my mind to ask him about 'Vincent'!" he said, the excitement now very evident in his voice.

"What did you say to him, Gene?" I asked, wondering if he told Clarence, how we 'met' Vincent.

"Well, I sort of said that you had a 'dream' and you saw a man that was dressed like a monk. I told him the color of the robe and that you thought his name was, 'Vincent'. I couldn't remember the name of the Hills. I said it started with a P something, and Clarence looked me right in the face without any hesitation at all and said, 'Gene, it sounds to me like it was St. Vincent Pallotti, from the Pallotine Hills of Italy'. As soon as he said, *Pallotine*, I knew it was him!" Gene commented.

"Oh my God!" I remarked. "Did he tell you anything else about him?"

"No. I asked him if he had any books or anything on him. He said he didn't, but that I should be able to find something in the bookstores." Gene said.

"I don't know if the library is open tomorrow or not, but you can bet first thing on Monday, I'll be searching for it! I can't believe it, Gene!" Tears filled my eyes, spilling over onto my cheeks. "Vincent *knew*! He knew! We just assumed it would be my friend! *He knew and he must have given the thought to Clarence to talk to you!* And now I have to research at the library!" I cried.

We couldn't wait for the group to arrive, to tell them of the latest developments. Tonight I would start the group with the meditation protection prayer, as well as some additional prayers in giving thanks for these precious gifts; the Spirit Guides.

The revelations of that night are also burned in my memory, as well as in all of the group members'. The information has been shared with everyone that has asked and offered to those who are eager to listen.

Vincent met with me in the 'library' immediately. The information that was revealed through me comforted us, enlightened us and prepared *me* for future 'negative' encounters.

"Greetings, my beloved children of the earth plane. I come to you from the realm of Our Lord and Saviour, Jesus. Christ. So shall tonight be a night of learning. In times of ere, I have revealed to you, in part, death of the physical life, mediums and their purpose and the existence of evil. So shall I enlighten you further. First so shall I say, there are those among you, including the channel, that question why is it so that she be utilized by the spirit world, as you know her shortcomings and she herself feels unworthy. Instruments of God-consciousness in times of ere were subject to the same frailties and human weaknesses as the mediums of today. So too, did they have their shortcomings and failings. Judge not, lest ye be judged, as only the Lord, thy God, knows what lives in the heart of another and so it is the heart that harbors the spirit of man. Now then, I shall expound of clairvoyance and clairaudience abilities. As I have stated, mediums possess the necessary energy for communication with those of us of the spirit world. So shall you come to understand this current is referred to as 'ode'. It is this ode in insurmountable supply that the medium possesses. In time to come so shall I explain of the **colors** of ode, its vibration, its scents and its purity. It is this connection that enables spirit to attune to the medium. Those spirits of the lesser realms can also attune to this energy source. So shall I now explain the gifts of clairvoyance and clairaudience. So shall I give an example that you will relate too and know to be of truth. In the channels visit with 'Jonathan' she was able to 'see, hear and experience his presence'. The same was true with her visit of the one you had known as her earthly brother, also including, scent. The degree and purity of ode as well as the mediums ability to release the ode are necessary to facilitate this connection and determines the depth of the spirit's communication. An example; some mediums only possess enough ode for a spirit to communicate through automatic writing, others for clairvoyance and so on. To distinguish properly a medium and one who has clairvoyant abilities is such; True mediums experience that which I have just said, those who are gifted with clairvoyance alone, only **sense** spirits about them. They cannot hear nor see, nor can they smell the ode of the spirit. Mediums with clairaudience, which means the ability to 'hear' the spirit, are true mediums, for they possess the ability to release the necessary ode that is *needed for the spirit to converse with them. So shall you learn more in time to come. In parting, so shall I leave you with these words; as I have said, spirits of the lesser realms can also attune to this power supply of ode. It is faith and faith alone that shall keep you strong in time of temptation. So shall you experience influence from the negative realms. Stand firm of your faith. As you draw nearer to God-consciousness so too shall you encounter opposition. May God continue to grant you His Love, Peace and Guidance."*

Gene rewound the tape, so I could hear it. We were all speechless. Everyone just sat in silence. We were all very emotional, whispering prayers of thanks and absorbing the wonderful enlightenment of this magnificent message. How blessed and humbled we all felt! And there were more *rewards* and *gifts* to come! So would the 'opposition'.

*   *   *

Monday morning, 9 a.m. October 15th. As soon as I finished with my morning runs, I headed straight to the Otis Library. Again I parked out in front. I went inside and spoke with the same young woman at the information desk. She tried to help me as much as she could. The library didn't have what I was looking for. She told me she would make some telephone calls to some of their affiliate libraries and would call me if she could locate a book on 'Vincent Pallotti'. I left her my name and telephone number and left the library. "Hmmm. More 'research' would have to be done." I pondered, as I drove home.

*   *   *

Wednesday morning, 11 a.m. October 17th. It was an unusually warm day, so during my morning break; I had decided to wash my car, inside and out. I was spraying my windshield with windex, when the thought popped into my mind, 'This would be a perfect day for divers to be in the water, it is so warm'. I glanced at my watch; it read 11:12 am. As I was finishing the cleaning, the memories of the entire episode of my visit with the detectives flooded my mind. I would soon find out why.

I finished the car and put all of my cleaning products away. I had to return to work and pick up my afternoon school children. The afternoon seemed to pass by very quickly and my thoughts continued to swirl around on the events of October 5th.

I drove directly home after work and was enjoying the bright sunshine and warmth of the day. As I drove into the driveway, another car pulled in behind me, it was Edie.

"Hey there!" I yelled, smiling. "Coming in for coffee?" I asked.

"Sounds good to me," she smiled, "I haven't really had a chance to talk to you in awhile, thought I'd drop by."

"Great. Come on in." I grinned.

Once we were in the house and sitting down over coffee, we started chitchatting about 'normal' things, our kids, school and subjects like that. It was close to 4 o'clock, almost time for Gene to come home, when the phone rang.

"Hello." I answered.

"Dennis here! Put your radio on! Hurry. W-I-C-H!" Dennis's voice commanded.

"What's going on?" I asked, totally surprised by his behavior.

"Can't talk now. I've only got a few minutes. Just put your radio on!" he repeated and hung up.

I walked over to the radio in the kitchen and turned it on.

"What's up?" Edie asked.

"I don't know. That was Dennis. He told me to put the radio on." I said, tuning in the station.

"Think it has to do with Eastman?" she asked, her eyes bright with excitement.

"I don't know. That thought occurred to me, too, but I would have heard from the detectives, don't you think?" I commented.

We sat down at the kitchen table and heard...

"Good afternoon everyone. It's four o'clock and I'm Dennis MacCarthy, W-I-C-H news. In New London this morning, at approximately *11:15*, police divers lifted a government car containing what is believed to be the body of a missing Coast Guard Warrants Officer—Richard Eastman. Eastman who disappeared some six months earlier…"

Dennis's voice seemed to fade from my ears. Edie and I looked at each other, tears rolling down our faces as we hugged each other and cried.

"Sources say a psychic was used in locating the man. However, no names have been mentioned at this time. Divers located the car in the murky waters of the Thames River close to the City Pier…" Dennis said.

"Pat, did you hear that?" Edie's shrill voice echoed in my ears. "I can't believe it! You did it! You were right!" she cried and hugged me again.

"No Edie, thank God!" I remarked.

The next few hours were like a dream. It was if I were watching and not participating in the actual events, waiting for someone to wake me up and tell me—it's all a dream!

Gene walked in and started rambling about the news broadcast that he had heard on his drive home. We didn't even have time to discuss it. The phone started ringing immediately, beginning with Dennis.

"Dennis here again! You can get prepared for the media to start hounding you for stories now Pat," he stated seriously. "If you would like, I'll come over and screen the calls for you."

"I-I am shocked. I still can't believe it!" I stuttered, "How did you find out? I wasn't aware of anything consciously. I-uh thought about it this morning,"

"We were tipped off. Someone called the station and told us there would be divers at the City Pier this morning. We sent one of the other newsmen to cover the story. The New London Day was there and the Norwich Bulletin, too", he said.

His voice rambled on to other details. I just couldn't comprehend everything at that moment.

"Pat? Are you listening?" he asked, bringing me back to the reality of the moment.

"Yes. Yes. And please come on over, Dennis." I said and hung up the phone.

As soon as I placed the handset in the cradle of the phone, it would ring again.

"Hello", I answered a bit leery, because of what Dennis had said.

"May I speak to Pat, please?" the masculine soft-spoken voice asked, which I thought I recognized.

"Speaking. Who's calling please?" I asked.

"This is Dick Rainville. I would have called earlier but we have been super busy. I suppose you've heard."

"Yes, just a few minutes ago. I'm still finding it hard to believe!" I commented.

"I owe you an apology and, by the way, a thank you. I want you to understand, Pat, I was told that that area had already been checked. After your visit though, Ed was quite impressed. He did some investigating as soon as you left. When it came right down to it, the divers hadn't gone into that particular vicinity," he said calmly.

"Oh, I see. Well, the main concern right now is for Mrs. Eastman and her family. They will be able to put the pieces of their lives back together, and I am grateful and thankful for that. And you don't owe me an apology, or thanks. I am happy that I was able to help," I answered solemnly.

The three of us sat around the table, Gene, Edie and I. I said a prayer of thanks and Edie and Gene offered their reflections as well. "Thank you Lord, for making me an instrument of Your Divine Love and Mercy. The spirit of Mr. Eastman can now be put to its final resting place. For this I am truly happy." The tears were now flowing. My body shook from all the pent up emotions. All the feelings that had been locked away for nearly two weeks were now being released.

Calls continued to come in. Dennis was there and answered each and every call for us. Dennis screened all of the media calls and said no comments could be released at that time, pending an investigation. Friends called in between and Dennis told those who could to just come over. The house was filled with family and friends; tears of joy were on everyone's faces! Dennis wanted to get an exclusive from me first. He seemed a little hurt that I hadn't told him that I had gone to the State's Attorney's office. I explained that I didn't feel I should, as I didn't want to break any confidences with the detectives. He smiled and seemed to understand.

"You know you can't do a story now, Den," I stated with compassion yet with conviction. "I gave my word that we would wait until the investigation was over."

"Pat. I admire your integrity, but someone has already tipped off the papers and the station. It will only be a matter of time before every news media around starts calling, especially from the AP wire. I would like W-I-C-H to be recognized first with the story," he commented.

"Dennis, you are my friend and I *trust* you. I will give you the story first, I promise." I smiled.

Unfortunately it didn't really work out that way. The next afternoon, the paper from New London had printed the story. They didn't have any details of the case, but they certainly did their homework on me! My name, address and even my place of employment were mentioned.

Dennis called and he was really upset. "I sat on the story because of my friendship with you, but now I guess we'll go ahead with the interview. We will still get credited, because the paper didn't give the important details", he said.

I was pretty upset too. I couldn't understand how a story was printed without permission. I was naïve as to just how the media worked, with ratings, competition and such. I learned very quickly and over the many years, that media can be quite beneficial as well as a deterrent at times.

"I am sorry, Dennis. I don't understand how they could print all that about me, without ever even talking to me." I said.

"Pat. I've been in this business a long time. No one is going to hold you responsible now for any news that will be aired. You have the right to tell your side of the story. You didn't get the media involved in the first place. The person who tipped everyone off said a psychic was involved. How do you think the newsmen that have been calling, got your name? Someone had to tell them. If you remember the broadcast, I said, 'Sources say a psychic was used'. When rumors like that hit the ears of a newsman, they do digging on their own and try to find out any information first, so that the organization they work for is credited. It's more or less considered part of the job. It shows they are performing well. There is also the well-known concept of freedom of the press. The public has a right to know." Dennis said with compassion and warmth.

Dennis asked me if I wanted to go to the station for the interview. I asked him to come to my house instead. I wanted to call the State's Attorney's Office first, to inform them it was going to be on the radio, as I was feeling torn between friendship and obligation.

"I'll be there shortly. Relax and stop worrying," he said and hung up.

Our telephone conversation truly bothered me. The only consolation I felt was that I would speak to Mr. Pickett, and tell him of the situation. If I didn't tell my side of the story, would the media continue to print what they wanted the pubic to know?" I wondered. "They have a right to know the *whole* story."

Dennis arrived and the three of us sat at the dining-room table, Dennis, Gene and I. Dennis had brought a tape recorder and he taped the entire conversation. He wanted to get right back to the station to edit and make clips that he would play during each of the news broadcasts. During our interview, and off the record, Dennis told me that someone informed him that Detective Rainville was a *radio DJ* and moonlighted one night a week. No wonder I sensed so many *speakers* around him!

For at least two weeks, the telephone never stopped ringing. Gene decided that I needed an answering machine, which he purchased for me. The media from everywhere inundated me! All the local newspapers wanted interviews and pictures. The Norwich Bulletin sent a reporter to W-I-C-H, where I had an interview on the Potpourri show, with Stu, in progress.

It was during this time that I had received a telephone call from Bob Bletchman, the attorney I had met at Betty Hill's home. He had left a message on the answering machine, first congratulating me and second to invite us to a party in his home. He asked me to call him back as soon as I could.

More plans and *gifts* were in store! The pebbles on my path were taking me, and all those close to me, and all the persons that we would encounter, to such glorious heights of awareness, experiences and most importantly spiritual revelations, that there are no words to adequately describe the impact it had made on all of our lives!

*   *   *

• Healing, Auras & Direct Voice:

I returned Bob Bletchman's telephone call. He asked if Gene and I would attend a small gathering at his home. He had invited several guests that were quite interested in making my acquaintance. It would be an informal affair, and perhaps I might consider doing some 'readings' as there would be some persons attending in 'need' of my help. The gathering would be in a couple of weeks. It would be another revelation! Another 'gift' from the spirit world! We accepted the invitation.

In the interim, we continued to meditate daily and more astounding revelations were brought to us! News of 'Vincent's' visits had spread quickly among our family and close friends. Many of the persons in our group asked if they could also join us during the week as well as other members of Gene's family. We were delighted to oblige, as spiritual insight would also benefit them.

Wednesday evening. The number of people that were gathered in our home had grown immensely! Besides the regular group of the six of us, were now, Gene's brothers, Frank and John, Gene's sister, Chris and other friends, Carole M., Sue and Edie.

Gene put both extensions in the dining room table and some of the guests brought folding chairs. The table was just large enough to accommodate all 12 of us. It was tight sitting quarters, yet cozy and comfortable.

The dining set, we sat around the table holding hands. Gene and I had spoken earlier and decided it would be a good idea to inform the 'new' members on what to expect, if 'Vincent' were to grace us with his presence.

"It is imperative, first of all," Gene began, "that we keep as quiet as possible. It doesn't take long for Pat to go really deep. I have to tell you the first time it happened, I was a little shaken up. Oh, and before I forget to tell you, expect the room to get quite cold. If you watch Pat, you can also expect a lot of different facial expressions, and sometimes she is crying. If the spirit guide comes through, she makes gestures with her arm too, and her voice changes. We are truly blessed," he smiled, and quickly added, "I won't stand for anyone making any comments or wisecracks," he said, looking straight at Johnny.

John was a younger brother and the 'comedian' in the family. Tonight's experience would give him a lot to think about!

We did our deep breathing exercises, and recited the protection prayer and the 'Lord's Prayer.'

This time while I was in the 'library room', Vincent greeted me with his face exposed. The 'gatekeeper' still remained in the background. I remember smiling and wondering if he *was* Vincent Pallotti. That's all that I remember.

When I 'woke' up, everyone was staring again. Johnny was literally 'white', his face was pale and he just sat like a stone. This is the wonderful enlightenment we were given.

"Greetings, beloved children of the earth plane. I come to you from the realm of Our Lord and Saviour, Jesus Christ. So shall tonight be a night of learning and preparation. There are those here in attendance that believes it is curiosity alone that has brought them here. And so I say it is the deep desire of your spirit to quench its thirst for spiritual knowledge and for the escalation to its soul. This was a request from the spirit prior to its incarnation into your

*physical body. So shall I enlighten you further in time to come. Of your conversations often you refer to all that you have experienced as **coincidence**. And so I tell you, coincidence does not exist in all that is planned from the spiritual realms. As I have stated in times of ere, there is much to be done in the preparation of a physical medium. Those of us here who have the tasks and duties of spiritual intervention with the medium may only offer guidance. You are given at the moment of your birth a precious gift; free will. When you reach the age of reason, the ability to make a choice is yours, by free will. There is much for you to learn on this matter, as there will be a need for you to understand the truth of why persons are borne with afflictions, physically or mentally handicapped and so on. So shall I impart this knowledge when it is necessary for your spiritual growth. Now then, so shall I expound on the matter at hand. In time of ere, I have told you of the power supply that is necessary for the medium to possess, and to what degree, in order to facilitate the need of the spirit that comes in contact with the medium. Of this matter, I am now speaking of a spirit that inhabits the physical body. Soon so shall you experience yet another 'gift' of the medium's ability when releasing and utilizing this ode. So shall you be a witness to God's Greatness in fulfilling the desire of a spirit to escalate on its journey toward God consciousness. May God continue to grant you His Love, Peace and Guidance."*

We had absolutely no idea that the 'gift' he spoke of would be so wonderful and so spiritually powerful that it would *change* the 'faith' of some persons instantly!

*   *   *

It is just a couple of days now before our trip to Bob Bletchman's house. From the night we had first learned Vincent's last name, besides going to the library, I had telephoned the only bookstore in our area that sold religious items, as well as the bookstores in our neighboring towns. No one had anything on Vincent Pallotti. I had to be 'patient' and wait with the *hope* that the library would come through.

I finished with my morning run and went directly home again. My reading appointments had escalated to such a degree that my mornings were filled every day. I allowed myself approximately forty-five minutes before I began with the first appointment.

As soon as I walked into the house, I made it a habit to check the answering machine first. The light was blinking and one of the messages that were left was from a woman at the library! She informed me that a book had been located on *St. Vincent Pallotti* and it would be available at the library on Monday; I could pick it up then! I was so excited! I would just have to be patient, but it wouldn't be easy!

*   *   *

Friday, the day of the party. Bob lived in Manchester, which was about an hour drive away. As we were getting dressed, Gene started talking about some reservations that he was feeling about going there.

"What's his real purpose in wanting you to meet these people?" Gene asked, while fixing his tie.

"What makes you ask that, hon?" I smiled. "Larry speaks very highly of him, they have worked together a long time on UFO investigations."

"I don't know. I just have an uneasy feeling. I am a little uncomfortable," he said. "You know Pat, he is of the *Jewish* religion, probably a lot of the people there will be too," he commented, putting on his jacket.

"I know. I thought about that too, but I don't think that there will be a discussion about 'faith' or our personal beliefs," I smiled, putting on my coat. "And if there is, who knows maybe it will be a *good* thing!" I laughed.

On the drive to Manchester we chitchatted about various personal matters and, of course, my anticipation of picking up the book on Monday at the library. Gene was listening, but he was preoccupied with his own thoughts. He didn't want me to be put on 'display' or any kind of exploitive situation. He was getting agitated almost to the point of wanting to turn the car around and drive back home! I told him it would be all right and we would just rely on our faith and convictions. This was just a small taste of what the 'opposition' tried to accomplish. If we hadn't gone that night, a wonderful experience would not have taken place!

Finally, we arrived. There were cars parked everywhere! "I hope all these people aren't attending his 'small' gathering." I remarked.

"If they are, I would hate to see what he calls a 'large' party!" Gene said, parking across and down the street.

Warm and pleasant greetings passed between the other guests and us. There were eight other couples besides Gene and I. Some of them were Manchester residents; others were from various other areas of Connecticut.

In the first hour of the visit most of the conversations and questions revolved around how I realized my abilities. Gene and I both answered the questions, and we spoke of Vincent. We talked about the contents of his visits, and the fact that I had 'seen' him, but not that he had channeled through me. It was obvious to both of us that some of those present were skeptics. Vincent was precious to us and we would not put ourselves in a position to have to defend *Him* or ourselves.

Bob approached me and asked, "Would you care to give a few readings to a few of the guests? Of course I have told them about your reading with my wife and the accuracy of it. There are a couple of people here that are anxious to 'witness' your abilities. I must warn you though, there are some mighty skeptical spectators here!" he laughed.

I knew that Gene was giving me that, 'I told you' look. I turned and looked him in the eyes and gave my, 'don't worry sweetheart, it will be okay,' look.

"All right, Bob. I will do a couple. But I am not going to do all of them. I don't want to deplete all of my energy. I am not going to go home exhausted." I stated.

"Sure. I understand. I'll send someone out here," he said, pointing to a closed-in porch. "It'll be much quieter in there and you won't be disturbed," he said walking with me to the area.

The room was beautifully decorated, and it had a wonderful atmosphere. It was so peaceful. There were many plants and the furniture looked like it was made to order. It looked like a room out of a home fashion magazine.

"Hi Pat!" a very pleasant woman's voice said upon entering the porch.

"How do you do?" I replied, reaching out and shaking her hand.

"I'm really excited about this! I'm a believer and I see 'mediums' all the time! It fascinates me the 'powers' you people possess!" she exclaimed, sitting down on the sofa.

I didn't like the word 'power'. It was a personal thing, and I wanted to share my views with her. "It's an ability. Not a power. A God-given gift," I said, politely and calmly, gently correcting her. "I offer it as such solely with the purpose of benefiting man emotionally, mentally and spiritually," I smiled. "I will not offer any insight for anyone seeking monetary gain. Also, please don't be concerned about hearing anything from me that you feel you can't handle. If I perceive something in your reading that I feel can be a benefit to you in the hopes of avoiding a detrimental situation, that I will tell you, as perhaps a warning. I will not reveal anything to you that would cause you to have an emotional burden that you can't bear. Okay?" I said, smiling at her and holding her hand.

"Okay!" she grinned. "You need an item, right?" she asked, taking off her watch.

"I will hold onto it just to make a connection with your energy," I smiled, "but I have 'already' picked up on some things just by the sound of your voice," I said, taking the watch from her.

"You have a sister that lives in another state. You haven't seen her in awhile, but you will be making plans very soon to visit each other." I said, smiling at her. "I believe her name is Sharon."

"Yes! Yes! That's incredible! How did you *know* her name?" she shrieked.

I just smiled at her and continued with some very personal information about some problems her sister was having in her marriage and that she should encourage her sister to seek some counseling. I had also revealed some personal information about her life, husband and two children. She was so delighted with her reading, she was crying, and so was I!

She hugged me and asked for my telephone number and then she left the room. In a couple of minutes another person entered the room, a man. He was around my age, tall and slender with brown hair and had nice looking features. It would be an experience that touched our lives forever! And another '*truth*' that we would witness, just as foretold by our beloved Vincent!

"Hi Pat. My name is Reed Kalisher," he said, his handsome face smiling. "I have to tell you, I am pretty skeptical about all of this, but I am willing to give you a shot at it. That other lady was pretty ecstatic about the things you told her and your abilities!" he commented, sitting on the sofa.

"She must have said something to him about the 'power'," I thought to myself and then burst out laughing.

"What's so funny?" he asked, a peculiar look on his face.

"Did she tell you to say that?" I asked grinning.

"No. She was very happy with the information you told her. She said you were very accurate in your information and descriptions," he said.

"No, that's not what I meant," I giggled again, "I mean did she tell you to call it an ability?"

"Why, yes, sort of. As I was walking toward the porch, she mentioned something about, 'Call it an ability'. I didn't get the drift. I still don't. What's so funny?" he asked again, grinning.

"It's nothing really. I just don't like that word 'power'. When she referred to the abilities as power; I just said I prefer the word ability. That's all." I smiled. "It seems as though most people that are uninformed in the area of the paranormal are of the mindset of everything being based on good or evil. It just has a negative connotation, I think."

"I'll certainly remember that myself," he smiled, "but you are right in your sentiments about persons beliefs on good and evil on areas they don't understand. If you can actually see various pictures in your mind, it's logical to assume that part of your brain is activated in an area where others' are not; right?" he grinned.

"More than you realize," I smiled, thinking of the messages and how the 'gifts' really do work. "It is God-given, Reed."

Reed handed me his wedding ring. I did my normal procedure and then began to describe a home and an older woman that meant a great deal to him. I was even given her nickname! I told him about a room in this house, where you could look out of the window and see the overhang of the roof right next to it. The woman was his grandmother and the room is where he stayed when he used to visit her!

"She isn't gone, Reed. She is still around you. There seems to be a concern, how can I help you, Reed?" I asked, compassion filling my voice.

"Can you tell me anything about my health?" he asked.

"I am not a diagnostician, Reed, but I have on many occasions been able to sense pain and symptoms. You asked me about your health, I can tell you this. The whole time I have been holding your ring, I have had no feelings in my legs. From my thighs down to my toes it feels like a sleeping sensation. You know, as if I had hit my funny bone. I know my legs are there, but they feel numb and tingly." I said.

Tears welled up in Reed's eyes. "That's exactly right. I haven't had feelings in my lower extremities for the past eight weeks and..."

"Just a minute, Reed," I interrupted. "Do you know why I am seeing a large stone building with many windows, a statue, and a fountain? As you're talking, I keep seeing this around you."

"No. I don't have any idea. It doesn't mean anything to me. I don't live near anything that fits that description," he answered.

"No. I didn't think you lived by it, I felt more like it is a place you are going to visit." I said, staring into his eyes.

"Really? That will be interesting. Maybe the building has something to do with my New Jersey position, the new job you told me about in the reading, remember?" he asked, with a note of humor in his voice.

"Maybe. Continue with your story please. Excuse me for interrupting, but I felt I had too." I smiled.

"Oh, that's okay. This has been a really interesting evening," he smiled, and continued. "I have been seeing two physicians for about three months now. Only a week ago I underwent a myelogram. The doctors feel I have one of three possible diseases; syringomyelia, Lhermitte's sign or viral myelitis. The fact is the myelogram has shown that I have a swollen spinal cord, which could be symptomatic of any of those. However, because of the numbness from my thighs down, and because the disease has been affecting my arms and hands, the doctors are leaning more toward the syringomyelia. If this is the problem, depending on how advanced it is, it is terminal. I am, in three days going to have one more test done; a scan. They are doing this to show the advancement of the disease. My spinal cord is swollen and continues to swell. As a matter of fact, I am in so much agony tonight, I didn't want to come. Mary, my wife, was so enthused about meeting you, however, that I just couldn't say no," he smiled.

"Reed I am so sorry to hear this. But you know, you were brought here for a reason tonight, a *purpose*. It wasn't just your wife's suggestion, either. I believe there is a God in heaven and that this whole night was part of His plan. I am not professing to be a healer, yet I *feel the need* to pray and do healing passes over you. I 'know' that some persons like myself, possess an inexhaustible amount of energy. I would like to try and use this energy for healing, Reed," I smiled, taking a hold of his hand. I know by the books I have read, these are called passes. A passing of the hands does this procedure over the entire body from head to toe, approximately an inch away from the skin. There is no actual body contact. The book calls them a clearing and healing pass." I said, looking into his eyes. His eyes held a look of doubt, yet I 'sensed' that he wanted me to continue.

"Reed, as I said, I am not claiming to have the gift of healing, but I am willing to try if you are," I said with compassion in my voice.

"Hey, at this point I am willing to try anything. The way I see it, I've got nothing to lose!" he stated.

We walked out into the living room together and took Bob aside and I asked him if Reed and I could go to another room in the house that could offer us total quiet. I told him what Reed and I were going to do and he offered his larger room upstairs. On our way to the stairs, Reed stopped by his wife and whispered in her ear. I looked at her and her eyes instantly filled with tears, as she smiled at me.

We went into a very large bedroom that also had a reading area. There was a small sofa and coffee table littered with magazines.

I walked over to the sofa and motioned for Reed to come and stand next to me. I asked him to close his eyes and that he should say his own prayers.

"I know that you don't believe that the Messiah is here, but coming, Reed. I do. I will be praying to the Lord, Jesus." I said, putting my hands up in the air, closing my eyes and taking a few deep breaths.

I started to say some familiar prayers, and then found myself saying these words, "Lord, make me an instrument of Your Divine Mercy allowing me the healing *energy* necessary to remove this affliction from Reed. If it is meant that he be healed, Thy Will be done. I ask this in Thy Holy Name, Jesus. Amen."

I started the 'pass' on the top of Reed's head and continued to follow the entire outline of his body. A tremendous heat was building in the palms of my hands. I continued praying and did the pass a second time, starting at the top of his head again.

Reed was swaying back and forth slightly, and then suddenly he exclaimed, "I feel so hot! Dizzy! I can feel this strange sensation going through my legs and feet! It's like blood rushing or something-I-uh can't really explain it! The numbness is gone in my legs!!" he blurted, bending over and rubbing them furiously with his hands. "I don't believe this!" he shouted, as tears were rolling down his cheeks.

I watched Reed sit down on the couch and rip his shoe and sock off with much haste. I was feeling quite tired and sat down a couple feet away from him, and began to cry as I watched him take a pen from his jacket pocket and begin to rub the bottom of his foot rapidly back and forth.

He looked at me, tears of joy flowing and exclaimed, "I can feel the bottom of my foot! I couldn't feel anything at all for eight weeks! This is incredible! Absolutely incredible! Bob! Bob come up here!" he shouted.

Bob, Reed's wife, Gene and several other people entered into the room. Reed was exclaiming the experience and we were all in awe and overjoyed.

"You are really something! You've got it, whatever it is! Thank you!" he said beaming and hugging me.

"You're thanking the wrong person, Reed. I am not responsible for the feeling returning to your legs and feet, it's by the Grace of God!" I said with tears pouring from my eyes, as I whispered prayers of gratitude for Reed and his family.

The experience had a great impact on everyone there. Many of the guests knew Reed. They were given much to think about, especially concerning their own beliefs!

On our ride back home, Gene and I discussed all that had happened at Bob's house. He and I were just in awe of all that was happening to us, and our lives. We had no idea of what was still in store, more which was to come! We pondered in depth the meaning of Vincent's last message to us, *'Soon so shall you witness yet another gift, a spirit's escalation on its journey toward God-consciousness.'*

*   *   *

On Saturday night Gene and I couldn't wait to tell the group about the beautiful spiritual experience with Reed, as well as the other events that took place at Bob's.

"It is all just so miraculous," Karen, said, "I think about all that has happened and continues to happen and I just can't comprehend it all."

"Believe me, Kay," I said, calling her by her nickname, "I know exactly what you're saying. When I reflect on everything, it's like watching a movie of my own life." I said solemnly. "I wonder many times, *who am I?* Why is this *happening to me?*"

We prepared our room in its usual manner for our session. Prayer was becoming very important and we always made it a practice before our meditations began. Everything was set. Although each of us tried not to anticipate another visit, it was a hope in all of our minds that we would be 'graced' by *brother* Vincent's presence.

"*Greetings, beloved children of the earth plane. I come to you from the realm of Our Lord and Saviour, Jesus Christ. So shall tonight be a night of learning. In time of ere, I have spoken to you about the existence of ode. So shall I now enlighten you further. Ode is connected to all things, spirit, persons, plants, animals, water and even the air that you breathe. It is in various forms and density, clarity and purity. So shall I give an example, mist and vapor is one form of ode, in a more condensed form, it becomes water. And so if you were to place one drop of water into a container of water, would it not become part of the whole? And the whole is that of God; which is ever present in all creation and thus referred to as the omnipotence of God. Purity and clarity of ode, color and scent, have much to do with the spirit's incarnations, as well as Karma, cause and effect, which has much to do with physical, mental and emotional afflictions as well. This I shall speak of in time to come. So shall I now speak of the matter at hand. Physical mediums that possess insurmountable ode are given the ability, as you have witnessed, to release healthy ode to physically afflicted persons. The healthy, or purer ode cleanses and restores the unhealthy ode, thereby healing the affliction. There is much else to consider, however, with some persons a healing may not occur, depending on the person's free will, attitude and the spirits prior request before incarnation. This I shall speak of in time to come. Your professionals refer to this gift as healing passes over the aura. The aura being the surrounding body around and about an individual. However, the correct term is the odeic body. Gifted persons can see the odeic body and its colors, which enable them to perceive much information about that person. Now then so shall I speak of direct voice, and how it is that the channel allows me to impart my thoughts and words to her. Through her willingness and desire she releases the ode that is necessary for my spirit to utilize the substance of her mind. What are thoughts? Are they not energy? Often you have heard the channel say, 'I don't know why I said that, it just came to my mind.' Soon so shall there be a need for much direct voice attunement. So shall you witness more of the Greatness of God-consciousness. It is also through this same willingness and desire that the channel releases nearly the entirety of her odeic energy so that my spirit may utilize much of the power current to facilitate my visits. Be not concerned that a negative presence shall invade or occupy her physical body, for this is the duty of the gatekeeper to keep the opposition away. However, the opposition will try to utilize this same power source with temptation through free will and thought. So shall you remember, that one negative thought may be replaced by another, a positive thought, the choice is yours. May God continue to grant you His Love, Peace and Guidance."*

We had no idea what Vincent was alluding to for the future or of the magnitude of the impact of *direct voice* in our lives and the lives of virtually hundreds of other persons around the nation!

*　　　　*　　　　*

Monday morning. I could not wait to go to the library to pick up the book.

As soon as my morning bus run was over, I headed straight to the library. There was a parking space available again right in the front of the building. I locked the car and hurried inside. The woman behind the information counter at the front of the library recognized me. By the time I approached her, she already had the book in her hand.

As she was handing me the book, I let out a gasp, "Oh my God!" I shrieked. There on the cover of the book was the **man** I had envisioned in the hospital room and in my meditations!! I stared at it and took in every inch of the description! His head was bald, except for the long gray hair combed back and over his ears. His eyes were deep-set and close together, his nose and thin lips were exact! And he had one arm extended from under his robe and across his chest with two slender fingers pointing upward and his thumb bent under!!

"Are you all right?" she asked, confused and curious about my outburst.

"Uh-yes. Yes. I am okay," I said embarrassed. "Thank you so much for finding this book for me."

"You are welcome. I am glad we were able to help," she smiled, still looking at me as though I was a little peculiar.

I left the library and headed home as quickly as I could. I wouldn't have time to sit and read, but I would peruse as much of the contents as possible. I would have to wait to read it tonight!

Gene and I learned about Vincent together. I read from the book and Gene listened very intently. We could not believe how this man had lived and how great was his devotion to God and to his people. Vincent was born in 1795 in Rome. From the time he was a very young child, he had a reverence and a love for God. His entire life was one of devotion, simplicity and humility. He is called a devoted and selfless servant of God and the Padre of *mystical gifts*. He had the gifts of healing, prophesy, discernment of spirits, and so much more. He was the founder of the Society of the Catholic Apostolate, and he had established many orphanages. He and his colleague and friend, **Bernado Clausi**, who in life, was **short** and **heavy set,** devoted their lives to the service of God. They died within a few short months of each other. Over the years to follow we found more books on St. Vincent Pallotti, one of which is entitled **Give Me Souls**.

We spent a relaxed evening Tuesday. I had prepared a special dinner, Gene's favorites. We were celebrating and giving thanks for all of the wonderful gifts and experiences that our beloved Vincent had brought into our lives. Just as we were about to get ready to retire for the night, the telephone rang.

"Hello," Gene answered. "Reed. Hi! How are you? Fine thanks. Sure. She's right here. I'll put her on," Gene said, handing the phone to me.

I said hello, but there was no response for a few seconds. And then I heard some sniffling.

"Pat. Hello. I just had to call you. I am calling because I want to thank you, and also because my wife and I would like to have you and Gene over for dinner. We are asking you to drive forty miles, but we want to show our appreciation and gratitude," Reed said, solemnly.

"Gratitude? You don't have to show us any gratitude. What's going on, Reed?" I asked.

"What's going on?" he asked, his voice now filled with excitement. "Do you remember telling me about the stone building with the statue and the fountain?"

"I think so. Why, did you see it?" I asked, curiosity rising in my voice.

"I guess I did! It's St. Francis Hospital. I had to go there yesterday for my scan. I got the results a short time ago. You aren't going to believe this! I know, because I am having a hard time accepting it myself! The scan showed that my spinal cord is *completely normal*! The swelling is totally gone! And I still have feeling in my feet! You really are gifted!" he remarked.

"I don't know what to say, but thank You God! I am so happy for you and your family. Both of us are. I don't want you to thank me. I am only a channel. Thank God. I am just so thankful to have been *directed* to you." I said, tears welling in my eyes.

"Please say you will come and have dinner with us. It will make us so happy," he said.

"We'll be happy too. But, I want it understood that it would be a celebration dinner in thanksgiving to God. Okay?" I asked tearfully.

"Yes. Great! How about Friday night, sevenish?" he asked excitedly.

We made the arrangements and Reed gave us directions to their home.

Since the night of that dinner party, which was over 20 years ago, we have all remained close and good friends. Reed is still perfectly healthy and continues to live a full, happy and productive life. The most remarkable outcome of all was Reed's change in attitude. He attended our prayer meetings and meditations as often as he could. He also brought people to our meetings who suffered various health afflictions. One such young woman had a severe case of lupus and was given instant relief of her suffering! That night, a *dripless* candle that we had burning made a long series of snapping and crackling sounds. By the time the meeting had ended, the candle wax had formed into an out-line of a woman holding a bouquet of flowers! We believed that this was a 'sign' of the Blessed Virgin, and that our prayers were answered. Reed and his family have since moved to Florida, but we remain in touch and make plans, when we can, for visits.

We continued with our meditations and the Saturday night group of regulars was now growing. There were 20 and sometimes more people attending, so we moved the location of our meditations to Frank's house, Gene's brother. We also started meeting twice a week, and we changed the days to Monday and Thursday evenings.

The way the 'newcomers' were brought to the group, in and of itself, is miraculous. All of them were *directed* there. Each person had been searching for spiritual knowledge and answers. Each of them had some-thing personal in their lives that wrought some kind of pain. Some had suffered losses of loved ones. Some had personal religious conflicts, while others had physical pain or disease. It was just wonderful to see, and *still is*, the greatness of God-consciousness. Through the intervention of our beloved Vincent, many afflictions were alleviated, emotional suffering was arrested, and personal conflicts were resolved.

*   *   *

• Guardian Angels & Spirit Guides:

Added to our 'regulars' were; Robin B., diagnosed with liver cancer, and her friend, Jackie L., both of them had to travel 40 minutes one way to attend; Valerie W., a lovely woman who has spent her entire adult life on dialysis, and still is, after rejecting multiple kidney transplants. Gene's other sister, Dolores (Del); Steve, Del's son; Cathy, Del's daughter-in-law, Gene's brothers Johnny and Jim, and Kathy, Jim's wife. Other members of our group were John and Arnette Hunter, Jan Grasso, Alice C., and her mom, Lucille, Carole F., Nancy G. and Dr. Nicholas (Nick) Scotto.

Each and every member of the 'Unity', which is what we now named the group, was *guided* to attend. I have been given permission to divulge some of their full names, and their remarkable stories. When Vincent told us '*there is much to do here on the spiritual realms in preparation*' we really had no concept of what he meant. We learned and understood by being witnesses to the magnificent outcome of spiritual intervention.

I need to jump ahead here in order to keep the flow of this chapter and its contents consistent. This will allow you, the reader; to fully grasp the wonderful and loving intervention from the spirit world and how *perfect planning* enriched all of our lives. I promise, there will be *nothing* left out!

I will begin with some of our family members first. My brother-in-law Frank and his wife, Mary, have spent their careers in mental health. Mary is a Registered Nurse, Certified in Psychiatric and Mental Health Nursing and is the supervisor of a crisis service for Southeastern Connecticut. Frank was a Mental Health Worker on an inpatient unit, with 33 years of experience. Their story is one of such profound spiritual revelation, enrichment and devotion, that they still share it to this day!

*　　　　　*　　　　　*

This is Frank and Mary's story:

At 5:30 in the morning, Frank was getting ready for work. Suddenly he experienced sudden and excruciating pain deep in his head. He *knew* what it was, as his good friend had died of the same affliction a few years earlier, an aneurysm. He woke Mary to take him to the hospital, as he waited for her, he sat on the sofa and prayed the rosary.

At the ER, Frank underwent tests, including a CT scan and neurological exam. Frank's brother, Bill, had joined Mary at the hospital. Dr. Sculco, a neurosurgeon, made the diagnosis. He took Mary and Bill into another room to explain.

"We need to be fatalistic about this," he said. "Frank has had an aneurysm partially rupture deep in his brain, in the area of the pons and the medulla. The build up of pressure from the blood in this area will cut off the vital functions of his brain. The aneurysm has leaked out a pool of blood, which can be seen on the CT scan. It could completely rupture at any time and he will die instantly, or he could remain as he is, and slowly fade away."

Dr. Sculco offered to have Frank transferred to a major medical center in order to have a neurological specialist evaluate the aneurysm in case surgery could be done to clip the bleeding vessel. Mary chose Hartford Hospital. Joined by Frank's three adult children, Mary sat in a waiting room while testing was being done. The surgeon, Dr. Goldman, told them ahead of time that there was a 70% chance that Frank wouldn't survive the test, that the pressure of the dye being injected would likely burst the leaky aneurysm. But, to Dr. Goldman's amazement, Frank *did survive*! And to Dr. Goldman's further baffling—while the pool of blood remained in Frank's mid-brain, the aneurysm itself *was totally gone*! It could not be seen at all in the arteriogram! Frank remained at Hartford Hospital's neurological ICU for a few days, in deep sedation for pain, photosensitive, and suffering from reactions to the pain medications. He was transferred back to the Backus Hospital in Norwich, and the blood began to be reabsorbed in his body, the pressure on his brain decreased, and the intensity of his pain decreased as well. After two weeks, Dr. Sculco released Frank. He told Mary, "You live close to the hospital if anything happens. If the aneurysm ruptures, he will be dead before we can get him to the O.R., even if he was here at the hospital." So an ambulance brought him home, with instructions that he was to remain in bed, only up to go to the bathroom. But Frank continued to improve and within just a *few days* was walking about, sitting outdoors, sleeping less, and taking less pain medication! Frank went back to Hartford Hospital where he underwent a second angiogram to locate the aneurysm. There was none to be found! Frank returned to work before Christmas. In December quite a few members of our family went to the Elk's Lodge for a New Year's Eve celebration. I approached Frank and said, "Frank you need to meet me at my office, as soon as possible." A couple of days had passed, and we all gathered at my office in the evening, Frank, Mary, Chris, Del and me. Gene had to work. There was a recliner in my office, and I was *guided* to lie down and go into a deep trance. Our beloved Vincent, through channeling, brought Frank this astounding message!

"Greetings my beloved children of the earth plane. I come to you from the realm of Our Lord and Saviour, Jesus Christ. And so tonight shall be a night of learning. I shall explain in detail the events that have taken place with the one called Frank. And so my brother, you have witnessed the Greatness of God-consciousness. For sent to you was a holy spirit of the highest order that healed you of your affliction so rapidly. And to the one called Mary, so have you blocked from your memory the location of this affliction. And so it was in the pons, the menganese and the medulla. My brother, why do you fear reoccurrence? There will be none. And so of your faith and the many prayers that have been offered in request of your recovery, so were you granted an extension of your physical life. So shall you read Kings II, chapter 20. In this reading so shall you learn of a dying king who was granted an extension to his physical life for the Glory of God. May all of you continue to be granted God's Love, Peace and Guidance."

For Mary, the words that she had heard from our Beloved Vincent were concrete evidence of the veracity of this communication, as *no one* but she and Bill had been present when Dr. Sculco had described the location of the aneurysm nor had she or Bill revealed them to *anyone* else. Vincent revealed the aneurysm's entire location in Frank's brain! And *only* Frank knew his fear of another episode! That was sixteen years ago! To this day, Frank is still completely well and has had no side effects from the aneurysm at all! Our lesson learned here, the spirit world is with us and watches over us even in our darkest moments, and there is tremendous power in prayer.

*   *   *

This is Del's story:

When Del first started attending the 'Unity,' as our prayer group came to be known, she had some concerns and pangs of *guilt* about being there and participating because the group was not formed under the auspices of the Catholic Church.

However, she and Chris had for many years shared a healthy curiosity and sought after whatever was available concerning the paranormal. They wanted to learn everything from crystal balls, to ghosts, guardian angels, and had even attended one service of a religious order that purportedly was officiated by persons who claimed to obtain information from inhabitants of another planet. Del could not have known back then that her healthy *curiosity* would be sated once and for all, that her *guilt* would instantly be alleviated and all of us would benefit by the contents of the revelation and the experience we all shared!

"Greetings my beloved children of the earth plane. I come to you from the realm of Our Lord and Saviour, Jesus Christ. And so tonight shall be a night of learning and experience. So shall impart the knowledge concerning spiritual guides. And so shall you learn of the truth of that which you seek and quench your spirits thirst for knowledge. In times of ere, so I have told you of the properties concerning ode and the connection of this current to all things in your physical world and in the spiritual world as well. First so shall I remind you, the purity of the ode determines its scent, form and color in all matters, physical and spiritual. Spirits have form, but are not limited by time and space. Your human bodies are shaped exactly as the spirit that inhabits it. Contrary to other beliefs, it is the spirit that creates the physical body with the aid of ode. How is it then, if it were otherwise, that the Arch Angels could recognize one another? The higher the evolution of the spirit determines the characteristics and form of the physical body. If the spirit is closer to God-consciousness, so then the physical body that it inhabits emanates this beauty, as well as scent and color. Beauty is harmony, the lack thereof is unsightly, this is a law that pertains to all creation. Think then of all the animals that roam the earth, and how hideous some of these creatures may be. The scent is

determined in the same way, the purer the ode, the sweeter the fragrance, and vice versa. Now for the matter at hand, in time of ere, I have spoken to you about the age of reason, which is seven to eight of your physical years. It is at this time spirit guides are sent to individuals that are able to make conscious choices concerning attitude and actions. The option of right or positive influence, or wrong or negative influence rests solely with the individual's acts of free will. So shall I enlighten you further in time to come. And now for the one known as Dolores, often you have asked about spiritual guides, and your wish to see one of us. That which you have asked in earnest, first so shall I say, 'Call unto me, and I will answer you, and show you great and mighty things which you did not know.' (Jeremiah 33:3) And so shall you all now witness spirit energy in one form, color and scent. May God continue to grant all of you His Love, Peace and Guidance."

When I opened my eyes, everyone in the room was crying, and intently tuned in on Del. In her mind's eye, she *had seen* Bernard! She was crying and trying to tell us how clear his image was! She said she could *feel* his love, and the words in the scripture brought her peace and understanding removing all doubts! And then another grace was given to us! Through direct-voice, I was *told* that a spirit form, 'Mary', would 'appear' in the room, and to have everyone look up in the corner of the dining room entrance. All eyes went immediately to the top and left of the entrance. Suddenly there appeared a beautiful brilliant glowing ball of blue light! It was about the size of a basketball. It moved away from the entrance, and came toward us. The scent that filled the room was like cinnamon and tangerines! It was absolutely incredible! As it slowly moved closer to the dining room table, I said, "Watch the chandelier, *she* is going to turn the lights on and off three times, for those of you who can't see her!" The fixture above the table was on a dimmer switch. It went completely off and then from the dimmest lighting to the brightest lighting, three times! Frank was the only one who couldn't physically see it, and he was mentally praying to experience something more. In that instant the spirit moved rapidly toward and then right through him, nearly knocking him to the floor! And then *she* was gone! It was an experience that humbled all of us, and one we would never forget and share to this day.

*   *   *

This is Steve's story:

When Steve had *thoughts* of coming to the Unity, he was going through a very rough time emotionally. He had been divorced from his wife, Sandy, and was suffering from much guilt over the separation from his daughter, Michelle. Steve was also searching for answers to a tragic accident that happened in his life that nearly cost him his life. It was his need for direction in his life that brought him to the group. Steve plays guitar, and his music provided a perfect vibration of harmony for the singing part of our meetings. The insightful message that he received again benefited all of us.

"Greetings my beloved children of the earth plane. I come to you from the realm of Our Lord and Saviour, Jesus Christ. And so shall tonight be a night of learning.

There are those of you here who have questions pertaining to your physical lives, and if then there is a purpose, what is it? And so I say, there is only one purpose, and that is for the escalation of your spirit to return to God-consciousness, as pure as it was at the onset of its creation. The Divine Design is without flaw and so shall I give an example in as simplest an explanation as possible so that you may comprehend. In time of ere, so have I explained of spirit guides, and tasks and duties thereof. To the one known as Steve, so you have questioned, was it a guardian angel that saved your physical life? So that you may understand, so shall I first make this analogy. The spirit world follows an order in much the same way as the physical world. We too follow a chain of command, such as the leaders of your government, to the chain of command exercised in your education. We as spirit guides are the teachers, the guardian angels, the superintendents. Contrary to what some authors have written, guardian angels are not with persons on a daily basis. The duties of the guardian angels are to protect the spirit as it proceeds along its journey of the physical life and to intercede only in situations such as that which you experienced when you were struck by massive bolts of electricity and left totally unscathed. And to further enlighten, so shall I repeat, the Divine Design is without flaw. The purpose of physical life is solely for the benefit of the spirit, which inhabits it. The spirit needs to learn and experience all that it can in the physical body for the escalation toward the soul, which rests in the Kingdom of God in all its purity. Your soul is the sheath of your spirit. When your soul was created, it was created in the magnificence and purity of God-consciousness; it is the blueprint of which the spirit was designed. When the spirit has achieved its nearness to God, then it no longer must incarnate and unites with its soul in God's Kingdom. So shall I enlighten you further in time to come on reincarnation and the hall of records. May God continue to grant you His Love, Peace and Guidance."

All of us were again in awe and very emotional. It took Steve quite awhile to regain his composure before he could talk to the rest of us. The experience that he had the day he was electrocuted was beyond the shadow of any doubt, *'miraculous'*!

Steve had purchased a kite for his daughter, Michelle. Someone that worked at a local shipyard had given Steve a roll of what he thought was thick cord material. Steve didn't know that the cord was lined inside with thin wire. He took his daughter to a field located across the street from where he lived to fly the kite. The kite flew toward a transformer and became entangled in the wires. The tremendous amount of voltage that went through Steve should have claimed his life. The electricity went threw his hands, arms and legs and out of his feet. There was so much power that a circle of fire started in the grass around him. The soles of his shoes were completely burned off and the top of one of his shoes was blown off! Steve didn't suffer any burns, injuries or any complications at all! Since the night of that powerful message, Steve has offered his talent of playing the guitar back to God as his way of giving thanks and praise and to glorify His Name.

*   *   *

• Soul Mates: Near Death Experience, Records, and Reincarnation & Karma:

On this particular night, before going into meditation and channeling, I had a question on my mind pertaining to near death experience and the 'library'. This was the revelation given to us about near death experience, and the records of life.

"Greetings beloved children of the earth plane. I come to you from the realm of Our Lord and Saviour, Jesus Christ. And so tonight shall be a night of learning. So it is that the channel has asked for enlightenment of the truth concerning what you term as near death experience, and so shall I impart of this knowledge. In time of ere, so I have explained of the different spheres of the spiritual realms. So I have touched upon odeic vibrations, color and scent. So shall I now enlighten you further. Often you have heard the channel speak of the 'colors' that she witnesses of her mind's eye. And so it is that when her own spirit combines with the ode of the spiritual realms, so does it pass through these spiritual spheres, thus attuning to each of the vibrations of these levels which consists of brilliance of color, scent and sound. So shall I impart the knowledge of those who give testimony of near death experience. So have you heard claims of those who have envisioned tunnels, brilliance of color and the white light. So it is that the spirit is making the same attunement, traveling through the spiritual spheres and ultimately reaching God-consciousness. Since the spirit is still attached to the physical body, so it returns with the knowledge and imparts its experience to the conscious mind. So also can the ode of the spirit attune to the odeic energy of the sphere from which it incarnated from in a previous life. Hence, it can obtain some knowledge of that life and bring it back to the subconscious in its present physical life. Each and every action, word, thought and deed of every physical life is recorded in the spiritual library. Thus you have heard in some of these testimonies, 'my life flashed before me.' So too have there been testimony of those who have had near death experience and have revealed horrifying tales. So it is that the spirit attuned to

the sphere of a previous incarnation from the lesser realms, and brought back with it some of its spiritual memory. May God continue to grant all of you His Peace, Love and Guidance."

That revelation satisfied all of our questions, not just mine, about near death experience, colors, and the 'library'. I hope it has for you as well.

*   *   *

This is Nick's story:

Nick met Mary while he was doing his residency at the hospital where Mary and Frank were employed. He just *happened* to be placed on the same wing that Mary worked on. One day both Nick and Mary *wound up* in the medical staff's lounge, sharing lunch together. Over lunch a conversation ensued between the two of them. At first the chat was about general 'getting acquainted' talk, but Nick found himself telling Mary about this *compulsive search* he had to find out the *truth* about mental illness. This need was the main reason he wanted to become a neuro-psychiatrist. He told Mary about a colleague of his that had committed suicide and the effects his death had on him, emotionally, mentally and spiritually. Nick explained that he had always been curious about spiritual matters and that his curiosity now led him on the path of learning about Buddhism, and the *need* he had to *experience* whatever he could to find answers. Mary, *knowing* it wasn't *coincidence* that the two of them met, invited Nick to our group. She briefed him that the group had a psychic that channeled information that he would probably find quite profound and may provide some answers to his questions. However, again *we* would experience and benefit by magnificent planning and the knowledge provided through the intervention of the spirit world!

*   *   *

The first night Nick joined the group he entered into the house and walked into the dining room where several of the group members were seated around the table. I was in the living room preparing the spiritual music tapes that we would listen to softly in the background, while we engaged in our prayers. When I walked into the dining room to be introduced, Nick turned to look at me, and when our eyes connected, there was an electric shock that was felt by both of us! Nick exclaimed, "You're Pat! You *must* be! I don't believe this!" Nick explained that he had gone shopping a week or so earlier, to pick up some decorations for the walls in his living quarters at the hospital. While he was in the home fashions department of the store, there was a poster type picture in a brass colored frame that was hanging on a wall amidst thirty or more of similar type pictures. He said he looked at all of the different posters one particular picture seemed to *jump* out at him. He tried to ignore the strong impulse to buy it, but he couldn't. He walked away and went to several other departments, but ultimately returned to that department and purchased that picture and took it back to his residence and hung it on the wall. He just kept staring at me the entire time he told this story. The connection between us was so *strong* it was uncanny! It was nothing physical; it was a much deeper spiritual connection. "*You*! It's *your* face in my picture!" he exclaimed. The next week, Nick purchased the identical picture for me, and the resemblance was remarkable! Even though it was a sketched type drawing, the artist certainly could have used my face as the model! There is much more to this story and the spiritual connection that Nick and I share. I will explain some of the experiences. Nick and I were able to finish one another's sentences. We would always pick up the telephone at the same time to call one another to share a spiritual experience that we both had. We could 'hear' each other's voices in our minds and *knew* exactly what each other's thoughts were. The most remarkable experience was the day I was driving in my car at approximately 2:10 in the afternoon, and I *heard* Nick asking me to call him, and the scent of his shaving lotion filled the entire car! I mentally sent him a message that I could not call at that time. Later, when I arrived home, he had left a message on my answering machine, telling me that at exactly 2:15 he *heard* me telling him I couldn't talk to him at that time. Many people associate the term 'soul mate' with romantic relationships. However, the true definition was explained to us. This is the message we received from our Beloved Vincent.

"Greetings my beloved children of the earth plane. I come to you from the realm of Our Lord and Saviour, Jesus Christ. And so tonight shall be a night of learning. And so I say there have been questions concerning that which you term as soul mates, so shall I expound on this matter and enlighten in this area. First so shall I say, there are male and female spirits in spirit-creation. They are perfectly matched according to God's law and are equal in amount. They share happily in the tasks that God has assigned to them. The correct term is double or twin spirits which means 'two who belong to each other', so shall you read; 'look upon the works of the Most High and there are two and two who are allotted to each other,' (Ecclesiasticus 33: 14). And so as I have stated, their works are united for the Greater Glory of God. To the one called, Nick, so I say, you have experienced with the channel, much of your spirit's familiarities and the connection thereof. Of your chosen profession and the knowledge that may be shared, so shall you be enlightened of that which you seek concerning mental illness and your quest for truth concerning God and the spirit world. So shall you be given in time to come, the understanding of negative influence from the opposition and its effects both physically and spiritually. So I say much of the journey is predestined of your physical lives, 'Whatever happens has been determined long ago,' (Ecclesiastes 6:10). Not all that an individual suffers is fate; much has to do with the acts of freewill. 'All the days of my life were foreseen by thee and set down in the book, all that took shape, all that was assigned to me and everyone of them was mine,' (Psalms 139:16). There is a general path and certain turning points that are predestined; at these crossroads it is then, by freewill, the individuals choice. Life has but one purpose that has been carefully planned, and that is to bring the spirit closer to God-consciousness. The path of life is filled with tests, and trials. At

the end death awaits. Depending on the course one has chosen, will determine the spirits escalation in the hereafter until it reunites with its soul in union with God. If there is failure then the spirit incarnates again. There is much to learn of this matter concerning natural causes of death and suicide. So shall I enlighten you further in time to come. May God continue to grant all of you His Love, Peace and Guidance."

After this magnificent enlightenment, Nick shared a lot of his personal feelings, his questions and curiosities about paranormal phenomenon, as well as his questions concerning the mentally ill. Since he, Frank, Mary and Del were all associated with the mental health field (*coincidence?*) they all shared a need to *know* if there was a connection with mental illness and the spirit world. If there was a connection, what was it? Often times we have said the words, 'God's Infinite Wisdom', and you yourself have probably said it, or have heard it too, but just like most everything else in life, experience is the best teacher. For us, it was so apparent that God in His Infinite Wisdom knew that we were not capable with our limited knowledge to truly understand; therefore we were always given the experience first, and received the profound enlightenments afterwards.

Again, through perfect planning of the spirit world, we would be given the understanding of reincarnation and karma, cause and effect.

Frank worked on a different unit than Mary and Nick. Two new patients *were transferred* onto Frank's unit, and Frank provided care for a little over a week. One of these patients, I will call him, John, was diagnosed with a paranoid schizophrenic disorder, as well as an antisocial personality disorder. This patient claimed to 'hear' voices and displayed random acts of violence. He was considered very dangerous, as he had murdered a relative, and at times he needed to be confined to a room and bound in what is termed as 'physical restraints,' which constrained his arms and legs. Frank, on a couple of occasions, had prolonged interactions in which he looked directly into John's eyes. Frank shared the story with us, after this revelation from our Beloved Vincent.

"*Greetings my beloved children of the earth plane. I come to you from the realm of Our Lord and Saviour, Jesus Christ. And so tonight shall be a night of learning. In time of ere, so have I told you of the opposition, influence of the negative realms; fallen spirits that have chosen to follow under the rule of Lucifer. So shall I enlighten you further on this matter in time to come. As I have also stated, laws governing your material world, apply to the spirit world as well. So have there been revolts and wars waged in our world, carefully planned and carried out, such as in the physical world. The fallen spirits are at liberty to tempt and corrupt individuals using their influence in anyway as the individual allows, through choices of freewill. So shall I also explain karma, cause and effect as to quench your spirits thirst of this knowledge. So shall I first say consider karma as the circumstance, cause and effect as action and reaction, as to better understand. All that you say and all that you do applies to this analogy. As I have stated in time of ere, the purpose of life is to bring the spirit closer to God-consciousness; if then an incarnated spirit follows a path of continuous sin in a physical lifetime, then it has incurred more karma and will return in as many lifetimes as necessary until it becomes good karma. Karma may effect more than just one incarnated spirit, there may be individuals that share a karma; example if in one lifetime two individuals have committed crimes against one another, so it may be in a next life, the spirits incarnate in different physical bodies, each as the other, but neither recognizing, and if both follow a path to God-consciousness the karma is finished. This applies to both good and bad karma. And to the one called Frank, so have you experienced looking into the void, the tunnel of despair, a spirit that reigns in what you term as limbo or purgatory. Of that which I speak, is the one called, 'W.J.' So shall I expound of this matter. Until your men of science concede and accept the existence of the spirit world, both good and evil, so shall they continue to explore and research in the wrong direction. Those that do not fear ridicule and take the right action will ultimately help the spirit trapped in this state and enable it to progress on its journey toward God-consciousness. And so you have at your disposal charts recording this man's actions since early childhood. So shall you learn that from the age of reason, through freewill he allowed opposition to rule over his physical life. The spirit that once inhabited this physical body became overpowered by the opposition; thus is lost in the void. Through the power in prayer, which elevates spirits consciousness, it may regain control over the body and continue on the path toward God. Much depends on what the spirit had experienced from previous incarnated lives, the karma that it may have incurred, which is now evident in the effects of this physical life. In time of ere, so I have also explained, spirits are not limited by time and space, so shall you read, 'One day is with the Lord as a thousand years, and a thousand years as one day.' (2nd Peter 3:8). May God continue to grant all of you His Love, Peace and Guidance."*

Frank was in total awe! First of all he had never spoken to any of us about the transfer of these patients, let alone mention their names! Patient confidentiality was something he honored diligently in his professional and personal life as well. Maintaining that confidentiality he told us the story. Frank had told us that when he looked into the eyes of his patient, he saw sheer emptiness and darkness. He described it as similar to looking into a deep pit, seeing nothing but emptiness, darkness with no bottom. He said that it sent shivers through his entire body. When he heard the word 'void' used by Vincent, he understood perfectly what he meant. It was another magnificent enlightenment for all of us. We also continued to offer prayers for this patient and others, at each meeting.

*　　　　　*　　　　　*

• Life Between Life & Afflictions:

These are combined stories of Robin, Val, Cathy, Jan & Kathy G.:

All of their accounts are remarkable each and of themselves, however, they all share a common bond. All of them were, and some still are, physically ill. We have since lost Robin, but it is a story of happy tears. We miss her physical presence, but *knowing* what happened to her spirit, gave us wonderful peace and joy!

Robin was a client of mine. Knowing her pain and suffering and her doubts concerning spirituality, as well as her distrust of humankind in general, I invited her to attend our Unity. She attended for nearly six months and her visits were pretty regular. She and her friend, Jackie, (who drove) only attended on Monday nights, but they were usually present every week. Robin suffered from liver cancer and the drive took its toll on her physically, but the peace, comfort and love that she felt would rejuvenate her and kept her coming back.

Jan has been a friend of mine for over 20 years. She was also searching for answers and has been a member of our group since the beginning. Jan developed a very serious condition in her esophagus. She was at the point where she couldn't even swallow water. She made an appointment with Dr. B., and went through a test called an endoscopy, that involved a long tube with a light and camera on the end of it, which was inserted through her mouth. The test revealed that her esophagus was almost completely closed off from scar tissue damage from gastric reflux acid burns. He scheduled her for one more pre-op scan to 'show' him the exact location of the problem and how much surgery would be involved. He prepared Jan; he would have to 'rebuild her esophagus.'

Val has no kidneys. She has been the recipient of two transplants, both ow which failed. Valerie was also a client first and was invited to our group. The length of time that Valerie has been on dialysis, which continues to this day, is very rarely heard of. It has been over 20 years. Her story is one of tremendous faith and trust.

Cathy D., joined our group shortly after it began. She had been a healthy, young and vibrant mother. Shortly thereafter, she began to suffer headaches, dizziness and loss of balance and coordination. Cathy sought the help of many doctors in the hope of finding out what was ailing her. One doctor suggested that she see a psychiatrist, as there was nothing physically wrong with her! Her story is not only incredible, but intervention from the spirit world proved to be absolutely critical in her life. I am sure it will have quite an impact on you.

Vincent personally invited Kathy G., along with her husband Jim, to our group. Kathy and Jim's accounts are also remarkable, and the intervention from the spirit world once again benefited all of us. However, her faith, devotion and gratitude to God serve as an example of standing firm in time of temptation and trial.

Kathy developed breast cancer after joining the group. After she was diagnosed she was given radiation treatment. Shortly thereafter the cancer was found to have metastasized. She was placed on four different series of chemotherapy. The oncologists prepared Kathy and Jim both; her life expectancy was limited to two years. Kathy was now faced with making a life threatening decision. She could allow the disease to take its natural course or undergo an experimental stem cell transplant; with the hope the transplant may add some years to her life. The transplant procedure could take her life due to the complications of the treatment.

*　　　　　*　　　　　*

This is Nancy's story:

Nancy G. attended our group initially at the encouragement of her friend, Arnette Hunter. Nancy had lost a young daughter to drowning in a terrible boating accident. Nancy had sought consolation for over five years, since the accident, through conventional counseling to try to come to terms with her loss. It didn't help her. Her pain and suffering continued on a daily basis. Not only was she given understanding, Nancy was also given proof positive concerning life and after life, through the intervention of the spirit world by the message she received from *her daughter* who crossed over!

I will share the rest of these stories following this message.

"Greetings my beloved children of the earth plane. I come to you from the realm of Our Lord and Saviour, Jesus Christ. So shall tonight be a night of learning and experience. In time of ere, so have I explained karma, so shall I enlighten you further of this matter. So shall I speak of your spirits requests prior to its incarnation of your material bodies and the lives you lead today.

Much of which I impart to you, I trust you will rely upon faith in your understanding, knowing all that I have told you is of truth. Much of the contents in the Bibles of today contain erroneous information. In the translations of eons ago, words were omitted; statements were changed, some completely deleted, as this was the work of fallen spirits at the hands of the authors. So shall I say there is little to be found in the New Testament concerning reincarnation and the creation of the spirit world, however, Paul, the Apostle, eludes to these truths through the letters, so shall you read, 'Roman 8: 19-24'. In this passage he speaks of the entire creation, the spirit world and the physical world, which means the plants, flowers, animals and men, all of creation. Thus as I have said, spirit inhabits all things clothed in different shapes and matter. As I have told you in time of ere, the purpose of all life is for the spirit to return to God-consciousness in all its purity. Now then for the matter at hand; at the moment of physical death, the band of ode is severed completely and the spirit is released. There are thirteen spheres in the spirit world. The lowest is what you term as 'Hell', but there is progress in this sphere as well. A spirit that has a change of heart will continue upward from this realm. Be not misled here, spirits that incarnate, do so from one form to the same form, they do not regress. A spirit in man, does not re-incarnate to plant form. Each progression depends on the spirits willingness to follow the act given to it by God-consciousness, prior to the incarnation. Also it may be that spirit will remain in one of these spheres performing tasks or duties before incarnating again into the physical body. In the case of afflictions, so it was that the spirit requested to experience pain and suffering, as to escalate quicker through these spirit realms, thus having less incarnated physical lives. So then when you ask why is this innocent child borne with such handicaps, or why has this young person suffered such a horrible death, so shall you realize it is for the escalation of that spirit and its nearness to God. When afflictions are healed, and lives are extended, so it is to give thanks and to Glorify God and spread the news of His Good Works. As for the one called Jan, so shall you experience this night, the Greatness of God! And so shall I leave you with these words, 'And yet what we say is true wisdom, although it is such only in the eyes

of those who are ripe to receive it.' So shall you read, '1ˢᵗ Corinthians 2: 6,7'.
May God continue to grant all of you His Love, Peace and Guidance."

I was again utilized as an instrument and performed healing passes over Jan. She was instantly healed that night! When she returned to Dr. B's office, and the scan was completed, Dr. B. could find absolutely *no trace* of any obstructions in her esophagus! Dr. B. commented that he *knew* he hadn't read the wrong tests. There had previously been an obstruction; he was perplexed. Jan asked him if he believed in the power of prayer, and in God. Jokingly he smiled and said that he prayed every month to meet his bills. There was no surgery and she continues her life in good health.

Val grew in her spirituality, and felt comforted in knowing that *she*, her spirit, was drawing nearer to God-consciousness. She continues to this day, sharing the *good news*. Val has been granted many of her prayers, first and foremost an extension of her physical life, and then the joy of becoming a mother. She could not have a child biologically, however, she and her husband were able to adopt a beautiful infant daughter, who has grown into a lovely young teenager.

My sister-in-law Kathy still continues to baffle science and the medicine as well. On many occasions she received physical intervention from the spirit world. A couple of evenings prior to Kathy's visit to her oncologist, Vincent revealed to her exactly what to expect if she were to choose to have the stem cell transplant. He told her that the first ten months would be the most difficult. He also told her there would be a new medicine introduced within the first three months and she would be a recipient for this drug. He encouraged her to rely on her faith and trust in that matter. As it turned out, Kathy did have the stem cell transplant; she physically suffered greatly within the first ten months. However, within the first three months, a *new drug*, 'gemcitabine' was introduced. As an experimental drug, recipients were to be selected by lottery. This meant a list of potential patients from all over the state of Connecticut would be put in a computer and only *two* names would be picked at *random.* Kathy *was* selected as a recipient! Kathy continues to astound and baffle the medical team, and her faith is unshakeable! She remains as a constant reminder to all of us, when the 'opposition' tries to weaken our defenses, to hold firm of faith.

A valuable lesson learned from this is and understanding that there is Karma behind illness and suffering helps us to accept it and be at peace in our suffering. Asking for the grace of God in our suffering allows us to harvest the fruits of it, to learn the lessons contained in that suffering. This is why some victims of illness often are grateful for their illness, as the spiritual benefits can far outweigh the physical cost.

Cathy D. suffered from headaches, dizziness, and nausea for three months. She had appointments with three different doctors; the third doctor recommended that Cathy see a psychiatrist, as 'there is nothing wrong with you physically'. One night in-group, and through me, Vincent told Cathy she would visit with a neuro-surgeon and it would be discovered that she did in fact have a brain tumor and that the location of the tumor would be difficult to perform for *their* surgical team. However, there would also be a *surgical team* from the *spirit world* that would intervene utilizing combined ode! And that is exactly what happened. Cathy had a tumor; the surgeon explained that the tumor had 'legs' and in the areas of the brain where these 'legs' were located, made surgery very difficult. Cathy entered into the surgery with faith, confidence and trust. The surgery was a success! Her story does not end here. She was still to witness the Greatness of God, in His Compassion and Love, and so would we.

In the interim some of us were planning a trip to Sedona, Arizona. We had heard about the vortexes there and we wanted to visit as a group. Again we would all share in the magnificent intervention from the spirit world!

Frank and Mary had just returned from a trip to Disneyworld in Florida. One week later, Gene and I were visiting at their home and telling them about our plans to go to Arizona. We were sitting at the dining room table and talking about how *we* were going to try and arrange the trip.

Frank and Mary both were expressing how 'there is no way for us to go now' as there wouldn't be anyone to watch the twins and money was tight. Frank said, "It would take a miracle for us to be able to go." He had no sooner said the words when there was a knock at the kitchen door and Mary's dad entered in. This was a complete surprise as unannounced visits were not his habit. He walked right into the dining room and said, "What's going on here? Planning a trip? How can I help?" Then he looked straight at Mary and said, "Do you need a sitter?" Mary looked at her dad totally astonished. When she asked him, why he stopped in and how did he know about the trip, he simply said, "I was passing by and *something told me to stop*, I didn't know about the trip, it just *came into my mind!*"

To say we were flabbergasted is an understatement! That was that! Frank and Mary would be going! Sixteen of us made reservations for the trip! There were absolutely no problems with anyone getting time off, or babysitters' expenses, or whatever else may have stood in the way!

Cathy wanted so much to go with us. She was still recuperating from her surgery and the trip to Arizona would have been too difficult for her physically. We would be climbing mountains and trudging through some rough terrain. The look of disappointment on her face tore at all of our heartstrings.

That next week, Del and Cathy went to a service in Worcester, Massachusetts. There is a well-known priest there who is utilized as a healing minister. Crowds of people from virtually every state on the east coast attend the services. At this particular service the number of persons in attendance was approximately two thousand. There was also a raffle; the first prize, an all expenses paid trip to Disneyworld. Yes, Cathy won! *Coincidence?* Never!

Nancy's daughter, I will call her, Lori, crossed over at the young age of 18. Her death caused Nancy, and other members of her family, extreme anguish, spiritual doubts and the constant unanswered question of 'why?' Along with the wonderful insightful message from Vincent, Nancy was also able to 'hear' from her daughter, via direct-voice through me. The information that 'Lori' revealed brought instant relief to Nancy's emotional pain and suffering. From that night on, Nancy has been able to 'let her daughter go' and continue on her spiritual journey. These are the remarkable events that took place:

Told through me, 'Lori' wanted her to remember a time when they all lived on the island. She was to recall the black and white cocker spaniel, the long dock and 'Lori's' bicycle. At these words, Nancy started to cry. She was also to remember the bangles, baubles and beads that meant so much to her daughter. Lori also told her that *'where I am now, I never have to be concerned about time'*. She also encouraged Nancy to live in happiness and in the joy of knowing that she is not 'gone' from her, only her physical body is absent.

Only Nancy knew of these very personal and touching episodes, while her daughter was alive and with her. She told us of the jewelry that Lori loved that belonged to her grandmother, which she had always referred to as *bangles, baubles and beads*. The dock, cocker spaniel and the bicycle was another situation that brought Nancy tears of joy and *proof* that only Lori could provide. She had thrown the bicycle from the dock into the water one day in an impetuous mood, and hadn't told Nancy about it for a long time. The cocker spaniel was a pet that was loved deeply, and had also died. Lori was conveying to Nancy that they were both together now. The reference to 'time' was that while Lori was in the physical, she was always late. No matter how hard she tried, she was always rushing. Nancy recalled that she was always bounding down the stairs and out of the door. This revelation satisfied Nancy and she was able to enjoy the memories of her daughter, pain free and her questions finally answered.

Robin was a very quiet person. She confided only in me, until after her death. Then one week after she crossed over from the physical into the spiritual, her spirit, utilizing me through automatic writing, graced us with this beautiful poem. All of us thank God for the peace He gave her and for the spiritual comfort she received. According to Robin's sister, this poem has brought consolation to the family as well.

"The Rescue"
I hear their weeping, their sorrow and pain.
If only I could speak, I would tell them to refrain.
For though I am here appearing lifeless and still;
My heart is racing and my life force is in His will.
He came on a white horse with such speed and such grace,
He said, 'Sleep my dear child, as we now leave this place.'
He took me with Him to a place all aglow,
I felt total peace and great love, and this I do know,
He rescued me from physical life and its pain,
So I could rejoice with Him and live free once again.
You may pray for my soul, but please don't be sad,
For now I am home, so rejoice and be glad,
He has rescued me from my sickness and pain,
And here I will stay, until we are together again. Amen."

*   *   *

• Opposition: The Negative Realms & Warnings:

Up to this point I have outlined many of the wonderful experiences that we have shared. We have also encountered the 'opposition' numerous times and still do.

My intentions are not to frighten you with these following revelations, but rather to enlighten, just as we were. Some of the experiences are graphic in detail and you may find them a bit unsettling, but nonetheless, they are true accounts of what has transpired and the revelations that were given to us. In sharing this knowledge, the hope is to benefit you with an understanding of your own questions and curiosities, as perhaps you can relate to some of these circumstances in your own personal lives.

In the very beginning, shortly after I had discovered my abilities, and before knowing about Vincent, I had a natural curiosity to want to

experience everything and anything that I could, which included divination boards and séances. Not knowing then, about evil influence or
of the existence of spirits of the lesser realms, I did just that.

One particular gathered in our home was, Gene, Fred, Karen, Edie,
Ron, Chris, and I. At the time, Gene and I had two Doberman dogs. At
nighttime, they were kept inside in the basement.

We lit candles in the dining room, and I placed a large bowl of water
in the center of the table. This was prior to our learning the importance
of saying protection prayers and we did not protect ourselves in any way.
All of us sat around the table, holding hands and we were all of the mind
set to let whatever may happen, just happen.

Within a very few minutes, right after I very stupidly asked, "Are there
any spirits present?" the dining room temperature felt like it had dropped
significantly. The dogs began to howl, a low moaning type howl and then
they made sounds of a warning type of growl.

What happened next, you would think, should have scared us
enough, to never participate in anything like that again! It didn't. Evil
influence is very strong and very cunning, and we were not wise enough
then to realize or recognize it.

A very loud and menacing sound like that of a beast echoed from out
of the kitchen and into the dining room! The only way I can describe it
is, at first it sounded like someone in a car stepping on the gas and burning tires, right in our ears, the screeching noise was followed by what
sounded like a door closing and a bolt type lock clicking, twice. At this
point, we all opened our eyes and Ron was staring into the kitchen and he
was completely pale. Karen complained that she felt sick to her stomach
and Edie was crying.

We did have enough wits about us that night to stop and we were
fortunate that nothing else took place. Not then anyway. We blew out
the candles, and turned the lights on, and we all sat there talking and
tried to figure out just what *that* was. Gene got up to make coffee in
the kitchen and let out a yelp! On our kitchen door was a dead bolt

lock. It had *two* lock functions; a slider lock and a large oval knob lock. *Both of them were in the locked position! We* had not previously locked the kitchen door.

Because we couldn't *see* any visual results of that evening, and because we were foolish enough to believe that there is *strength* in numbers, we didn't stop there. Unknown to us at the time, each of us were, in fact, having *negative* experiences, all that next week.

Edie was suffering from nightmares, and she and Ron were arguing a lot. Chris was having difficulty with her daughter; Karen and Fred were having trouble communicating and Gene and I had another frightening experience!

Gene had gone to bed early one night, and I stayed up in the living room to watch TV. I had fallen asleep on the couch. I was abruptly awakened by the sound of three very loud raps on the living room window. I got up off of the couch and looked outside of the window. I could see nothing. A very uncomfortable feeling, however, came over me. I looked at the clock and the time was 2:30 in the morning. Within a few minutes of my experience, Gene came out of the bedroom and into the living room. He told me about a very weird dream he had. In telling me the chain of events, he kept saying, 'But I wasn't sleeping. I was aware of what was going on, but my body felt like it was frozen, paralyzed! I couldn't move. It's like my mind was awake, but my body wouldn't move. Pat, I was in a place like darkness and then I saw this thing; it looked like a gargoyle! It was huge and it was dark greenish brown and it had wings, big wings, and it was making this *screeching* noise, and I kept thinking I wanted to beat it away from me. I thought about taking my shoe off and striking it.'

Gene was visibly shaken by his experience. We sat on the couch and talked for about an hour. I told him what happened to me with the raps on the window, and then we both went into the bedroom. I flipped the light on so I could see to put on my pajamas. When Gene walked around to his side of the bed, he hollered, 'Ow!' There at the very corner, at the bottom of the bed, was his *work boot*! The other boot was near his night table, up near the head of the bed, where he always kept them.

As I said, we were foolish. Even though we were scared, the *persistent thoughts* that nothing would happen to us, and *our acts of freewill*, kept us engaging in very unwise endeavors.

Carol M. called me and said she had found a divination board at her Aunt Kaye's house. Of course we experimented with it. Once and only once! But it was only the protection of my spirit guides, which I didn't know then, that we escaped this experience without further harm or serious repercussions!

Present on this night were Carol M., Kaye, Gene, Chris and I. Again, we didn't say any protection prayers, or protect ourselves in any way. It literally gives me the shivers as I recount these episodes, knowing the danger, our utterly stupid behavior and the foolishness of our actions.

Kaye at that time was probably in her early sixties. She was a very sweet and gentle woman. The divination board was very old, and according to Kaye, never used. Someone had purchased it years before, she didn't even remember by whom, and it was just kept in a closet, until now. After this night, however, the divination board was burned and thrown in the garbage.

We sat around the dining room table and placed the board in the center of it. Of course to add to the suspense, again we lit candles and placed the large bowl of water on the hutch. According to some information I had read in one of the books, water attracts spirits.

According to the 'instructions' of the board, persons were to lightly place their fingertips on a small wooden device that was shaped like a teardrop. It had three peg feet underneath it with felt tips so it could slide easily on the board. This device was called an 'oracle'. The board itself was approximately 18 inches in width and length. The board was made up of the letters of the alphabet, black in color, in a circular fashion and the words 'yes and no' were written at the top, one word in the upper left hand corner and the other word in the right corner. The background color of the board was brownish mahogany. The object of using this board was for a person to ask questions and the '*energy*' present would answer either by moving toward the yes or no response, or by moving to a letter of the alphabet and spelling out responses.

Kaye and I placed our fingertips on the oracle, while the others each held their hands around us forming a circle. Kaye began to ask questions, she wanted to 'reach' her mother. Evil spirits are clever and very cunning, and will tell you what you want to hear, just to gain confidence and trust. The oracle began to move, very slowly at first, and then more rapidly. My fingertips were on this device, and it was very evident there was another 'force' moving it, neither Kaye's nor mine. Tears welled in Kaye's eyes as the oracle moved over the letters, spelling out her mother's name. Thinking of course, that she had made 'contact' with her mother, she began to ask *her* questions of a personal nature. Suddenly the oracle in swift motion flew off of the board and somewhere onto the floor! The room filled up with an awful putrid odor! It so startled all of us for a moment that we were unaware of what was happening to Kaye! Gene let out a gasp and we all looked to see why. Kaye was slumped crooked in her chair and we literally watched the color draining out of her. It started from her hands and moved upward to her neck and face. She was turning completely gray in color. Her eyes rolled up into her head, and she began to mumble in a very strange unintelligible voice, and then the tone became louder. It all happened so quickly we couldn't react immediately! Kaye's body then began to shake, uncontrollably. I screamed at the top of my lungs; 'God! Please! Please! Help us!' Kaye slumped back into the chair and her color began to return. Kaye had no recollection of what happened to her. She sat there as though she were made of stone. The *thought* to pray was powerful in my mind, and that is exactly what we did. We prayed continuously until everything felt normal again and Kaye was all right. I took the board, and the oracle, which was lying on the floor, near the telephone table, along with a box of wooden matches outside to the garbage barrel and set them on fire. That night put an end to our curiosity and foolish behavior, but it didn't stop evil influence. However, we would come to know the difference between unwittingly inviting the opposition, and understanding how fallen spirits tempt, corrupt and can also utilize ode to carry out the destructive planning for their leader, Lucifer.

There will be more details outlined in the following chapter, **Cries For Help**, concerning events and circumstances that beleaguered us. However, faith, strength in prayer and the unity of One Mind and Heart of Jesus, in our group prevailed and continues to this day.

Once our Beloved Vincent enlightened us, the fallen spirits did their best to try and scare us, especially me, from continuing along my path. I will admit I almost reached the point when I wanted to move away, change my name and just lead a simpler life. Of course that would have been exactly what the 'opposition' would have liked.

This following account was the most frightening of all. It happened one night at Frank and Mary's and in the presence of most of our group members. The intention was to terrify me enough, and for everyone else to witness, so we would stop our Unity meetings and thwart all the good works that were ahead and planned by God's spirit world.

We were all seated around the dining room table and holding hands in preparation of prayer. We did this before entering into the living room in order to create harmony and high vibration, to set our minds on spiritual thoughts and to rise above our concerns of physical life.

Gene always sat on my right, and Chris to my left. The same applied to all of our regular members, each sat next to the same person every week, and thus the harmony of the circle remained the same. The order never changed unless someone wasn't present at the meetings or a new person was in attendance.

Within just a few moments after joining hands, closing our eyes and bowing our heads, this terrible feeling came over me and my entire body became ice cold! In my mind's eye the most horrifying scene appeared! It happened so fast I was unable to break from it! Even now as I recall the memory, my fingers shake. I *saw* the most hideous looking animals, and what looked like deformed humans in what reminded me of a cave, very dark and musty smelling, and then suddenly these dark piercing eyes, just two large eyes appeared, but I could see through them into that cave, and I heard these words that were said in a very deep gruff and menacing tone, 'Do you think you are a match for me? I will show you!' and then I felt stinging pain in both of my eyes and on both sides of my ribcage! I winced from the pain, and broke my hands away and tried to open my eyes. Chris became nauseated and Gene experienced an instant headache. Mary who was sitting directly across from me experienced cold sweats and clamminess in her hands. She was staring at me and shrieked, 'what happened to you? Your eyes are all red and blood shot! They look *scratched*!' The realization of what happened made me start to cry, and the tears added to the pain in my eyes. I was wearing a cotton sweatshirt and I lifted it up. There on both of my sides were *long deep scratch marks*! Everyone became panicked. I tried to convey to the best of my ability, what had transpired. Words do not adequately express that horrifying vision and those occurrences. Then these soothing words came into my mind, 'Pray, do not give in. This too shall pass.' I reached out for Gene and Chris's hands and everyone followed. As soon as we started the prayers, followed by Mary starting us off with a hymn, the pain and everything that was visible disappeared.

There were many revelations that were given to us concerning Lucifer and the spirits of the lesser realms. They are as follows:

"Greetings my beloved children of the earth plane. I come to you from the realm of Our Lord and Saviour, Jesus Christ. So shall tonight be a night of learning. So shall I enlighten you with knowledge of creation. So shall I impart as much wisdom as you may comprehend with your limited capacity to understand fully. In time of ere, so have I revealed laws of nature and the existence of ode both in the physical world and in the spirit world. So shall I expound on this matter. So shall you recall to your mind, all is made of spirit first. God being of the most intelligent and purest spirit of all and everything created from Him is also spirit. First so shall I say, God created all things small and great within the Grand Design of His Wisdom and observance of laws conceived thereof. So shall I give an example, one single seed produces plant life

form, trees, flowers and so on. Many seeds produce an entire variety of the same. So it is with the spirit world, all laws pertaining to the physical world, exist in the spirit world as well. God in His image created spirit beings in such large numbers that there are no figures available in your physical world to count. As I have stated in time of ere, there are equal amount in male and female. Among these He created what you would term as 'sons'. The first being, Christ, whom He made in as near a perfect image of Himself. So shall you read; (Colossians 1: 15). Christ is the highest and most perfect spirit created. So then there was a second creation, Lucifer, the light bearer, the second greatest of spirit creation and also the one to turn against God. In your world you appoint a leader, 'head' of government, along with a staff that share duties and tasks all for the common good of the people. So it is in the spirit world. God anointed Christ as King; along with other spirit beings with allotted tasks and duties all to work for the good of the whole of spirit creation. So shall you read; (Colossians 1: 16,17). Just as in your world, freewill was also given to the spirit world as well. Lucifer decided he did not want to be second glorious, but rather King. With careful planning, deceit and cunning he formed his own legion and waged war against Christ. He and the spirits that have joined with him caused a separation in the spiritual spheres, thus creating the lesser spiritual realms. So shall I explain more in time to come. May God continue to grant all of you His Love, Peace and Guidance."

This following message enlightened us on temptation and how spirits of the lesser realms can influence us through our *thoughts*.

"Greetings my beloved children of the earth plane. I come to you from the realm of Our Lord and Saviour, Jesus Christ. So shall tonight be a night of learning. In time of ere, so I have spoken of the creation of the lesser spirit realms. So shall I enlighten you further. As I have stated, Lucifer and his followers formed their own spiritual realms, created in darkness, as they were now absent from the brilliance of the purity of Ode, and where there is absence of Light, there can be only darkness. Just as your leaders choose to wage war, so the planning begins in the minds of those who are in control, then the ideas are presented to the followers and carried out. Lucifer made many promises of high

positions of power to his subordinates in order to gain their trust and to carry out his plans. So it is still today that the spirits of these lesser realms influence through thought to the spirits inhabited in your physical bodies. So have I stated in time of ere, one negative thought may be replaced by yet another, a positive thought. Negative influence from these spirits will be cunning, enticing and contain half-truths. So shall I say, the nearer your spirit draws to God-consciousness, so shall the negative influence become greater and more cunning. Keep your faith close at hand, and be always prepared, in the blink of an eye, so can you be ensnared. In your most vulnerable of emotions and your weaknesses, so they will strike. So I say, curiosity can be for you or against you. Curiosity in those of little or no faith, become easy prey for these spirits. So shall I enlighten you further of this matter in time to come. In time of ere, so have I spoken concerning guilt, the weakest of emotion, making one most vulnerable to the influence of these spirits. May God continue to grant all of you His Love, Peace and Guidance."

This following message is not only very enlightening, but powerful as to the warnings of divination boards, and seeking out persons who claim to have spiritual gifts.

"Greetings my beloved children of the earth plane. I come to you from the realm of Our Lord and Saviour, Jesus Christ. So shall tonight be a night of learning. In time of ere, so have I imparted to you the knowledge of influence through thought, both negative and positive. So shall I enlighten you further of this matter. So tonight shall I expound of curiosity, and the dangers therein to those persons of little or no faith. Recall to your minds for a moment, that which I have told you in time of ere, concerning karma. In each physical life there will come a time when the spirit reaches the crossroad and seeks answers, as I have explained. It is at these times when spirit will choose a path closer to God-consciousness, or incur more karma. Here the influence of the spirits of the lesser realms will use whatever means available to them to ensnare the spirit. You have tools of your physical world that make entrapment easy. So shall I speak of that which you call the divination board. So this device was created by influence of the powers of darkness. So were negative thoughts in the

mind of the designer of this board and then carried out. This tool is an open portal to the spirits of the lesser realms. Those who take part in challenging these tools are opening themselves up to great dangers. Only persons whose lot in life, such as the channel, has gatekeepers, to keep at bay negative influence, and this can only be if freewill does not dictate otherwise. All others are without protection and are subject to any and all influences from the powers of darkness. Persons that have participated in use of this device have suffered from possessions of evil spirits, driven insane and have followed falsehoods concerning spiritual matters, instructed by the lesser spirits. So have you touched upon this of which I speak, in time of ere. So in continuing of the matter of curiosity and emotional vulnerability, this same applies to persons who seek counsel from those who claim to have possession of spiritual gifts. So it is that there are those who have allowed utilization of ode to spirits of the lesser realms. Some of these instruments have done so willingly and others have fallen prey to the guise of the spirits of lesser realms. To the one known as Kathy, so have you experienced that of which I now speak. So then, you must ask self, what was the benefit? If the knowledge imparted from this source only satisfied simple curiosity, conveyed news that you wanted to hear and served no purpose toward your spiritual growth, what then were the fruits? So I say, does a parent instruct a child by satisfying the child's wants, or by enlightening him with wisdom that may encourage a foundation of security and stability for his growth? May God continue to grant all of you His Love, Peace and Guidance."

Kathy was in awe of Vincent's comment! She hadn't told any of us yet about the experience he was referring to! She planned on sharing it that night, and she did. Kathy told us that she had attended a psychic fair a couple days earlier. At this gathering, many of the persons occupying booths claimed to have different psychic abilities. Kathy stopped at one booth, and a male psychic told Kathy she needed to purchase some kind of stones that would align her body and spirit and balance her 'aura'. He then proceeded to perform an auric pass over her and told Kathy that he *saw* an 'Indian' behind her, that was her guide. Then quite abruptly he said the 'guides' were having an argument! Allegedly the psychic's guide and the Indian were in conflict. He then told Kathy that her Indian guide was inexperienced and needed more instructions. Kathy walked away at this point and left the fair. Kathy admitted that hearing about 'her guide' intrigued her, (*news you want to hear*) but she immediately dismissed it after the 'argument' happened. Kathy also suffered from depression for those two days.

*   *   *

• Suicide and Power of Prayer:

In reading this following information, again the intention is to enlighten you. If perhaps you know of someone that has committed suicide, or if you just have questions, hopefully these revelations will offer you understanding, consolation, and a renewal of faith.

One of the greatest gifts that our spiritual teachers enlightened us with was knowledge of the power in prayer. We were given the understanding that prayer creates a harmony and vibration, which raises spirit consciousness. When this elevation occurs the spirit then may receive the benefits from the Holy Spirits' kingdom, such as healings, and extension of physical life. Prayer offered for the spirit of someone who has died has profound effects on that spirit's escalation. The spirit may move upward through the spheres toward God-consciousness, especially in the case of suicide.

At the hospital where Frank and Mary worked, a young male patient committed suicide by jumping out of a window. He was 30 years old. I will call him, Joe. News of this prompted a revelation from Vincent, and the beginning of our adding a 'book of names' to our meetings. We refer to this book, with all the peoples' names in it, as our 'Prayer Book'.

This is one of the revelations that we received.

"Greetings beloved children of the earth plane. I come to you from the realm of Our Lord and Saviour, Jesus Christ. So shall tonight be a night of learning. And so it is that I shall impart knowledge this night on the power of prayer. So

shall I enlighten you on the matter of spiritual death, separation from God-consciousness. In time of ere, so have I explained of the spiritual spheres. And so to continue so shall I expound on the sphere referred to as 'Hell,' the lowest of the spiritual realms and in which reign Lucifer and his followers. As I have also stated, there can also be progression upward from this sphere as well. So shall you learn the power in prayer elevates spirit consciousness to the harmony and odeic vibration of the Light Of Christ. It is then the spirits choice whether to remain in darkness or journey upward. So it is that ultimately all spirits, including Lucifer and his followers, will return to God-consciousness as ordained by Him, 'For thou sparest all, for they are thine, Oh Lord, thou lover of souls;' so shall you read; (Wisdom 11:26). So have you questioned what happens to the spirit of one who takes his own life. So shall I remind you of that which I have explained in time of ere. So I have stated; at the physical age of reason, choices are made from positive or negative influence. Reason; defined as the ability to make a rational and logical choice. So then if a person of right mind makes such a choice, so shall he either benefit or suffer from his decision. So shall I impart this knowledge by example. For the one called Nick, as in the death of your colleague, D.D., so did he willfully and of right mind take his own life. So then shall his spirit suffer the consequences of its actions, which I shall explain. And to the one called Mary, so did the patient, J.W., take his own life, however, so he was not able to make a rational and logical decision, as his mind was altered from the use of prescribed medications, thus the punishment of this action will be according to the crime. God is Just. Be not misled here, if a person so chooses by willful intent to first become intoxicated as to falsely supply courage for this deed, so then shall the spirit suffer the consequences of this action. So it is that the spirit that willfully interrupts the journey of this physical life, so does it continuously relive the experience of that physical death, in the spirit realm. Thus you have heard the words of Christ; 'Cast him out into the outer darkness; there shall be wailing and weeping and gnashing of teeth.' Those spirits that were severed from God-consciousness was a result of their disbelief while inhabiting a physical body on earth. Since they are unaware of their physical identities of former lives, they do not know of the horror that awaits them in the darkness. God in his Infinite Mercy will grant the spirit redemption, prayers offered by those of the living is most powerful in His granting this petition. The more frequent the prayers, the numbers of persons praying, help the spirit to escalate from the realm of darkness. Each realm of progression begins with the deepest black to the most brilliant of hues to the sphere of God-consciousness which is brilliant white, thus this sphere is what you call, 'Heaven'. And so it is that true mediums see into these spheres, as you have witnessed by the channel. May God continue to grant all of you His Love, Peace and Guidance."

This following message is also quite powerful. The contents contain past predictions of mass suicide, children murdering children, and the evil that prevails in our world. However, understanding the power in prayer, and full of faith in the unconditional love of God-consciousness, we continue to hope and pray for *'inner attitude changes'* in all of mankind.

"Greetings my beloved children of the earth plane. I come to you from the realm of Our Lord and Saviour, Jesus Christ. So shall tonight be a night of learning of that which has passed, and of preparation of that which is to come. In time of ere, so have I imparted the knowledge of spiritual death; severance of the spirit from the realm of Light. So shall I enlighten you further of that which you now seek. So you have questioned mass suicide, and those who have fallen prey to the so-called Messiahs. So shall you read; (Matthew 24:6) 'Many will come in My Name, saying; I am the Messiah, and they will mislead many.' So as you have witnessed in your earth year of 1978, with the one called, Jones. So shall you still witness in time to come, more of the same. Lucifer has waged greater war upon the spirits, as he knows his time grows short. 'Then I saw an angel come down from heaven with the key to the abyss and a large chain. He overpowered the serpent and chained him up for a thousand years,' so shall you read; (Revelations 20:1) So shall you also witness in time to come much human suffering, as children turn against children. So it is that the powers of darkness rule with a mighty hand, and influence the minds of those who are in authority. So shall you see the cleverness, and so I say stand firm of your faith, 'So you have the image of the Lord Jesus in your

hearts, follow this example, see to it that no one captivates you with science or with foolish and misleading theories which are based on human traditions and derive from the evil powers that rule the world,' so shall you read; (Colossians 2: 6-8). So shall the powers of darkness use trickery and strike in the most vulnerable of your leaders, as they all worship power, the greatest weakness and Lucifer's easiest mark. So shall church and state be of issue and the power of darkness shall prevail. And so I say, those who pray together stand tall in the time of temptation, all else falters away. So shall I say from the words of Our Saviour, 'Woe unto him who sins, and causes others to sin, for great will be his punishment in the beyond.' May God continue to grant all of you His Love, Peace and Guidance."

Many messages, poems and prayers were given to us concerning the 'fate' of man and the corruption and destruction that has become so painfully obvious in our world today.

Events that were foretold and have come to pass include Waco, Texas, David Koresch and the Branch Davidians-April 19, 1993. The Oklahoma bombing, the same day, two years later-April 19, 1995, that claimed the lives of 168 people; and Hale-bop in March 1997.

The most alarming prediction, *'the issue of church and state and darkness will prevail'* is so painfully evident in our education system today in the negative effects it has helped to promote amidst our youths. Was it *necessary to remove prayer* from the classrooms?

We were given revelations pertaining to gangs, cults and religion. On religion as it was relayed to us, *'much of the religion that is offered today contains contradictions, promotes doubts and causes great confusion within the minds of persons who are seeking the truth, thus enabling the powers of darkness the tools to influence.'* We were also enlightened as to, *'those who are in official religious positions are in need of much prayer. As the right Justice judges what truly lies in each and every heart of man. Judge them not, pray for them. So it is, when you are employed, you must follow the rules of your employer without question. And so the same holds true for those who choose to instruct of religion. They must follow the rules of those in authority.*

And let me say further, where there is prayer, there also shall you find Holy influence. The 'fall' of some of our religious leaders was one of Lucifer's greatest achievements. In the minds of many people, fuel was added to the fires of *doubt, confusion and contradiction.*

On cults and gangs we were offered much of the same enlightenment along with this knowledge. *'So then do not children learn from example? When planting a rose bush do you not apply support so that it will continue growth upward and flourish? In the minds of your youth, what is there for nurturing and promotion of good fruits? So it is that the foundations for your offspring's arise from the examples set by adults consumed with negative influence. So then separation of parents, lack of supervision and violence, are these not the poorly laid plans in which they are to build from? If you offer no **light**, no supervision, nor tend to the other needs of your rose bush, it will surely perish. The minds of children offer a great playground to Lucifer and his followers. Children that already live in the absence of light—without prayer and spiritual direction—are easy prey. Curiosity, a need for recognition and mental stimulation are the greatest weaknesses and tools for the powers of darkness to ensnare the spirit of your youths.'*

Although these revelations contain saddening news, they also offer us an understanding of mercy, forgiveness and hope. Vincent didn't just tell us about the *power* in prayer, he also shared with us *how* to pray. And by utilizing me through automatic writing, we have received many, poems and prayers. I will share some of these magnificent writings later on in the book.

But for now, I am going to end this chapter with a poem that was given to me, through automatic writing:

"From the Eyes of a Child"

Can I go out to play?
Will it be safe today?
In my classroom there is an empty chair;

A short time ago, a friend of mine sat there.
He went outside to play a while,
In just a few moments there was havoc,
And then gone was his smile.
I remember people shouting and lots of noise;
His mother was crying—"It's my boy! My boy!"
There is so much misery, hate and pain;
Will it ever end? Couldn't we all love and refrain,
From all the anger, racism and sin,
Does it stem from a need to belong? Lack of confidence?
Where and when did it begin?
I want to be a child and to grow;
Please help Dear Lord and make it so.
As children we need to be loved, hugged and cherished;
By our parents, friends and prayer so we can flourish.
Please God; I just want to play.
Will it ever be safe again? Will it come—that day?

7 ▶▶

Cries for Help

On February 19th, 1980 the story of my involvement in leading the authorities to the location and discovery of the missing Coast Guard man, Richard Eastman, was published in the National Enquirer. The New London Police Department became inundated with telephone calls from private persons and police officials from all around the nation seeking information on how to get in touch with me. Telephone calls, letters and parcels containing pictures and personal items of missing persons and victims of crimes started to arrive at my residence within the first week of the national publication.

My telephone would start ringing as early as 5 am and continue all day long and into the night, sometimes until 2 or 3 in the morning. The frantic cries for help were coming in from all over the globe! The calls remained steady for a period of two weeks and then slowly tapered off.

When I would arrive home in the morning after work, I would find the tape on my answering machine half full of messages. The emotional pain and anguish in the voices of these people as they left their message and the reasons for their calling me was overwhelming. I did my best to answer all the calls as they came in, however, I placed a priority on missing persons. I would answer those calls first. Missing animals, pets, and robberies would have to be secondary.

It was during these calls that the gift of 'direct-voice' would be utilized. The odeic vibration and connection that I was able to make with voice contact alone also produced other astounding events to happen! And some of these remarkable accounts are recorded on tape.

This is one of the very first phone-calls I returned and the details are absolutely heart wrenching!

"Mrs. Sterling. This is Pat Gagliardo. I am returning your call."

"Hello. Thank you so much for returning my call. But, even though I am desperate, I must first ask you what your fee is. We have exhausted pretty much all of our financial holdings at this point," she commented, anguish very evident in her voice.

"Mrs. Sterling," I replied with empathy, "there is no fee. Please tell me how I may help you."

She started to cry, and with her words breaking up by her sobbing, she began to give me the details.

"My daughter and another girl have been missing for eight months. There has been no word, no sign, nothing about them. They were at a rodeo. This was on the twenty-fourth of June. The other girl's mother and I would like to know if there is anyway possible you could help us?"

"I will do all that I can. Please continue. I am taping this call. I will attune to your voice—if I interrupt, it will only be because I am receiving information. Okay?"

She continued with the details. "The girls are young. And neither one of them drive."

"Just a minute. I am picking up on a small Volkswagen. I believe a young man picked up the girls. I'm also getting the name, Randy. They haven't gone very far."

"I believe I have heard that name before," she remarked, "but I am not sure about the car."

"All right. Please continue."

"There were five children together. My oldest daughter, and a few friends. Somehow, they were split up. When my oldest daughter realized they were not all together, she began to look for her sister."

"Can you tell me why I am picking up two different times?" I asked. "One time is six o'clock and the other time is eight o'clock."

"Yes. Yes I can! The last time I saw my daughter was six fifteen that night. And my other daughter noticed her sister missing at about eight thirty."

"I see. Okay."

"My daughter said she would see me later. I haven't seen her since," her voice now broke into heavy sobs.

"Mrs. Sterling, my impression is not of a detrimental nature. I don't feel as though any harm came to the girls. I feel as though they have run away—probably looking for some excitement. I want you to be honest with me. It is imperative that you tell me the truth. It will affect my vibration and attunement. I am not going to pass any judgments. I want to help you. Okay?"

"Yes, Pat, I will. But I don't feel that they ran away. Why? We have been good parents."

"I am sure you have. But, I am getting a strong impression of an argument. Did your husband recently lay down some new rules?"

She was hesitant to answer and then she said, "Ah, well, yes. Yes he did."

I reiterated, "I am not going to pass judgments or form any opinions. Please, I need you to confirm my impressions if you want me to help you," I said solemnly.

"I know you do. Thank you," she replied, her voice cracking from her sobbing.

"I am getting the name, Jenny. I am sure she is a friend. I feel that she knows where the girls were going."

"I'll check on it, Pat."

"I am *picking up* on a freeway, near the rodeo. It is under repair. If it isn't now, it was when the girls disappeared."

"Yes, there is a highway like that. It's approximately three miles from there, and it was and still is under construction."

"I am sensing them traveling down this highway. I *see* a ski lodge, and I am getting a restaurant with the word, 'apple' in its name. It's a well-known ski area…Also…"

"Wait a minute!" she shrieked, interrupting me. "I do know a Randy. He's about eighteen. He lived in Carson City—and he was into drugs."

"This is what I believe happened. The girls are trying to get work at a restaurant—something with the apple, I mentioned. They are near a well-known resort, a ski resort. And there is also an Indian lake in the vicinity. I also perceive the number eighty-nine. Does this mean anything to you?"

"I don't know. You said you didn't think it was too far away, right?"

"Yes. That's my feeling. You're in Nevada, right? I think you should look at a map. I believe you will find that eight-nine is a route number. If you find out anything let me know. I will check a map also. Please give me your phone number again."

"Thank you so much, Pat. God Bless you. I will check into all of your information."

After we hung up, I went into my car and took out the Rand McNally Road Atlas. I found route 89, which lead from Nevada to California, right on the line. I also found the ski resort, and the name of the lake was Tahoe.

I called Mrs. Sterling back immediately. She said it was some distance to travel from her home, but that she would make the trip. I suggested that she leave as soon as possible as I felt they would continue to travel, and in the not too distant future, either. She said that she and her husband would leave the next morning.

Four days later, I heard from Mrs. Sterling again. She had wired the photos of the girls to a runaway center located at Lake Tahoe. The girls were there! They would be coming back home that weekend. She informed me of the conversation that had taken place with her and a gentleman from the center. She asked him if there was a restaurant there with the word, 'apple' in it. He told her that on route *89*, there was a French restaurant with the word 'apple' in it! And that is what led to finding the girls! Tears were streaming in Nevada and Connecticut!

She said something to me that day that *connected* both of our lives.

"God has touched your life. What a beautiful gift! You must be a very special person. I'll never forget you. Thank you so much!"

"Mrs. Sterling," I said sobbing, "you are right. But God has also touched *your* lives. It is Him, you must thank for His messenger that He has sent to me."

This next case brought about another aspect of the gift that I would soon discover and learn about!

"Hello," I answered, when the phone rang.

"Is this Pat Gagliardo?" the pleasant voice asked.

"Yes it is. Who's calling please?"

"My name is Mrs. Rotcha. I am calling from California. I got your phone number from Larry Fawcett. His name was in the Enquirer article. It said he was from Coventry. They gave your address as New London, not Norwich."

"Yes. I understand. The article didn't mention that I was from Norwich. How may I help you?"

"My sister-in-law, Delores, has been missing for nearly a year now. The police have done all that they can. We need your help...."

"I am seeing a house. It's on the corner of the road. There is a row of trees too, I believe, the left side of this house. There is also one bush in the front. Something took place—a bedroom—a fight. She was wearing something yellow. I, uh—ohhh, no," I stammered, "I think she is buried. Behind this house, under something cement and there is water."

"That's her house!" she exclaimed. "It is on the corner and there is a row of pines on the left side. She was wearing a light yellow nightgown!"

"Is there a lot of land?"

"Yes, a little over five acres. And the problem is the police can't get another search warrant. They don't have any hard evidence. You see, the oldest boy heard the mother and father arguing that night. That's why you picked up on the fight. He left the house at approximately eight o'clock that evening. He stayed out very late. The next morning around eleven, he asked his dad where Delores was. He told him that she had taken off about ten o'clock the night before. Her car, belongings and wallet were still in the house! And the yellow nightgown has never been found either. The police searched her husband's car and found some blood and hair samples. They matched Delores's. He told police that she had had a bloody nose a few days earlier. The police did, however, get a search warrant on suspicion. They went over the property with some kind of equipment—something like a metal detecting device. And they came up with nothing. Without sufficient evidence, they can't return."

"Hm-m-m. Is there a basement in the house? I am feeling she is under cement."

"No. There isn't a cellar."

"How about a patio?"

"No."

"Could you please send me some photographs of the house? It's going to be tough to give you a location. You just can't dig up five acres of land. You know, I am also getting the impression of something wood and metal—some kind of a homemade structure in the yard—and are there tractors being used on any portion of that land?"

"He had an old tractor. It isn't running anymore, and hasn't been for a long time."

"By the way, I am taping this call, Mrs. Rotcha. I do this so I can listen to it later and see if I can pick up on anymore impressions."

"That's fine. I don't mind at all."

"I do want you to know that I do feel her husband is responsible. It could have been an accident. It's possible he simply panicked."

"We think he is responsible too. Listen, Pat. Would it be better if you came out here to California? We will take care of all of your expenses."

"I would rather you send me something by mail first. Hopefully we can avert my having to come out there and avoid the expenses."

"Well, as far as I am concerned it won't be a waste of money, no matter what happens. You've already convinced me of your credibility! I will speak to my husband and call you back."

"It's up to you. I will come if you insist. But, I want it understood that I will pay for the hotel and car rental if I need it."

"We'll discuss that later. Good-bye and thank you so much."

"Who was that, hon?" Gene asked, as I placed the handset back onto the telephone cradle. "Was that another missing person?"

"Yes. It was a lady from California. Her sister-in-law is missing. I am going to play the tape back. Maybe I can get some more impressions."

"Z-z-z-z-z." the recorder sounded as I pushed the rewind button. I stopped the tape near the beginning. I listened with my eyes closed, hoping to perceive more visions and impressions. Suddenly a very weird noise was coming from the tape! It sounded like a motor! A sound of a small engine motor! We had in the past, during meditations, experienced moaning and other strange sounds that appeared on our tapes. But this was a first with direct-voice! I rewound the tape again and Gene and I both listened intently.

There it was again! "P-rup-prup-p-rup!" The sound appeared as I was asking her about the tractor. I sat and thought for a moment. 'Why did I ask her about the tractor to begin with? I must have gotten an impression about a portion of the area. Maybe, just maybe, it had something to do with where she was buried—possibly near the tractor!'

While I was waiting to hear from her during the next couple of days, more calls were coming in and more letters.

Larry was among the callers. There was an eighteen-year-old boy missing in Coventry. Larry asked me if I would meet with his family.

"I have his wallet in my possession, Pat. How about if Lois and I take a ride to your house and you can try psychometry there?"

"Sure Larry. How about on Saturday?"

"Sure. We'll see you then."

*   *   *

What a change was taking place in my life and in those lives that connected with mine! There was so much joy in helping people. Knowing that faith was being born or restored in their lives gave me such comfort and inner joy. At the same time, it was also angering the 'opposition', and the encounters with *it* would be fierce and difficult!

The first signs of the 'opposition's' influence were with people at work. Usually, everyone was pleasant and we chitchatted over coffee in the mornings before we all set out on our bus runs. Once the article was published in the National Enquirer, some of the drivers began acting cold and indifferent toward me. It was difficult to deal with. I enjoyed my time in the office and the laughter, joke telling and conversation we used to have. I started to say some prayers, before entering into the building. I would always say, "Help them, Lord, show them the *good* that Your gift can bring. If some of them are jealous and envious, please enlighten them."

I felt that my prayers were answered. Upon walking into the building, some of the co-workers that had in the past acted indifferently were now speaking to me! Some of the drivers told me how much they enjoyed listening to the 'Potpourri' radio programs. If they asked me questions, I happily responded. I wouldn't ever bring it up first, though.

On Saturday I anxiously awaited Larry and Lois's visit. In the meantime, Mrs. Rotcha called back. She and her husband had decided that they wanted me to fly out to California.

"Mrs. Rotcha," I began, "I replayed the tape recording of our conversation, and there was a funny motor sound, from a small engine that appeared on my tape. I thought at first it might have something to do with the tractor, but when my husband listened to it, he said it would be a small vehicle. Is there any portion of that land where a small vehicle is used?"

"The only thing I can think of is the lawnmower," she replied obviously confused about my remark.

"I would think the lawnmower is used on the entire property," I said.

"Oh, wait a minute! The boys have dirt bikes! And they are only allowed to ride on the right-hand side, and to the rear of the property—because of the tracks they leave!"

"I'll bet that is the connection. Maybe we can narrow it down from there. When I come out there, I will bring the tape. I know you don't understand what I am talking about. I have had similar experiences before, during meditations. I have not experienced strange sounds by phone contact, though. Yours was the first."

"When will you be able to leave Connecticut? Just give us the date and we'll get prepaid tickets here."

"Let me see what I can arrange for next weekend, and I will get back to you."

"Beep! Beep! Beep!" came Larry's trademark. He always honked the horn as he entered into the driveway. He and his wife Lois, and my family had become good friends. They are the greatest people! Larry devoted a lot of time to the UFO Center he was affiliated with, and Lois was right there by his side to help and support him. It was a friendship of mutual respect and admiration and, of course, fun times!

"Hi ya sweetheart! What's been happening?" Larry smiled, walking into the kitchen.

"Lots of wonderful things," I grinned. "How about with you, Lois?"

"Oh, just fine. I got a raise last week and I am wondering how I can spend it!" she laughed.

We sat around the dining room table and Larry began to give me some details about the missing youth. His father, a reverend, was concerned about the boy emotionally. He felt very strongly that the boy could have seriously harmed or even killed himself. I concentrated on Larry's words while holding the boy's wallet and began 'tuning in'. My impressions led me to believe otherwise.

"Larry, I am seeing a white house. It has dark, black trim. There is a convenience store very close by. There is also a school. I think this boy stayed at this house for a while. And I keep seeing a lunch box! What on earth could that be a symbol for?"

Larry started to laugh. "You know—you're something! You really are something! This kid used to eat there! It's a restaurant—called the Lunch Box!"

"I am getting a feeling that this house is connected with that place. Do you know where the owner lives?"

"Yep. I sure do."

"It's possible he liked this boy and wanted to help him out. And by the way, there are two dogs tied up out back."

"Isn't she something, Loie?" Larry laughed, calling his wife by her nickname. "That's his house all right. And I believe it's two shepherds tied out back. He's been known to have kids in and out of there all the time."

"Well, this is what I believe. I think that this boy has really been hard on himself. He makes too many demands that he can't keep up with. He has some really strong values, Larry. I think he has simply left home. If you don't find him in the area, I feel that within a few weeks he'll be found out of state. Do you know why I am seeing a structure like the Eiffel Tower? I have a funny feeling it represents two different aspects."

"I do," Lois commented. "That school you mentioned has a structure on top of it that looks like the Eiffel Tower. And Larry, didn't his father tell you that they had relatives in France? I thought that he had mentioned to you that his son wanted to go there again."

"Yeah, that's right, he did. And she's right about the school, too."

"If you still would like me to visit with the family, I will, but I really don't think it is necessary, though. What I perceived from his wallet should be sufficient enough to give you something to go on. I really don't feel as though he is dead."

"I think you're right, too. It's just the family is very worried."

"You're going to talk to them, aren't you? If they would like to meet with me, I will go. No problem."

"Okay. We'll leave it at that. Well, Loie, we had better be going. I'll call you, Pat, and let you know."

"Okay. Oh by the way, Larry, I saw a canoe behind a red house, too. And I saw a ship—it was made out of shells, I think. It was accompanied by an impression of where the boy lives."

"I am not sure about the canoe, or the ship. But I do know the boy's house is red!" He just shook his head from side to side, an expression of sheer amazement on his face.

Later on that evening, Gene and I discussed my going out to California. At first he seemed a little reluctant. He was worried about my safety, and I knew it.

"Honey, I am not afraid to go out there. I really think I may be able to help that family. Please don't worry."

"When do they want you to go?" he smiled, his eyes filled with love and pride.

"Next weekend. I guess I should leave either Friday night or Saturday morning."

The telephone call was made and the plans were arranged for me to leave the following Saturday morning.

*   *   *

On Monday morning, March 3rd, I received a telephone call from the Willimantic Police Department. The police officer I spoke with, Officer Griswold, was a friend of Larry's. He asked me if I would consider helping his department out on a case. He said it did not involve a missing person and he would prefer to give me the details when we met. I agreed to meet with him and assured him that I would do the best that I could to help. We made arrangements for Friday morning.

A day didn't go by without someone calling for help. I prayed every day for God to help me through the intervention of the spirit guides. I felt that I had been given such a wonderful and useful purpose in my life.

During this same week I had my first contact with Nancy Ritter. It had been predestined although neither one of us knew at the time, Nancy said she got my name from the article in the Enquirer, and my address and phone number from Dennis at the radio station. She and her friend, Doug, called me.

She went on to tell me that her husband, Larry, was missing. He had taken a private plane from Montego Bay, heading for Florida, and had never arrived—no sign of him or the plane. It was her understanding that the Coast Guard had searched the waters with no sighting of wreckage. Would I please help?

She left me her telephone number and I told her I would get back to her as soon as I returned from California. She was obviously distraught over her situation, but there seemed to be a feeling between us that we *knew* each other and were friends. I had never heard of her before, and could not have known that I would be seeing a lot more of her in the future and for another very *necessary* reason!

This same week, I would experience the 'opposition' again. This time it would happen through my son. David was the light of my life, and a son any mother would be proud of. Naturally, love of my son, would be a target for the 'opposition' to try and get to me.

*   *   *

Snow was falling. It was such a beautiful sight! We had seven big pine trees that lined our driveway and they were lovely covered with snow. School had been cancelled, so I made out a schedule for my activities—including baking. David wanted to scout the neighborhood in the hopes of getting some shoveling jobs.

"Hey Mom! I am going to get the shovel and head up the street, okay?" he asked, his handsome young face beaming in anticipation of making a little money.

"Sure. Just be home for lunch, okay?" I smiled. He was such a good boy. At times we had our disagreements. It was *that* age; junior high school. David also had a lot to contend with. He was shorter than average and he was picked on by his peers. They would call him names such as, shrimp, half-pint, short-stuff, etc. Most of the time he just shrugged it off.

In no time he was dressed and out the door. "Dave, if you get cold come back here!" I yelled after him. "And be careful!"

"Don't worry, Ma. I'll be back at lunchtime!"

I went on to do my chores, but I had this *nagging* feeling inside of me. It wasn't a feeling of panic; it was more like anxiousness. I would soon find out why!

I had just finished putting the clothes in the washing machine when I heard the kitchen door slam upstairs.

"Is that you Dave?" I yelled from the bottom of the stairs.

I didn't hear a response, and then I heard another door slam.

"David. Is that you?" I asked again, heading up the stairs.

I looked in the dining room, then the kitchen and walked to the bathroom and opened the door, calling his name. I walked through the living room and toward his bedroom. As I approached the door I heard him whimpering.

"Dave, what's the matter?" I asked, entering his room. He was lying across his bed; face down.

"Want to talk about it?" I asked, sitting down next to him and gently caressing the back of his head.

"No!" he shouted. "I hate those guys!"

"What guys?" I asked, my concern growing. "Tell me what happened, David. Please."

He turned over on his side to answer me and I let out a gasp! All around his left eye was redness and it was puffy! "David! What happened?" I shrieked.

"You'll get mad at me. I couldn't help it!" he began sobbing. "That kid said some rotten things! So I punched him and he punched me back."

"Let's go get some ice for that eye. And I want you to tell me the whole story."

I was unprepared for the reason of the fight. At first, I thought it had been only a squabble between the boys, maybe about a shoveling job. But that wasn't the case.

"He said you were a kook! Nuts! He told me you belonged in the mental hospital along with all the other crazy people! I told him to shut up. That's when he said you were the *devil*. That's when I hit him," he cried.

Cradling him in my arms, I sighed, "I'm not mad at you, sweetheart." Tears welled in my eyes. I didn't want my son to have to suffer for my actions. I began to cry and thoughts of '*is it worth the risk?*' entered into my mind.

"Don't cry, Mom. I know that you're trying to help people. I can take care of myself," Dave said smiling through his tears, his brave tone breaking my thoughts.

He hugged me then and scurried towards the bathroom. In a few seconds he returned, the washcloth with the ice in it was removed from his eye.

"Please don't go back outside, David." I sighed.

"Mom. I'm okay. I want to shovel the walk and the driveway. I'll stay in the yard. Don't be afraid." And then he was out the door again.

I walked to the window and watched him. My eyes searched wildly for signs of the other boys. I looked toward the hedges and saw three youngsters approaching the top of the driveway. My heart leaped! I ran to the door and heard...

"Hey sissy! Had to run home to your mother, the witch? Is she going to brew up something and turn us into toads!" They laughed hysterically.

I opened the door quickly and was about to yell at them, but they saw me and ran. I stood frozen to the spot. I looked at my son, and started crying. Dave just continued to shovel. He was ignoring them. And they didn't come back.

All my intentions of baking and the other chores were shot! I made a pot of coffee and continued to go back and forth to the window. I poured myself a cup and sat down and begged for strength and protection for my family. I recalled to mind the words '*the closer you draw nearer to God-consciousness and the good works done in His name, so shall the opposition grow stronger.'* Silently I whispered, "Please help me to be strong in my time of trial." This passed, but there would be more to come.

*   *   *   *   *   *

It's Friday. The snow was still on the ground and the wind was howling and it was blustery and cold! I called Edie and asked her if she would take the ride with me to Willimantic to meet Officer Griswold. The trip took about half an hour.

We pulled up to a parking space close to the police station.

"Do you know what this case is about, Pat?" Edie asked, searching her purse for change for the parking meter.

"Not really. He didn't tell me anything other than it wasn't a missing person. I felt it was a rape case, though. At least that is what came to my mind, when I talked to him over the phone."

Officer Griswold greeted us at the door. "Thanks for coming," he smiled and led us into a conference room.

He asked me if I preferred to be alone to do the psychometry, as he handed me a red bandana and a couple of items of costume jewelry. I told him it would be best if he did.

"Pat," he said, walking to the door, "I did tell you it was a rape case, didn't I?"

I glanced at Edie, turned my head to look at him, and said, "Not out loud, but I probably read your mind, because that's what I felt it was."

Edie also went out into the lobby with Officer Griswold. I picked up a ring from the pieces of jewelry belonging to the victim, Nancy S., took a deep breath and waited just a few moments before a couple of visions appeared. This would be the first experience of many to come, in which, I would physically *feel* what a victim felt! I wasn't prepared for it! It would be another phase of learning for me, and one that I could never get used to, but accepted.

The first vision was of a dark green van. Then I saw a man with a ruddy complexion, medium build, dark hair and eyes, and a little taller than average height. I saw a young woman, early twenties, light hair and thin in build. I kept getting the name, Alan, but that it was a street name, not a person. I also perceived the name, College Square, or College Park. I felt it was outside of the city limits, and a nearby 'green' and area with park benches. I perceived an elderly woman, Hispanic or light skinned black woman, on a dead-end street, near an establishment that sold donuts and coffee. There was also a place that worked on cars and a junkyard. Then I felt terror going through my body! I felt such fear I was overwhelmed by it! By my impressions, I sensed that this cruel act had been performed in that van! I felt that the young woman knew the perpetrator, and was afraid of him. I believed that he was stalking her. Then when an opportunity arose, he had grabbed her, put her in the van and taken off to a wooded location. I felt she was beaten and brutalized and then raped. And then I sensed that there would be another victim—if the perpetrator wasn't caught soon! There was other information pertaining to the man that Officer Griswold would later confirm. It took several months before I learned that the perpetrator been caught and held responsible for his crime.

Later that evening Gene and I were discussing the events of my trip to Willimantic, when the phone rang.

"Hello," I answered.

"I'd like to speak to Pat Gagliardo, please." A very pleasant man's voice said.

"Speaking."

"Hi! I am Mark Wile from, "P.M. Magazine," Channel 10 out of Providence. We've heard a lot about you and would like to know if you would consider appearing on our program?"

My heart was racing and excitedly I replied, "I would love to! What is it that you would like me to do?"

"I understand you give lectures and appear on radio talk shows. What I had in mind was taping you doing a show and a lecture—possibly on the same day."

"I see. Well I am scheduled to do a lecture for the Women's Auxiliary on March 10th and I have just recently appeared on 'Potpourri'. I can give you the names and telephone numbers of the contact people at the radio station and you can see what you can work out with them."

"That will be just great! I will try to get something together for April. I will be back in touch with you soon. Thank you."

I gave him Dennis's and Stu's names and phone numbers. After we hung up, I called Dennis. He said he would make the arrangements with Stu and Mr. Leonard from the Otis Library, and hold a lecture there.

"P.M. Magazine! That's great, Pat," Dennis said. "That is quite a popular show and a well respected one."

"I know. I feel so honored to be asked to be a participant on the program. Okay Dennis, speak to you soon, I am leaving for California tomorrow and I have got to get packed."

"Hey just a minute! I hope you don't cause them any electrical problems! You did mention the *power surges* that happen every time you do radio shows—didn't you?" he laughed.

"Very funny. No. I didn't," I remarked. "I have to go. I'll talk to you when I get back."

I was doing 'Potpourri' with Stu on a weekly basis. I enjoyed the exchange with the listeners, and being able to offer helpful insight gave me such a wonderful feeling as to the purpose in and of my life. Mr. Reed, the head manager, liked me well enough and was pleased with the response for his station. But, he was always a bit reluctant I had been told, to have me there, as *every* visit caused some kind of electrical mishap! The copiers would stop first. The FM alarm sounded, usually within just a couple of minutes of my passing by and walking upstairs. It got to be a real joke for Dennis. Then one day he told me I had better learn how to 'control' that! I did eventually learn how to make myself relax and balance the transmission and receiving of energy, but never completely, as it was not in *my* control. It was the odeic energy that I possessed. Dennis had made the comment to me jokingly, however, there *would be* electrical mishaps with the taping of 'P.M. Magazine!'

After I had hung up the phone from speaking with Dennis, I filled Gene in on all the details of what was going to be planned for the taping of the show. I then resumed my conversation of my visit in Willimantic earlier that morning.

"You have had a long and busy day," Gene smiled. "Now let's get to bed. We both have to get up early tomorrow morning. And you need to leave a little earlier, so you don't get caught up in the Hartford traffic."

*   *   *

The flight was scheduled to leave at nine o'clock. The airport was an hour's drive from my home. The traffic traveling through Hartford was usually pretty heavy, no matter what time of the day! I also needed to be at the airport at least forty-five minutes before departure time.

The long term parking section was nearly full when I arrived at the airport's parking terminal. After about ten minutes of searching, I finally found a spot. I locked the doors of the car and opened the trunk for my luggage.

It was miserably cold. The wind was blowing with raging force. It slapped my hair into my face and my eyes. By the time I reached the door of the lobby, I felt like a human ice cube! My face was beet red, stinging from the cold, and frozen!

I walked up to the Delta counter, placed my suitcase on the ramp and approached the man behind the desk.

"Good morning. I have reservations on the flight to California. The ticket is prepaid."

The young man smiled and pleasantly asked, "Your name, please?"

"Pat Gagliardo."

"Would you spell your last name, please? And I will need some identification."

I spelled out my last name and searched for my wallet and driver's license.

"Okay. Here is your ticket, the plane will be boarding approximately fifteen to twenty minutes before take off, at Gate 12."

"Thank you."

At the desk at Gate 12, I had asked for a window seat. I was hoping to get a view of the Rocky Mountains. Once aboard the plane, I sat down and buckled the seat belt. I pulled a magazine out of the rack in front of me. As I flipped through the pages, Mrs. Rotcha came to my mind. I closed the book and began to think of my conversation with her. I felt good about the information. She had confirmed my impressions and visions. As I recalled the incidents, I noticed a flickering of light on the magazine cover. I looked to my right and then to my left. Where was it coming from? Then I looked up directly above my head. My overhead reading light was flashing on and off! 'Oh no!' I thought. 'Relax! Think of something else and calm down!' I pushed the thoughts right out of my mind and started to count down and told myself to relax. It worked! Within a few minutes the light stopped flashing.

Fortunately, I did see the Rocky Mountains. What a beautiful view from the sky! It was a marvelous spectacle of creation! How I wished Gene and David were there with me and under different circumstances.

Mrs. Rotcha and her husband, Mack, were waiting for me in the lobby at the airport. She was holding up a sign with her name on it. We made formal introductions and then Mack said he had made reservations for me at a hotel nearer to where they lived. It was about an hour trip by car.

"Normally the weather here at this time of year is warmer and nicer," he said, "but I can't say that for today."

It was overcast and there was a definite nip in the air.

"It's warmer than Connecticut," I smiled.

"Pat, you are probably tired from your trip. If you would like to go directly to the hotel, that will be fine," Mack said, as we pulled out of the airport parking lot. "We have food prepared at the house though, if you're hungry."

"We can go to your house first, if you would like to. I am not really hungry, but a cup of coffee would be great," I smiled.

Their home was lovely. They had acres and acres of land. Horses were carousing in the fields and goats, chickens, and pigs had a home there too. The people themselves were very nice. It was difficult for me to push aside my own feelings of empathy. If I didn't, my emotions would get in the way. I told myself that I had to, in order to help them.

"Pat. We would like you to stay here with us," Mrs. Rotcha said sweetly. "We have plenty of room."

"Thank you. But, it's best that I don't. If I become too emotionally involved then my own sensitivity will get in the way. I won't be able to help you. The less I know about you and your family, the better it will be. You do understand, don't you?"

"Of course. Maybe someday we'll meet again under different and better circumstances," she smiled.

She had made a lovely lunch. Over lunch we discussed some of the same details. She told me that she and her husband had driven by the missing woman's house again since my phone call with her. She also told me that she had contacted Ron Heileman, the sheriff of the county that the missing woman was from. She told him I was coming out there and of the information that I had given her over the phone.

Around nine o'clock that evening they drove me to the hotel, which was approximately twelve miles from their home.

The weather remained overcast the next morning. As I was driving to their home, I took in the lovely scenery. It was so pretty in this part of California. How I wished I were there for other reasons!

I pulled up the long dirt driveway and parked close to the house. I got out of the car and looked at my watch. It read ten o'clock. Amused, I thought, 'Connecticut time, its only seven here.'

I knocked on the door and Mrs. Rotcha greeted me.

"You are early. Did you sleep well?"

"Like a baby. Am I too early?"

"Not for us. We are usually up around 5. Would you like some coffee and breakfast?"

"I have eaten, but I would like some coffee," I smiled.

"Sure thing, come on in the kitchen and sit down."

While she prepared the coffee, Mack and I sat down at the kitchen table and discussed the possibility of my gaining access to walk on the property of his missing sister.

"It won't be possible. Her husband still lives there. We tried having his son convince him to go away for the weekend, but it didn't work. He hasn't left that house since my sister's disappearance. I think he stays there out of guilt or maybe suspicion that someone would snoop around if he were not there."

"Is he aware that you feel he is responsible for her disappearance?" I asked Mack, nodding at his wife as she placed the coffee in front of me.

"You better believe it! All he ever says when he is questioned, especially by the police is, 'I haven't done anything wrong.' They flat out asked him if he killed her and he just kept saying, 'I haven't done anything wrong.' In his sick twisted mind, he's made excuses and has convinced himself that he was justified!"

Carefully I took in every word he said. I didn't comment one way or the other. "Can we at least ride by the property? I may be able to get some more impressions by being in the area."

"We sure can. And if we use the rental car, he won't recognize us. By the way, Pat, Ron Heileman is coming out here to meet you. I have to call him when we get back. That is okay with you, isn't it?"

"That's fine."

His sister lived a little further than ten miles from their house. It was ten miles of curving and winding roads. As soon as we approached the road that her house was on, I recognized the house immediately! "That's it! Isn't it? It's exactly as I saw it in the vision," I said, pointing up to the house on the *corner*.

"Yep, that's it," Mack said, driving a little past it and pulling the car off to the side of the road.

He parked the car at an angle that allowed me to see a good portion of the backyard. Then I *saw* the wood and metal object that I had tried to describe to Mrs. Rotcha over the phone. It was a homemade teepee.

"I have to get out of the car," I remarked.

I got out of the car and stood there for just a few minutes, staring at the teepee. I felt the same uncontrollable vibrations as I had with the missing Coast Guard man. A *voice* inside my head was saying, 'She's buried there, under the cement! And there's water, too!'

I got back into the car and told them what I sensed.

"Well, there is water on the property. It runs to the left-hand side, facing the house. That doesn't coincide with the motorbikes. They are on the right," Mack said.

We drove back to their house and tried to figure out the puzzle. Mack, in the meantime, had telephoned the sheriff, Ron Heileman. Nearly an hour had passed when there was a knock at the door, and a tall dark haired young man walked in. They introduced us. He was the son of the missing woman.

"Maybe he can help," I said, taking his hand and *feeling* his emotional pain. "I know this is difficult for you, and I am sorry. I do need to ask you some questions, though."

He just nodded, put his head down and then looked at his uncle.

"Do you know where there is any cement on your property? It would be somewhere near your motorbike route."

The young man sadly replied, "Uncle Mack has asked me that before. I really can't think of any place."

"All right. Let's try a different approach. The cement would have water around it. Try and think back. I know it was a long time ago, but maybe something will *pop into your mind*. Do you remember any part of the yard being dug up for any reason?"

His tall slender body was leaning backward against the kitchen counter. He pulled a pack of cigarettes from his shirt pocket, lit one and stood there quietly for a few minutes. Abruptly he shot forward!

"Wait a minute!" he yelled. "Some time later that afternoon when I was out riding my dirt bike, I do remember seeing a hole dug. Well, actually it was loose dirt. The ground had been dug up. When I asked dad about it, he said the *septic tank* was clogged up and that he had to fix it. I didn't think anymore about it! And it has *cement* and a round metal cover!"

"Also," I interjected, "there is *water*. What side of the property is it on? And where?"

"It's to the back and right-hand side. As a matter of fact, it's right *under* the dirt bike track! Uncle Mack, it is directly across from the *teepee*!"

"The only thing now is, how to get back on the property and dig it up. Also time is against you," I stated sadly, "if he used any lye or chemicals there may not be a trace."

I looked at the clock on the kitchen wall. I would have to leave soon, to catch my plane back home. As I was getting up from my chair there was another knock at the door. Mrs. Rotcha opened the door and a man in a tan uniform stood there. He was of medium build, brown hair and about five feet ten inches tall.

"Pat, this is Ron Heileman."

"Good morning. Nice to meet you."

"Same here. Were you able to come up with anything out at the house?" he asked.

"Pat has given us a location for Dolores. I am *sure* of it!" Mack interjected.

"I hope so. All of my visions and impressions lead to one place on that property, in or around the septic tank. I am just concerned that if her husband used any lye or chemicals to destroy the remains, you may not find her. I am sure that the Rotcha's will fill you in on all the details. Unfortunately I must be going, or I will miss my plane."

"You just leave that to us. God bless you, Pat! Would you please stay on a little while, we'd love to have you," Mack smiled.

"I wish I could, but I really need to get back home. I have a lecture tomorrow night. I need to rest up for it," I said, returning the smile.

"Here Pat," the sheriff said, handing me his calling card. "I have your name and phone number. Thank you for all of your help," he smiled.

"You're welcome. I pray that everything works out."

Mack reached for my coat on the back of the chair, and as he assisted me in putting it on, he remarked, "You have a son, don't you?"

"Yes I do Mack."

"Does he like baseball?"

"I'll say he does!" I laughed.

"Well I am a coach in the junior league, and I'd like to give you a cap to take home to your son."

"Thank you. I'm sure he will be pleased."

On the flight home, I was thinking, 'How thoughtful of Mack to think of my son.' I took the black cap out of my carry on luggage bag, held it and sighed, 'Please help them, Lord.'

Gene and my son were anxiously awaiting my arrival. They were all ears wanting to hear all the details of the trip. We sat down in the dining room and I explained everything that happened in California.

"I am worried that time is against them. If he used any chemicals to dispose of her remains, they may not find anything. I *know* she is there. I *felt* it so strongly."

"You've done all that you can, hon," Gene smiled, hugging me. "Whatever is meant to be, will be."

"Yes. You're right. I will leave it in God's hands now."

We went to bed early that evening as I felt a little jet lag and emotionally drained. I had the lecture the next evening with the Poquetannuck Women's Auxiliary and I needed to be as refreshed as possible.

It was nearly six months before I heard from the Rotcha's again. After my visit the police finally were able to get another search warrant. The area around the septic system was dug up. Through the lab, it was determined that harsh acid chemicals had been used, but there were some hair, teeth and nail fragments that remained. Thankfully, from this evidence they were able to convict and sentence Dolores's husband for her brutal murder.

*   *   *

My morning runs went by rather quickly it seemed, and in no time I was back at home and checking the answering machine. There were at least ten more messages that had come in while I was in California. I picked up the yellow pad and pen from under the telephone table and began to write the names and telephone numbers of the people that had called.

In looking at the pad, I saw the note that I had previously written; 'call Nancy Ritter'. I was just about to pick up the telephone and call Nancy, when the phone rang.

"Hello."

"May I speak with Pat Gagliardo, please?" a woman's voice asked.

"This is she. May I ask who's calling?"

"Hello. My name is Linda Flayer. I'm calling from Massachusetts. I read your article in the Enquirer, and I got your number from Officer Fawcett."

"Uh-huh. How may I help you?"

"I know that it was a missing person that you assisted the police with, however, I really need your help. I have two horses and a pony missing. They are valued at over ninety thousand dollars! My main concern, though, is for my two teenaged daughters. They love those animals so much. I think I know who's responsible for taking them, I just don't have any proof."

"Mrs. Flayer—does the name Rick mean anything to you? He has red hair, maybe five feet nine to ten inches tall and of medium build?"

"Oh gosh, yes!"

"All right, I see a large truck, white with red lettering painted on the side. The cab of the truck is a dark green, I believe. I feel the horses are in the back of this truck. That guy Rick is somehow affiliated with it. The horses are going across water, a lot of water, like the ocean. I am also getting 'cherry', the word 'cherry' keeps coming into my mind."

"My goodness! I didn't know you could get information right over the phone! I know that truck, and yes, Rick is affiliated with it—the water you see is heading them straight to New York! There are stables there. I'll check my book and find out if there is a stable with the name cherry in it. Thank you so much!"

"Mrs. Flayer, the horses won't be there long. I would suggest you leave as soon as possible."

"I'll check on it immediately! Thanks again."

"I hope it has been of help to you. Good-bye."

I was expecting my morning client now, so my call to Nancy would have to wait until later. As it turned out, I didn't have an opportunity that whole day to phone her. It would now have to wait until after the lecture.

The Poquetannuck Recreation Hall was packed! All women. There were approximately one hundred and fifty people there! What a warm welcome I received and what a super crowd of people! They were very congenial and the excitement on their faces made me feel so pleased. Questions were being asked from every section of the hall. I enjoyed sharing and enlightening, especially with those who were skeptical. If I was able to reach one person in the audience, by bringing them closer to God, it made me feel as though a true mission was accomplished. When the forum ended, I received a standing ovation with an overwhelming round of applause.

"Thank you! Thank you for having me tonight! Sharing my experiences and hopefully enlightening you has been *my* pleasure!" I remarked, tears spilling out of my eyes.

I drove home on cloud nine again. It was offering my gifts to help people individually and in groups like these, which gave me the strength to overcome any pitfalls. And there would always be '*pitfalls*'.

When I arrived at home. I telephoned Nancy Ritter.

"Mrs. Ritter, this is Pat Gagliardo, from Connecticut," I said when she answered the phone.

"Oh yes. Thank you for returning my call."

"I want you to understand, I can't make any promises about finding your husband, but I'll do the best that I can."

"I understand that. We're at a dead end. We have nowhere else to turn. Anything at all will be most appreciated."

She began to tell me the story. As she was speaking, over and over in my mind, I saw a small plane crash-landing over some very rough terrain and mountainous area. I didn't feel as though the pilot died from the crash. I did feel the area was very remote.

"Mrs. Ritter, can you send me something that belonged to your husband?"

"Oh Dougie and I would much rather fly you down here. We feel that if you're in the surroundings, it would be more beneficial."

"I don't want you to have to do that. Why don't we try by mail first? It's less of an expense, and could quite possibly provide the same results."

"Listen, Pat. My husband is missing, the father of my child—I am not concerned about the money!" she said, with a pleading in her voice.

"I didn't mean to sound like I wouldn't come, it's just that I didn't want to burden you with expenses on top of your situation."

"Let us worry about that, okay? And we also *insist* on you bringing your husband."

"Well, I will have to make some arrangements on my end, and my husband works rotating shifts. However, he does have two and three days off together on certain shifts."

"Fine. I will get back to you tomorrow."

Nancy was a very determined woman. I had no idea then that this was all part of a plan from the spirit world, and her involvement of what was to come in the not too distant future.

Gene and I discussed our going to Georgia. The next weekend was his 'long weekend', three consecutive days off. The plans were made and we would leave for Atlanta, Georgia, the following Saturday. I called the members of our group and asked that we meet on Thursday night instead of Saturday. That was all set too.

On Wednesday, a woman from Norwich telephoned. She informed me that her fourteen-year old son had been missing since yesterday.

"Can you please help me?"

"I am getting the description of a dark haired boy, with a small build, and he's not very tall. Was he wearing a light blue jacket?"

"Yes. He was mad at us because of his smoking," she cried. "My husband yelled at him. He left the house slamming the door! I'm so worried..."

"Do you live on a dead-end street?" I interrupted. "I feel the road is on an incline—lots of trees. There is also an old shack, it's in the near vicinity—I believe the kids hang around there."

"Yes! Everything you have said is correct! Do you see my son?"

"I believe he is close by, and spent the night with a friend. And I think he's at a big field of some kind, maybe baseball, I am not sure. I also feel he will be coming home soon."

"Really? He's all right then? You don't see him hurt someplace or worse?" she asked, anxiety very noticeable in her tone.

"I think he is simply cooling off. And if I were you I would give him a heck of a talking to!" I remarked lightheartedly in the hopes of calming her down.

"Okay. Thank you," she replied and hung up.

Two hours later, I heard from her again. The police had found her son. He was in the *baseball* field with some other youngsters. It was a few blocks from their home.

On Thursday night we prepared the room in the usual manner for meditation. The experience of this night was more visual enlightenment and confirmation of what lay ahead.

When our meditation ended, I began to verbally express the events that took place in my mind, and it was recorded on tape.

"The first thing I saw was a small plane. I saw it crash on a plateau somewhere. There was one man in the plane. I got the feeling the area was not in the U.S. I felt it was out of the country and remote. I *heard* the engine cutting out—and maybe that's why it crashed. I didn't sense the man dead, though. And a name like—Windward. I don't know what it means yet, but I am sure I'll find out."

I rewound the tape and we listened to it while we were having refreshments.

About halfway through—we heard it! There were some very definite moaning sounds! And then what sounded like someone calling my name! It was in a strained whisper, and then it was gone! There was nothing else but silence for a while, and then we heard my voice. I was talking about seeing the plane and then we heard...

"Putta-putt-putta-putt-putta!" It sounded just like a motor cutting out! And it was loud! We would understand very soon who and what that phenomenon pertained to.

On Saturday morning our flight to Atlanta was taking off from Hartford at seven am, and returning that same night at eleven pm. Our flight was booked solid. There wasn't one unoccupied seat. We found our seats, sat down and buckled up. Gene was nervous. This was the first time he had ever been on a plane. I told him how amazing and beautiful the 'sights' down below were when viewed from the sky, in the hopes of calming him down. The flight was great. I was glad that his first experience flying went so smoothly.

We arrived at the airport in Atlanta at 9:50. In the lobby we saw an attractive, slender woman, wearing glasses and approximately five feet six inches tall, with long dark brunette hair. She was holding up a large white sign with our names on it. Next to her was a man about five feet ten, with blonde hair and of medium build.

Formal introductions were made between the four of us and then we were on our way to Peachtree City. What an absolutely beautiful small town! It looked like a resort from a magazine! The homes were all gorgeous. Everything was split into little villages. Mrs. Ritter lived in Glen Loch.

Once we were inside the house, we didn't waste any time. Gene and Mrs. Ritter stayed out in the kitchen and Doug took me into another room of the house. It was a guest room.

He had handed me some various items belonging to Larry Ritter, the missing man. Among the items was some jewelry. There was a gold ring with black onyx and a couple of small gemstones in it. I decided I would hold this piece to perform the psychometry.

I sat down on the edge of the bed and Doug sat across from me in a chair.

I closed my eyes, took a deep breath and began the psychometry. The colors instantly appeared. The next thing I envisioned was a small plane. I also sensed that it was raining, and the plane was caught in it. And then I saw the pilot. I began to describe the visions to Doug.

"This man that I am seeing has blonde hair, but dark, not light like your color. I really can't tell how tall he is, I am sensing about five feet ten. I see a light blue jacket. There is also a turtleneck—a shirt—hm-m-m. Tell me, did your friend wear his shirt sleeves rolled up to about the middle of his forearm?" I asked, opening my eyes and looking at Doug.

"Yes. Yes he did. That's the *only* way he wore them. And your description and clothing is right."

"I feel he had to crash-land the plane. He ran into some problems. I can give you a description of the area. I felt it's in Haiti. It's very remote. I sensed a mountainous region, a plateau. Another plane there too, but not belonging to the missing man. I am not sure why I sensed that, unless it's another missing pilot and plane in that same area. I don't know. As for Mr. Ritter, I also picked up on some serious injuries. I felt he had hurt his leg. The wound was open and bleeding heavily. Doug, he may not have died as a result of the crash, but with this wound, I-uh, and the area, I am really not sure now what may have become of him," I said sadly.

"I understand," he said solemnly. "Is there anything else?"

"I don't think so. That's all I perceived."

We left the guest room and joined Gene and Mrs. Ritter.

"Doug, where does she think Larry is?" she asked.

"Somewhere in Haiti. She feels he had to crash-land the plane. She doesn't think he died in the crash though."

I was a little surprised by his last statement, but understood why he may have said that to Mrs. Ritter. I guess he wanted to offer her some hope until all efforts were exhausted.

"Mrs. Ritter," I began.

"Call me Nancy," she interrupted.

"All right, Nancy, does the name Windward mean anything to you?"

"It sure does!" Doug hollered, "There's a Windward Pass that Larry would have had to fly through! Why? What do you feel about it?"

"I'm not sure, but I felt he may have been in a storm through there."

"That's more than likely. There are storms through there all the time. And they can hit all of a sudden, without any warning."

"Oh, well that probably explains why I felt he veered off course and somehow landed in Haiti."

"I have some maps. Let's circle the area you feel it is. I will gather a search party and we'll start looking," Doug said leaving the room to get the maps.

In just a few minutes he returned. In his left hand he had two maps rolled up and secured with a rubber band.

He stretched one map out across the dining room table. I looked at the map and pointed to an area that I felt might possibly be where he landed. Doug circled it with a black pen.

"I don't know if you are going to have much success with air visualization alone," I said. "Searching by foot would also be extremely difficult, even if you could safely land a plane in there," I stated empathically.

"You're right," Doug sighed, "I've been over parts of that area myself. I am going to make some calls, Nancy. We have to try."

Nancy smiled at Doug and nodded. Doug went into the other room again and Nancy made some refreshments. We engaged in conversation about our personal lives. She wanted to know about my life, how I began, etc. She told us about her life, husband and her son, Larry Jr. By the time we left her house to head back to the airport, a friendship had developed between us. Unfortunately, Larry and his plane were never found, but I would be seeing a lot more of Nancy in the future, but it would be under different circumstances. And, we would become friends!

We slept late on Sunday. Gene and I were both exhausted from the trip. I needed to just relax, emotionally and physically. So we planned the day to do just that. That evening, I heard from Mrs. Flayer again.

"Pat! I've got good news!" she said, when I answered the phone.

"Do you remember telling me where you thought the horses were?" and then she added, "Well, you were right! They were there! You told me to leave right away, but I couldn't get anyone to watch the stables right then. I had to wait a few days. I checked my book, as I told you, and there was a Cherry Hills in New York! I went there with pictures of the horses and a ranch hand identified them!"

"That's wonderful!" I exclaimed, "I am happy for you and your girls. Did you get them?"

"Well, that's the problem now. They were moved from there. That's why I am calling. Do you think you can tell me where they are now?"

She no sooner got the words out of her mouth, and sorrow overcame me. The impression I received was not good. I felt the horses were disposed of—and the meat sold, in another country. I couldn't tell her that over the phone. I asked her to send me pictures of the horses by mail, and then I would write to her. How I wished she had been able to leave immediately and retrieve the horses. It was now out of both our hands.

*   *   *

The weather was breaking now. There was a definite scent and feeling of spring in the air! And tomorrow was April 1st. A thrilling and exciting day was in store for my family and me! Today was the day I would spend with Mark Wile from P.M. Magazine. They would be filming the Potpourri Show and later that evening, a lecture at the Otis Library.

The van pulled up in front of my house. It was white, with red, blue and yellow printing, "P.M. Magazine, Providence, Rhode Island.'

I greeted both gentlemen at the front door.

"Hi!" I called, excitement in my voice.

"Hi. I'm Mark Wile and this is my associate, Mike Casierri."

"How do you do?" I smiled and shook their hands. "I am really excited about the events today. We have to be leaving here very shortly. The broadcast starts at 10:05."

"Fine. We'll follow you. And it's our pleasure to have you on the show, Pat. A psychic phenomenon is a very interesting topic. And if we have time later, I would like to speak to you privately, okay?"

"Sure," I smiled. "We had better be going now."

Once we arrived at WICH, all the staff gathered around to meet Mark and Mike. The girls all oohed and ahhed, and with very good reason! Mark was even more handsome in person than on television. He had dark brown hair, gorgeous blue eyes, striking facial features, and was of medium build and height. He was also very charming. Mike was also nice looking with dark brown hair, brown eyes, a full beard and of medium height, and was a little overweight. Both of the men had a great sense of humor.

The show got underway. Mark sat in the booth with me, while I performed readings over the phone and answered questions. Mike was standing outside the glass door, filming. After the broadcast, we stayed and had light conversation with some of the employees. Then we left the station for my home, for the interview. Dennis came too.

We sat around my dining room table. I gave Mark some of the details of my 'new' life. How I became involved, my skepticism, and the details of some of the cases I had aided in.

While we were talking, Mike was setting up his equipment. There were two very tall lights. One was set up to the left of us and the other one was placed directly in front of me. He had placed umbrellas on top of both of the light poles. The lights gave off a lot of heat. He explained that that was the reason for the umbrellas. Mike picked up the Panasonic video recorder and began taping my conversation with Mark.

Within just a couple of minutes, Mark asked me, "Pat, do you think your powers are connected with the devil?"

I was prepared for the question. As I was about to answer, he interjected...

"Let me rephrase that question. Do you feel your powers are Satanic?"

"POW!" The light bulb on the fixture in front of me blew right out! Mike's eyes were as big as saucers! "That's a brand new thousand watt bulb!" he shrieked. "I don't think it has an hour's use on it! It must be a fuse."

He walked over to the pole, removed the umbrella and to his amazement, realized it was not a fuse. He threw his hands up in the air and rolled his eyes up towards the ceiling and said, "Okay. We understand. We *know* it comes from you!"

Mark just looked at him peculiarly. And then he looked at me, total confusion on his face.

I began to tell him of the past electrical disturbances that have always occurred in my presence. Dennis joined in, "Believe what she's telling you. It's the absolute truth! I have witnessed it many times!" he laughed.

There was a very definite look of doubt that crossed Mark's face. But, then he said, "Hmm, that was a new bulb, and we haven't ever experienced that before."

Mike, on the other hand, believed! He was making comments about the incident, "Forgive us! We won't say that again." He told us a few stories he had heard from his family, when he was a child. He was a believer in God; no doubt.

He began to rewind the tape in the recorder to view it. His intention was to restart the videotape at this new juncture. He let out with another squeal, "Look at this Mark! Tell me this is *coincidence* too?"

The videotape was brand-new. Yet, there were wavy lines, and it was extremely fuzzy. "It looks just like it does, when the *battery* is going dead!" Mike exclaimed. "How can that be when I am using the AC outlet!"?

Dennis just giggled. Then he said, "Once she calms down, everything will go back to normal. Her *energy* is still high from doing the show and all the excitement."

I made some coffee. We talked about different matters, and when we resumed the interview, everything went fine.

I had to return to work that afternoon. Mark and Mike followed my bus routes with their van. Mike was taking pictures from the rear of the van. My students loved it!

Most of them wanted to cram in the front seats.

I had layover time at one of the schools and there were other drivers, too. Dennis also accompanied us. All of them climbed onto my bus. The drivers were asking Mark questions. Everyone truly enjoyed the visit.

We returned to my house and ordered some pizzas for dinner. I had to freshen up and change for the lecture. At six thirty, we left for the Otis Library.

People had already begun to gather in the lobby. The lecture was scheduled for seven to nine. I searched the aisles, office and back section for Mr. Leonard. Finally, I found him downstairs. He was setting up chairs and putting them in rows. He was using the conference room— seating capacity, approximately seventy people.

"Mr. Leonard, excuse me," I said, walking up behind him. "I don't think using this room will be feasible. I have a *feeling* we are going to have a good size crowd."

"Really?" he asked, turning to face me. "Lectures have always been held in this room. And I don't recollect it ever being full," he said with conviction.

"Okay," I replied, with a note of, I-think-you're-wrong in my tone.

Fifteen minutes later, the entire children's library, which took up three-fourths of the downstairs, was full. There were enough chairs for two hundred people. The rest were standing everywhere!

Smiling, he approached me. "I don't know why I didn't listen to you!" he laughed, "You're psychic after all!"

What a *feeling* was present in that library! As I continued with the forum, my eyes roamed in every direction. There were men and women, young and old. Most of them seemed engrossed in the questions and answers. The interest was overwhelming!

It was nearing nine thirty, and the questions were still coming.

"Ladies and gentlemen. Please allow me to take this opportunity to express my gratitude and sincere appreciation for your attendance this evening. It's been my pleasure to share tonight with you."

The audience rose from their seats and began clapping. A few from every corner began shouting; "Longer! Longer!" I was delighted by their enthusiasm.

They didn't want it to end! I was so taken by their response that I began to cry. Silently I whispered, "Thank you Lord. Thank you so much."

Dennis stood by the door, counting the people as they left. He was also thanking each one for coming. Two hundred and forty four people had attended the lecture. Mark, Mike, Dennis, Gene and I were thrilled by the turnout. We left and drove to my house.

Mark was absolutely ecstatic over the day's events. He and Mike stayed for coffee and dessert, and then had to leave. He thanked me for the day and said, "This is going to be a real pleasure for me to air on the program. I hope to call you in the future, and we can do an update."

"Thank you Mark," I replied, and gave him a hug. "Thank you too, Mike. It was a pleasure meeting you."

"You too," he smiled and gave me a hug.

We said our good-byes and they were gone.

*   *   *

I was still daydreaming about it all the next day. I couldn't get the events of the night before out of my mind. So much was happening in my life! Me—housewife—ordinary person had been chosen to have such beautiful gifts! It was overwhelming.

At five thirty that evening. I heard from Larry.

"Well, you were right on again!" he laughed. "The boy that was missing was found in Alabama! It was nearly three weeks to the day!

"He's okay, isn't he Larry?"

"Oh yeah. Just tired and hungry."

"That's great news. Thank you for letting me know. You made my day!"

"Did you hear from the UFO center, Pat?"

"No. Why was I supposed too?"

"Well, I gave them your name and phone number. There is a man that is going to phone you from Australia. A young man, twenty-one years old has been missing for two years. It's an alleged UFO abduction case."

"Really? That would be interesting."

"Yeah. Dr. Hynek and I talked about you. Some folks are going to be sending you an item to perform psychometry with."

"Okay. If I get anything in the mail, I'll let you know, Larry."

I checked the mail every day. Nothing had arrived yet. It was Monday, group night. I was looking forward to the meditation, hoping I might perceive some impressions about the UFO case. It would prove to be very interesting and enlightening if indeed, this young man *was* abducted by a UFO!

What did happen that night was something, though. It didn't have anything to do with UFO's, but it did revolve around flying objects! Police cars!

Everyone arrived for meditation. Edie's sister, Donna, and Dennis, attended the group also. Gene was at work.

In my meditation, I perceived the following information.

The first thing I had sensed was the name, Jefferson. Then I saw two men standing near the water's edge, and they were fighting. They appeared to be in a cove. I saw a red colored building and the impression that I received was that it was a mill. And then the word 'falls' kept repeating itself in my mind. I also felt there was a small park up the road from this area. It had one table, and I had the impression of 'green', perhaps it was referred to as the 'green'. The vision then returned to the two men arguing. The next impression was that they were fighting over a body in the water! Then that scene disappeared very quickly, and I saw an elderly man in a boat! He had his back to me and he was wearing tan khaki clothing. I knew he wasn't fishing—I didn't sense a pole, or see one. I kept thinking of the word 'Jefferson' and felt that it was the key to finding out where this area was and of the events that had taken place.

"Jefferson Avenue is well-known in New London," Donna said.

"Yes. Yes it is. I am going to call my cousin, Sam. Maybe he'll listen to me, now," I smiled.

I telephoned the New London Police Department to find out if he was working.

"New London Police Station. Sergeant Johnson speaking."

"Hello, Sergeant. My name is Pat Gagliardo. Is Officer Sam Grillo working?"

"Just a minute, please."

"Hi cuz! What's up kid?" Sam's gruff voice asked.

"Hi Sam. I think I-uh saw something happening or something that has happened in New London." I gave him all the details and prepared myself for his little quips. Even though he always teased me about it, I really felt that down deep, he believed.

And to my surprise, he said, "I know that area you're talking about. And the reason you're getting the word 'falls' is that there is a buoy out there called, 'Outfalls'.

The station received a call about an hour ago about that location. Some guy called and said there was a *baby* in the water. We took a ride out there and searched with a flashlight, but we didn't find anything though."

"A baby? I sensed a body, too. Hmm, I wonder why I would have envisioned all of those details and that area, if it doesn't mean anything."

"Look, Pat. Why don't you take a ride up here and we'll check it out again. Bill Gavitt and Sergeant Lynch are both on tonight. We'll take you out there."

I looked at the clock. It was eleven o'clock at night. I asked Edie if she would ride up there with me. She nodded.

"Okay, Sam, Edie's coming with me. We'll be there in a little while."

We said our good-byes and Edie and I were on our way to New London.

I pulled the car over to the sidewalk, in front of the police station. It was nearly midnight now. The street near the station was deserted. New London was a typical old New England town. Some of its buildings were quite old, and some very dilapidated. Being that it was a Navy town, there was always some kind of action going on. So I was somewhat reluctant to be on the street at this time of night.

In the station, Sam and Bill were waiting for us. We walked into a small office to the right of the front desk.

"Pat, you'll have to run all that information by me again, okay?" Bill asked. "I have to make a report."

By the time we left the station, and proceeded to the area, it was nearly one o'clock in the morning. We all drove out in the cruiser. Sergeant Lynch was driving, Edie and I were in the front and Sam and Bill were in the back seat. Sergeant Lynch parked the car and took out a large flashlight from the trunk, and turned it on. When we approached the location, my body began to tremble. It was just as I had envisioned it! We walked to the cove's inlet. As I walked closer, my eyes were scanning every inch. In the meantime, Sam and Bill went in another direction. I zeroed in on two huge rocks jutting out of the water—they were in my meditation! I had forgotten about them until just then. "The body is over there! In between those two rocks!" I shouted to Sergeant Lynch.

The ground was very mushy. We could not walk out to the two rocks. The tide *had gone out*, and left the sand too soft to walk on. Sam and Bill had walked way out to the point.

"Sam and Bill are too far out, Sergeant. If I had a flashlight and boots, I'd be walking out there to those two rocks," I told him, pointing.

He was looking at me curiously. I think that he felt he was wasting his time. It was written on his face. He had been present in the room, when

I gave Bill the report. I even mentioned the man that I had seen in the boat. I was glad that I had.

"Pat! Look!" Edie bellowed. She was pointing to the right of us. I was quite a few feet away from her, so the sergeant and I walked over to where she was pointing. There with *his back to us*, was the man in the boat! He was rowing towards us. He was only a few feet away now, so we could see him very clearly. He was wearing tan clothing; he didn't have a fishing pole, because he was crabbing! When the sergeant looked at the elderly man and his clothes, he simply shook his head and said, "I don't believe it! What's the chance of finding a guy in a boat, at this hour! Young lady, you've just made a believer out of me! Ever consider joining the police department?" he asked, shaking his head from side to side.

A call came over the radio. All three of us returned to the police car. Sam and Bill were still somewhere out on the point. The call was for a robbery in progress! The next thing we knew, we were flying down the road in the car. A package store was being burglarized and we were on our way to it! Edie and I were scared to death! It was a bit more than we had bargained for.

Thank God other patrolmen had apprehended the suspects. They were already handcuffed and placed in another cruiser when we arrived.

While we were at the crime scene, Sam and Bill had been walking down from the point. Sam had injured his hand jumping a fence. We drove him to the hospital. The injury was not serious. It was bandaged and he was released.

Sergeant Lynch told us he would have someone thoroughly search the area where we had been in the morning.

Sam called me the next afternoon. A large black plastic bag had been found. There were bloodstains and other fragments inside of it. It had been wedged between the *two rocks*. They felt that if it had, in fact, contained a small baby, it could have fallen or been pulled out by crabs. The tide would have carried it out to sea. The bag was at the crime lab, and would be analyzed. Two weeks later, the skeletal remains of an infant were washed up on the New Haven shore. The case underwent an investigation; to my knowledge, it remains unsolved.

*   *   *

The next day a small manila envelope arrived at my residence. It was from the center for UFO research. Enclosed was a short letter, and three items—a driver's license with a snapshot of a young boy, an empty pack of cigarettes, and an envelope. I telephoned Larry and told him I had received the information from the center and would work on it that day and return it as soon as possible.

The letter was cordially written, asking me to handle the items and to please send the information that I perceived to the address in the return enveloped enclosed.

I performed psychometry on the license first. I envisioned a home, its surroundings, and different landmarks in the area. I sensed some characteristics of the individual and some information pertaining to his health. I was a little ambivalent to reveal the latter part, as I was unsure if anyone knew of his health problem. Not being a diagnostician, I could not tell the exact nature of the disease; I could only perceive its symptoms. And my impressions were that it was incurable and would lead to an early death.

The cigarette pack I felt belonged to a woman. I was able to describe her in complete detail. She was approximately five-feet 4 inches tall, medium length hair; light brown in color and petite in build. I had perceived her first name, Anne, and a description of her vehicle and some personal information about her.

The envelope, I felt, had a connection with this woman. I felt sadness, and strong emotional turmoil. It also enabled me to learn certain facts about a young man who might be involved. I perceived some other personal facets of the case, as well.

Later that week, Larry telephoned. The information had been verified. The envelope was the property of the woman's daughter. All of the information was correct. The young man was suffering from Leukemia; it was not a shock to anyone to learn of this, and Larry assured me that no one had been upset by the report.

"Pat, I want you to understand that your abilities weren't being tested out of skepticism on their part. And they certainly were not judging your credibility. There are a lot of scientists affiliated with the center. I think they just wanted to look into the psychic aspects."

"Larry, you don't have to explain their motives. If I didn't want to do it, I wouldn't have."

"It's for a good reason. I am sure you'll be getting involved with that Galentich episode. The one I told you about. It's a big story, and there's quite a bit of controversy over it."

"I'll do whatever I can, Larry." He didn't give me any details at that point. We exchanged good-byes and hung up.

It was this same evening that I heard from Andy Rebmann, a state trooper, who also trained and worked with tracking dogs. He told me he was affiliated with the Colchester, Connecticut State Police barracks.

"Hi Pat. My name is Andy Rebmann. I work with special tactics; tracking dogs. I'm working on a missing person's case from Maine. A woman has been missing for twenty-two months. Is there any way we could meet? I thought possibly you might be able to help me out."

"Mr. Rebmann, does this woman have psychological problems? I'm feeling she was under a doctor's care and on medication." I replied.

"Uh-why yes. I believe so," he answered; bewildered by the information I was able to perceive right over the phone.

He continued to speak, but I had already attuned to his voice, and I said, "I'm seeing a wooded area. And I'm getting the impression it's a place she had been familiar with. It's within only a mile or so from where she lived. There's a shack on top of a hill. Two broken trees, slender trunks, on the decline from the hill—about half way down. At the bottom you'll find two large, very large, either rocks, or pieces of ledge jutting out. My feeling is—ohhh, I believe she has committed suicide. And up near that shack, the ground will be concave in a small area. I'm sensing bones there."

"Okay! Wow! I'll certainly check it out! I'm going up there this weekend. The only problem we're faced with at this point, is time. There are a lot of wild animals in the woods. They could have carted those bones to Timbuktu by now! Thanks so much, Pat. I'll call and let you know."

That was the first time I had ever heard of Andy Rebmann. I had no idea then that I would be working with him again and on many different cases. I found him to be pleasant, sincere, willing to go above and beyond the call of duty, and with a good sense of humor. His personality rang out in his voice. We all eventually became friends.

In the not too distant future, Andy would be directly responsible for organizing a lecture/seminar at the Day's Inn in Mystic. The persons invited would be local and state police officials in every capacity, as well as other law enforcement officials from around the nation! He would introduce me as a 'reliable and credible source of information' and a 'gift' to law enforcement personnel.

*   *   *

Summer was around the corner! It would be here in no time! Already we were into the last week of May. New England was so picturesque this time of year. Flowers spread their fragrances everywhere. Soon the swimming season would start. All of us loved the water! The pool in our backyard always had someone in it every available minute! When I could, I enjoyed it for relaxation and meditation.

I had just finished reading the morning paper when the telephone rang. It was a call from an Officer D'Mico of the Groton, Connecticut Police Department.

A young girl of fifteen had been missing for a week. The only clue that they had was that she had telephoned her brother on the evening of her disappearance. There had been no further word, or any trace of her since. She came from a broken home, and her mother was extremely worried and upset. She felt that harm had come to her daughter. She expected to hear the worst.

In speaking with the officer, and making an attunement with direct-voice, there were several impressions coming to me. I saw an embankment, the river, railroad tracks, and a man in a tower of some sort. I told the officer that there was a school in the vicinity. I felt that she had been talking to the 'man'. I told him I felt she was in New London, the next town over, and only a few miles away. I felt she was staying with someone. I gave him the description of a house, somewhat run-down, and on a dead-end street. There were junk cars and some other debris in the backyard.

He said the first area was familiar to him. He would also talk to the man in the tower, a railroad employee. Later that day, I heard from the officer again. He had spoken with the railroad employee and showed him a picture of Carol, the missing girl. The attendant acknowledged the fact that she had been there. He asked me if I would please come to the station to help further. He would have the missing girls mother present. I agreed.

When I arrived at the station, introductions were made. The mother was about my height, five feet two inches tall, heavyset, and of foreign descent. My heart went out to her. Pain and anguish distorted her lovely features.

As I looked at her, she asked, a very noticeable accent in her voice, "Do you think my daughter is okay? I am so very worried."

I smiled and patted her arm. "I'll help all I can. I do think she is okay at this point."

Officer D'Mico wanted to take me to the area. I asked him not to have the mother accompany us. I felt it would only upset her. He agreed.

We left in the cruiser and he drove me to the area of the tower, and a small beach. It was a place the girl frequented quite often. As we drove to several different locations, I perceived the names 'Brown or Brainer'. I still felt she was in New London. It was out of his jurisdiction. We drove back to the Groton Station, and he told me he was going to contact the New

London Police Department, and ask them to check on it. Before I left, I told him he shouldn't be too concerned, I felt there would be word from the missing girl herself.

A couple of days later, her picture appeared in the Bulletin newspaper. The officer telephoned me and said he had heard from the girl. She called him and said that she was all right, but she wasn't going back home. She wanted to stay where she was! However, someone recognized her from the newspaper photo and called the police—the New London Police! She had taken up residence with a friend who lived on a dead-end street and worked on junk cars!

*   *   *

That evening I heard from Andy Rebmann again.

"Hi Pat! Just wanted to let you know, by the description and details you gave me, that wooded area in Maine was laid out just like a map for me!" he laughed. "I did find a bone, or I should say, my dog found the bone. It was in the area of that shack. It's at the crime lab now. It was pretty good size, I'm sure they'll be able to determine something from it. Thanks a lot. I'll be calling you again some time if that's okay with you."

"I was glad I was able to help you, Andy. Call any time. And also, thanks for letting me know."

"Great. And by the way, in case you didn't know, when I first spoke with you, you made the hair stand up on the back of my neck! I wasn't prepared for you to just start telling me stuff like that right over the phone!"

"Yes, I know. It's called direct-voice. I really can't explain it to you. It's like a switch in my mind that takes me into another dimension, with the help of spiritual guidance. Some day maybe we'll have the opportunity to have coffee together, and I'll tell you all about it."

"We'll make that soon, Pat. My wife, Jan, wants to meet you."

"I'll look forward to it, Andy."

My faith was growing in leaps and bounds. How I thanked God every day for these wonderful 'gifts', and the benefits everyone received from them. Every opportunity to share them and to enlighten other persons concerning faith gave me immeasurable pleasure and happiness.

Naturally, I had some rough moments as well. Each time I became involved with missing persons, or crime related cases, it created some tension and pressure. It was a great responsibility! The people who took action—searchers, authorities and families—did so all on the strength of my information. I tried to always rely on my faith for every outcome. Still, at times I dealt with frustrations, despair and other human emotions, and the greatest test of my faith was yet to come!

I received another call from a local authority, Officer Mike Duthrie, from the Ledyard Police Department. Mike was also the son of my sister-in-law, Del. Two girls were missing from the town of Ledyard. I told Mike that I felt the girls had hitchhiked to the beach. However, I wasn't sure which beach, Ocean Beach, in New London, or Misquamicut Beach, in Westerly, Rhode Island. I did feel that were in the amusement section of the beach. Mike said he would call both authorities and ask them to check it out.

Within a couple of days Mike called back. The girls were located in New London at Ocean Beach Park. They were at the amusement section and then were traveling toward the beach section. They were apprehended by the local authorities there and returned to their homes.

Things began to quiet down some for a few weeks. At least with the telephone, that is. Mail still continued to come in on a regular basis. Most of the mail consisted of people asking for help with missing jewelry and pets. Some wanted winning lottery numbers, and other gambling information! There were also letters from persons just wishing to express warm and congenial thoughts of a personal nature to me. And there were those who just felt a 'need' to share there religious views; positive and negative.

I welcomed the change of pace. My mind needed the rest. And it allowed me more time with my family. However, I believe it was more planning from the Holy Spirit world for what lie ahead. I would need to be completely refreshed and very aware! This would be the first experience to alert me to the very real dangers and risks to my own personal safety! And it wouldn't be the last!

Earlier I mentioned how the 'opposition' tried to deter me through my son and co-workers. It's important to note here, that all through this time there were many 'scare tactics' that were used to deter me from continuing on my path.

The first incident was a fire that started in the furnace of our basement. When we called our oil service man, and he came out and checked it, he was perplexed as to what may have caused it. There was no explanation! The furnace had been cleaned a couple of months earlier. The fire frightened me beyond words, as it was the cause of my brother, Jim's death.

In another incident *three* pipes had burst in the ceiling above our hallway closet! The damage was extensive. Reason? None. You might expect this if it was wintertime and cold; this was not the case.

Both batteries in our vehicles turned up completely dead at the same time! Both of our vehicles were only two years old! Again, it was not wintertime, nor was it cold.

Our beloved pet, King, a Labrador retriever, well behaved and well trained, disappeared! Even with posters up, and ads in the newspapers, he was never found.

Before you even consider the word 'coincidence', or think 'those things may have happened anyway' let me say this; in *all* these situations there wasn't one *human* explanation, of why or what the cause was. They all happened within a very short period of time. However, I would not let it deter me!

We persisted, continued with our meditations and extending our prayer time. It was during a meditation that I perceived visions of another missing person, and a new awareness! This case would take me to Tennessee…

*   *   *

"I am seeing a house. It's sitting up high on a hill. It looks like an older home. I'm getting the name, 'Ridge' something. The house is white. There is a porch with a swing hanging from it. Hmm, there is a sailboat coming into view—it's tipped on its side. Now I see a badge or a pin with a design on it. I am getting a strong impression that I am going there. Yet, I am uncomfortable about this for some reason."

Within two weeks, I knew the reason for that meditation.

I received a telephone call from a Kevin Kelly. His wife had been missing for about a week. He was telephoning at the request of his mother-in-law, Patricia.

"Ms. Gagliardo, my wife's mother is wondering if you would come here to Tennessee, and help us out here?" the young man asked.

In speaking with him, the previous visions of the meditation entered into my mind. I asked him if he could send me something belonging to his wife. He didn't allow me to finish the sentence, when he said, "She wants you to come here."

Something was nagging at me and I said, "I will have to bring someone with me."

Arrangements were made—I would leave July second. Edie would accompany me, as Gene was scheduled to work.

The trip to Tennessee was a couple of weeks away. In the meantime I had heard from Andy Rebmann again. He asked me if I could help him locate a woman who was missing from a nearby Connecticut town. I was able to describe her, her car and her home to him over the phone. I told Andy that I sensed she was the victim of a brutal beating and that she was buried near the residence, and close to water. Andy said he was going to the police department of that town the next day. I asked him if he had any idea what they were going to give him belonging to the woman, to provide his tracking dog with her 'scent'. He answered, no. I described a brown pair of shoes with some kind of buckle or clasp on them. He assured me he would let me know, and thanked me for the information.

Two days later, Andy called back.

"You and I have to meet, young lady!" he snickered, when I answered the phone.

"Did you hear the news yet?"

"No, I haven't Andy. How did you make out?"

"She was there all right—buried under a brand new patio! Right next to the pool! Her husband has been arrested for the crime. But, that's not the only reason I called you. Remember telling me about the brown shoes? Well, that's what the chief handed me in a plastic bag! Brown shoes with buckles! As I told you, you raise the hair right off the back of my neck! And I haven't even laid eyes on you yet!"

"I'd like to meet with you too, Andy. And I am sure we will someday soon."

"I hope so. Thanks again, Pat."

"Andy, thank God."

*   *   *

Early in the morning of July 2nd we left for the airport for our two-day excursion in Tennessee. This trip was one of great emotional stress and a frightening new learning phase for me!

We were met at the airport, by Pat, the mother, and her husband, Fred and the missing woman's husband, Kevin.

The first thing Kevin said to me made me very uneasy immediately.

"The media is all over this case. I've picked a hotel that's remote. No one will know where you are," he said, picking up our suitcases and heading toward the exit of the airport's lobby.

"I don't think so, Kevin. You *do* have the police involved, don't you? I want to call them and let someone know I am here, and where I will be at all times."

"Yes, the police are involved. The Constable, John Brown, knows we've called you," he answered.

"I'd like to meet with him."

"I'll arrange it," Pat said.

We drove out to the hotel first. I suggested that Edie and I would like to freshen up, and then I would give Pat a call and, if she wouldn't mind, she could pick us up to go to her home. She said that would be fine.

Once inside our room, Edie and I shared our unsettled feelings.

"What do you think about her husband?" she asked. "He doesn't appear to be too emotional or concerned, does he?"

"No. And he sort of gives me the creeps."

"Well, I shouldn't think about it. I don't want it to interfere with the psychometry I have to do. But, I do know one thing for sure, I want to speak with that constable as soon as we get to their house."

"No kidding! I mean we don't know what happened to her, or why!" exclaimed Edie.

I didn't even have time to call. In about an hour, Kevin arrived at our hotel, alone. He had a lot of food with him. There was sliced ham, potatoes, beans, rolls and several desserts. He said that Pat had made the food for us as she figured we would be hungry from the trip. He placed the box of food on the dresser and sat down on the bed.

"I thought I would take ya'all in my jeep and check out a few areas that I think she might be in," he said calmly.

"Kevin, we don't even know anything yet. Why? Do you think something has happened to her?" I asked curiously.

"Uh, well, she's been missing over a month now, and no one's heard from her. I am assumin' the worst," he said, looking at the floor.

"Well, I need to do some psychometry first. I will do that at Pat's house. She said she had a picture and some items belonging to your wife, Laura."

"All right then. Since I'm here, I'll drive you there."

"Okay. I will call her and let her know we are leaving with you now."

He seemed agitated and very nervous. It put me on guard, and Edie too.

It took approximately twenty-five minutes to reach Pat and Fred's home. Kevin turned right and the road sign said; West *Ridge*. The road was winding and went straight up. There was an older white house that sat at the very top of the hill. There was a *porch* in the front with a *swinging chair*.

Kevin pulled the jeep up the long dirt road and parked close to the steps of the porch.

Pat met us at the door. "Have you eaten?" she asked.

"No, not yet. We will have it later this evening. Thank you so much. It smelled delicious," I said, and Edie nodded.

"Well come on in. Ya'all can have something here for now, while we talk," she smiled.

We entered into the dining room. What a lovely Victorian home! Everything was in perfect order, nicely decorated and very clean. I noticed an 8x10 picture frame on the dark wooden hutch. It contained the picture of a beautiful young woman about twenty years old. She was blonde, with beautiful deep blue eyes and she had a gorgeous smile.

"Is that Laura?"

"Yes." Pat answered sadly.

We had coffee and sandwiches. Pat talked to us about Laura. She was an emergency room nurse. She showed us her *pin* with a design and inscription on it, and a badge with her picture and identification. She worked the late shift, and disappeared on her way to work. There was a witness who said they saw her drive into the hospital's parking lot that night, but she was never seen again after that.

"I need to go there," I said. "I would like to speak with the constable though, first."

"I've already called him, Pat. He is going to meet with you later. I told him where you were staying. He will call you."

"Thank you," I smiled.

Kevin insisted on being wherever we were. We all rode together to the hospital. Kevin drove.

We entered into the parking lot of the hospital and drove to the left and rear of the property. There was water, and a dock that was further back and across from the emergency room entrance. Edie and I walked down to it. And there on the sandy shore, was a *canoe, tipped on its side*! I felt that Laura was distracted on her way into the hospital, by someone she *knew*. Someone had called out her name. I sensed a white or light colored van, with writing on it. I felt an argument, and then a struggle. I would need to do psychometry now and hopefully perceive more information.

"We need to return to your house. I would like an item of Laura's, preferably a piece of jewelry that she wore often."

"Okay," Pat replied.

On the twenty-minute drive back to the house, Pat asked, "Did you feel something happened to Laura there?"

"I'm not real sure. I want to put all the pieces together, Pat. I will tell you what I feel once I have completed the psychometry, okay?" I couldn't bear to tell her what I really felt had happened. I would talk with John Brown, and I would let him take care of it.

The psychometry provided a lot more details. I sensed that Laura was indeed taken from the hospital parking lot, beaten and murdered. I saw an old mill, which hadn't been in operation for a long time. There was a wooded area close to it, and running water, like a creek bed. I also envisioned culvert type piping within that vicinity and Laura somewhere near there. I felt that she was covered, but I couldn't distinguish whether it was dirt, debris, or what. I just knew that she was covered. I didn't reveal this to the family. I just said that I needed to take a look at some areas that I had envisioned.

Kevin insisted on taking me to look at some areas that *he* felt fit the description. I was very reluctant to go with him, but I didn't want to arouse any suspicion at that point either.

"Okay Kevin. Let me call John Brown first and I'll let him know where we are going. Maybe he can join us. It's the way I always work on cases. In case we find something, it's best that the police are there," I said faking a smile.

"You won't get him now. He's out of the office, for sure," he said.

"Well that's okay. I am sure someone can take a message and get it to him," I replied, walking toward the telephone that was hanging on the wall in the kitchen.

As it turned out, the constable was out of the office. However, I left a message with the dispatch person.

Edie and I drove around alone with Kevin for nearly three hours. He had taken us to many different areas, none of which had an old mill or any of the other land markings.

Finally nearing seven pm, I said, "I think it's time to go back, Kevin. I don't feel anything in these areas. Maybe it's just not meant to be," I said, trying to stay calm and not cause any suspicion in him.

"Okay. I'll take you to the hotel."

Back inside the hotel room, Edie said, "You think he did it—killed her. Don't you?"

"I'm not a hundred percent sure, Edie. But I know that I am very uncomfortable around him. And if he didn't do it, I think he may have had someone do it."

"My God! We were alone with him, Pat! Didn't you think he might kill us too!" she shrieked.

"Edie, of course I did. That's why I called the police first and told Kevin that story. I didn't want to make him suspicious. We have to sleep here alone tonight! I want to wake up in the morning. Hopefully right now he thinks nothing is going to come of this," I remarked. "I'm going to call the constable again."

I spoke with a Mr. Robert Gill. He told me that he and John Brown would meet me in the morning and we would drive to the location of the mill. Edie and I were scheduled to leave late that afternoon. If we didn't make that flight, there wouldn't be another one for two more days! All flights were booked because of the 4th of July holiday.

Bright and early the next morning the two gentlemen were knocking at our door. Mr. Brown was dressed in a light brown suit. He was approximately five feet ten, and slender in build. Mr. Gill was dressed in more casual attire, about the same height as Mr. Brown and stockier in build. He also had darker hair.

When I had mentioned the area to Mr. Gill over the phone, he felt that he was familiar with the location. We drove right to it. Everything was there! We only had to walk a little way to find the creek and the cement culverts. The two gentlemen looked around a bit, and then John said, "We'll get some people on this today."

On the ride back to our hotel, I asked him, "Do you feel that her husband is a suspect in this?"

John and Robert exchanged glances and then John replied, "We have our suspicions, but without a body there's not much we can do. We just have that one witness who saw her driving into the parking lot. We're hoping this new information will give us some clues or more."

"I certainly hope so too," I said. "He makes me nervous. There is just something about him. Did I tell you, I kept seeing this van, and it had writing on it. I just couldn't pick up details about the driver. It was strange to me."

"Do you know what Kevin does for a living?" John asked.

"No. We never discussed it."

"He drives a *van* for a *soft drink* company," he replied very calmly

Edie just gasped and said, "Oh, man!"

*   *   *

It took nearly ten months before I heard any feed back on this case. Pat telephoned and gave me all the details. First of all, Laura's body was located, sixty miles away. She was *wrapped* in a plastic body bag, the kind used for people who die in the hospital and taken to the morgue. In light of the positioning of the body, it was determined that the body had been moved. Dirt and other samples were examined at a crime lab. These samples perfectly matched with samples that were taken from an area near the old mill. Kevin finally confessed to the murder of his wife; the motive, a ten thousand dollar insurance policy—which he used to purchase a condominium in another state!

*   *   *

Larry telephoned again. He asked me if I would pick up a gentleman who was coming in by train at the New London station on July 7th. The man was from Australia and wanted to meet with me. In his possession there would be some articles belonging to a young pilot that was missing. What happened to this young man? Had aliens in a U.F.O. abducted him?

"The train is pulling in now, Gene. Why don't we meet him outside?" I suggested, walking to the glass doors that led to the tracks.

"We don't know what he looks like, Pat. Are we going to ask every male passenger his name?" he asked, wrinkling his brow.

"Let's see if we can pick him out."

The passengers were getting off the train and all going in different directions. But when I *saw* him, I knew by the way he walked and appeared, that this must be Mr. Fogarty.

Walking up to the man, I asked, "Mr. Fogarty?"

"That's correct…Pat?"

He resembled my brother, Jim. If his hair were darker, they could have passed for brothers. He was the same height and build and his features bore a shocking similarity.

On the ride to our home, we engaged in idle chatter, to become acquainted. He was a charming man, and his accent added a stunning note to his personality.

Turning into my driveway, I saw Larry's car. I was glad that he had arrived early.

Introductions were passed around again. And then we settled down for the matter at hand. Quentin Fogarty would be leaving soon. Time was of the essence.

He showed us a poem that the missing young man's father had written. It was very touching, and quite sad—a nostalgic type of story that involved another missing person.

"How old is the missing pilot, Quentin?" I asked, passing the poem to Gene.

"He's twenty-one, Pat."

"I'm feeling he had a lot of problems within himself—not being accepted by others, at least, that was *his* viewpoint. When Larry first mentioned this case to me, I felt he was having problems with his job. I had the impression that he had taken a test and failed. I believe that I also felt it was no more than three months prior to his disappearance."

"Well, as far as I am aware, that's true. I am not sure, however, what test he failed. I know that he tried to get into the Air Force, but he failed to meet the requirements. And I believe that the flying he was doing was an attempt to gain experience. I think he was very frustrated that they wouldn't accept him as a pilot," he stated, his face looking very serious. "And I believe it *was* within the three month period. I could stand to be corrected, however, because it was a long time ago that I spoke to the father about these specific things."

"Quentin, would the father have told you honestly of his son's reactions after he had failed the test? I mean, he may not have wanted to put his son in a 'poor light' in your eyes. You see, as you're talking I am picking up these impressions, and it may be quite helpful in finding out what really happened to him. I believe the failure made him withdraw and made him want to be more alone."

"I believe his father expressed to me that his son was very disappointed. But, as far as his father telling me his true feelings about his relationship with his son, I don't know. If I was in the same situation, and I was being questioned about my own son, as you have said, I would naturally have wanted to present him in the best possible light. 'Tis very natural."

"Yes, of course. I think the majority of us would feel that way," I smiled.

"I've a little box of things here, Pat, which I will give to you. The father has written on the objects." He reached into his suitcase and pulled a small box from among its contents. His facial expression remained stern and serious. It was evident that he wanted to help the family in any way that he could. I felt that his motivations were strictly ruled by his compassion and empathy, and not for recognition or monetary gain.

"This is a tie, obviously. He's actually written on it, what it is, and when he wore it. I believe it was while he was in the Air Training Corps. Here," he said, handing it to me.

On the tie was a small piece of masking tape. It read; 'The Training Center, night of October 20, 1978'.

"That's the day before he disappeared," Quentin reported.

I held the tie for a few moments, closed my eyes, took a deep breath and then I asked, "Have you seen his bedroom?"

"I have, yes."

"Is there some type of very large map?"

"There's a big globe."

"Where is it?"

"Just a minute. It's either a globe or a map, now I really don't remember," he frowned.

"Do you remember seeing some markings on the map?"

"Let me think a moment..."

"There are markings—I feel that he had marked something on this map, in red. There is also some paper, the size of manuscript paper, next to the map. It's possible he marked the paper...and..."

"I'll certainly check it out when I go back," he interjected.

"Okay."

"I'm not really sure, Pat. It could have been a globe or a map on the wall, I really don't remember."

"I'm picking up on a small table, by the bedside. That's where those papers are, too. Do you remember seeing those papers?"

"Not offhand."

"Do you remember the description of the clothing that he was wearing? Do you recall a checked, or plaid, some type of print shirt? And very dark trousers—not blue jeans."

"I can't recall."

"Okay. I'm feeling they were a dark blue or black."

"Here again, I'm unsure, Pat. I will check it out."

"Okay. I'm sensing that he was very uptight—tense. Either the day before he disappeared or on the day in question—super uptight. And I feel that he had made several phone calls. If I'm not mistaken, one was a long distance call. Do you know anything about that?"

"No. I didn't get into this sort of detail with his father," he said, reaching into the box again and handing me a steering wheel cover. "This could be interesting, this is the steering wheel cover of the car that he drove down to the airport. So it's probably one of the last things he touched—just before he disappeared."

As I held the cover, Quentin broke into a smile and said, "Sort of a bit nerve-wracking for me. I'm not quite used to this—a new experience for me."

"Did he have a box aboard the plane with him—a small box? Something he would have had to have with him?"

"Here again, I'm unsure. He had to have some kind of container to carry his papers and the like in."

I stayed with the impressions, and I was sensing quite strongly that he might have planned this whole ordeal.

"The plane that he took, I am sensing that it was worked on. That the engine was overhauled—either earlier that day, or the day before."

"I will check. It was a plane that he had hired from the aviation school. And they would have records of that. It is something that can be checked out."

"How long after he was in the air did he report that he saw the flying saucer?"

"I am not positive. But, I believe it was about forty minutes."

"Okay. I have a very good reason for asking you that. This may sound strange to you, but—did he bite his nails?"

A frown crossed his face. It was evident that he didn't see the connection. I did! My impressions led me to believe that he had contemplated for some time on whether or not to radio the tower about 'seeing' the alleged saucer. While these thoughts were running through his mind, I sensed him biting his nails nervously.

He answered quickly and obviously bewildered by my question, "No. No, I don't."

"I sense him being very nervous."

"He had to fill out a flight plan before he left," he stated calmly, reaching into the box again. "I believe this is the pen he used. His father felt that possibly it was the same pen used in filling out the plan," he continued, handing it to me.

"The only thing about the pen is that you don't know how many people have handled it. I'd rather stay with the item I'm using. It has been helpful so far."

"All right, Pat. It's up to you."

I laid the pen down and returned to the cover. I then began to envision the airport.

"Do you know the layout of the airport?"

"Reasonably well," he said. "I've flown out of there many times."

"Good. From the position that I am looking," I began making gestures with my hands, "I know that there are hangars over here and planes here. And it seems to me I'm seeing the backside of the airport. Would he have had to travel in this direction?" I asked, circling my hands above my head, making the location from right to left.

"He could've done so; if the wind was in that direction. You can take off from both ends of the airport," he stated.

"Okay."

"Let me get myself in your position. Please show me the directions again."

"Quentin, I am seeing the building straight on—where the majority of the activities are going on, is to my left."

"Are you standing on the tarneck?"

"Excuse me? I am standing on tar, the runway if that's what you mean."

"Ah, well yes. The runway, I guess you'd call it," he smiled. "I'm not a hundred percent sure. But, it sounds right."

"Well, I'm sure you can check it out. And by the way, I feel this is a good size airport. I've never been to Australia, but if you had a picture of this airport, I would recognize it."

"You are right. It is fairly good size. It's in Melbourne."

"I feel it's important to tell you the direction I believe he headed in. It may prove that he had plans to go to another area—different than what he recorded on his flight plan."

"Well that can be checked also. The airport will have records of the prevailing winds that night."

"In any event, I am picking up the fact that after he was airborne, he went to the left and headed in that direction."

"So you're feeling is that he took off towards the sea and veered left? Was he going right around, do you know?"

"I'm not sure. I don't think he made a whole turn, just sort of bore to the left."

"I wish I could have brought his flight pattern. I don't believe however, that I could have had access to it. I have another item, here, Pat. It's a badge of some sort. Would you like to hold that?"

"Not yet. Let me stay with this."

"All right. I'm unsure if he even wore it the night before he left. He could have simply put it in his pocket. I don't know."

"You know, I feel like I want to handle his tie again," I said, placing the cover down and reaching for the tie. "I'm going to try and get an area, if I can." I took a deep breath, closed my eyes and began to perceive more visions. "I'm seeing two bridges. They look as though they are constructed of steel—very similar to the design of an erector set. The metal appears to have large circles, and the one bridge itself is curved like a half circle."

"Can you give me a bridge that is well-known, so I can compare it?"

"It's the same construction as that of the Eiffel Tower."

"Yes. I know what you mean. Go on."

"Ahh, I'm getting the feeling they run between two large mainland's. I feel it's in between, over water." I was again making the gestures with my hands. "Do you understand? And are you familiar with the bridges?"

"Right. I don't know about the actual construction of the bridge. But, there is a bridge. It's called the Whiskey Bridge. If he were heading toward the area that he was supposed to be going to, yes, he would have crossed that bridge. You don't have to pass over it. But, it is sort of on the flight path. It straddles the mouth of the river."

"Fine. Okay. If you go over this bridge, and here again, Quentin, distance is difficult to perceive in a vision; it may seem like a mile in the vision, when it could be five miles in actuality, especially over water, so please bear with me. But, I know that the body goes around. I see a large island. The body of water goes around to the right, and this large island is to the left but straight out. Do you know where that island is?"

"Well that could be Tasmania, or King Island. Because, see, Tasmania..."

"That's where he went," I said, opening my eyes and reaching for a piece of paper and a pencil. "I am going to draw, try to draw, exactly what I envisioned. I'm not an artist, but you will get the general description."

"I will show you some maps, soon. But, you are getting the area, right."

"I don't want you to show me any maps until I draw what it looked like to me mentally."

"All right."

As I was drawing the vision, I was explaining at the same time. "Over the bridge that I told you about, the plane went to the right. The mainland curves around to the right; there is a large island—right here," I said, drawing it. "I mean you have to see it from the plane. You see I am getting that description from the 'air', more or less from inside the plane itself. Here is the water. And here is that large body of water. Now this is land, and over here is land. And the bridge is here. There is the large island right here, and there are little ones here, three of them—shaped like this," I said, drawing them. "What is this large island?"

"I believe its Tasmania. May I get the map out now?"

"Okay. If that's Tasmania; that's where I feel he landed the plane—up in this portion of it," I said, making a mark in the northwest corner.

"Here we are," he said, stretching the map on the table.

"In fact, before I see your map, let me define that one island more clearly, it's very oddly shaped—something like this," I said, defining the lines. "And right here, in the water, there is a seawall or something that juts out. Fishermen or boaters would have to be careful not to run into it."

"May I ask a question, Pat?" he smiled. "You aren't terribly familiar with the geography of Australia, are you? And I don't believe you have ever seen any maps of these islands, have you?"

"No, to both questions, Quentin. I put my heart and soul into what I do. Just as I am sure you do," I smiled. "My abilities and gifts are very real. They are God-given, and I treat them as such."

"And I didn't mean to imply otherwise. I am very much taken by what you have said and done thus far. The questions were asked in earnest, not for any other reason," he smiled.

"I believe they were," I smiled. "Now let's take a look at the 'real' map."

"This is sort of a large map. Let's turn it around. Okay, here we are. As you can see, this island is Tasmania," he said, pointing at it with his pencil.

I looked at the entire area. Its shape was exactly what I had seen, mentally. And then I saw the three little islands that I had drawn. "What are these three islands? They are like the ones I drew."

Quentin looked at the map, and then at my drawings. Then his expression totally changed! "Woe, you've got them dead right, Pat! One, two, three; and perfectly shaped to those on the map! Right where you said they were! That's amazing, Pat!"

"Well, I feel he veered around this island, and landed up here. I'm getting the name, Stone—Rock, something like that. Let's look up in the northwest." After a few minutes of searching the area, we found an airstrip, in an area called Stony Point. Just below it was—Pebbly Point.

"That's got to be it! I believe the rock and stone were meant for stony and pebbly. That town is called Burnie. Quentin, are you familiar with the geographical features of this island? I also picked up on what the area looks like. It's hilly and wooded in some areas. But, there is also a large grassy plain—like a huge lot or a field. But, the hilly area is not close to the water's edge. It's back farther. I feel he could have landed unnoticed and camouflaged the plane up in the hills, by trees. It's not extremely hilly; but enough so that it would have given him a bumpy ride. The land is remote. And I feel it has a harvest color, and the trees are very green. I also felt he had to hike quite a distance to a neighboring town. And he would have had to climb *two* good size hills to find some kind of inhabitants— a community. There was something else that stuck out. Something that was pronounced—some kind of structure; something everyone recognized. Not a statue, but something similar. And also a tower. And I felt the road was under construction, the road to the tower."

I also explained in detail the condition of the plane's interior and exterior. I told him that I felt the inside was in need of some repairs, like torn seats and such. I also spoke to Quentin about the young man's likes and dislikes. I told him I didn't feel he was much of a sports enthusiast. I did feel he liked motorcycles, but he was much of a loner. We stopped for a while and I served coffee and sandwiches. Then I began psychometry again.

"I feel he was carrying a sufficient amount of cash; a couple of hundred dollars or more. When I asked Quentin, again he was unsure.

"I wish you knew. But I am sure you will check this all out. If this were planned, it would certainly fit into the puzzle. I'm also getting a very large structure; it has many windows—and also a castle. And I am getting the name, 'Richardson'. Oh! Before that, I kept getting the word, 'key'. I think it's a symbol. The plane he was in was blue—I'm sure of it."

"Pat, can you tell me why you think he may have arranged a hoax?"

"Well, my feeling is that he didn't feel as though he quite measured up to certain expectations. He was having problems with his job, and he was very upset over the failing of the tests. I think he may have wanted to get himself noticed. And it's quite possible that after he arrived in Tasmania, he liked it there. And after so long a period of time, it was too late to come forth. Speaking of which, a lot more time has now passed, and he may be in an entirely different area by now. If that town is a small one, he may have moved on to a bigger city."

"Yes. However, you *do* feel Tasmania, right?"

"Yes. Yes, I do. And I bet you'll find out that he had a strong interest in U.F.O.'s. I sensed that he read as much on the subject as possible."

We drove Quentin back to the station. I waited anxiously, day by day, for his reply. Nearly three weeks later I received a letter. The contents were very rewarding! Quentin told me he had verified everything that I had told him. The *clothing*, the fact he did *bite his nails*, he was carrying a lot of cash, he did have a *motorcycle* and he followed the loner pursuit. He didn't enjoy sports, the plane had undergone an *overhaul* the day before he left, and the inside needed repair. There was a huge map in his room on the bedside table. And he was a UFO buff! But the most important information was that the missing man's girlfriend had approached his father and asked him to fly her to BURNIE, to search for the missing pilot! Also, the mother had overheard a rumor, in the store where she was employed, that her son was in Tasmania working in a gas station! Quentin informed me that a search would be undertaken in Tasmania. Several months later, I received a report.

He had spent two days on a search. Every piece of information had checked out. The landing strip was exactly as I had described it. There were *two hills* between the two towns. There was a tower and the road had been under construction. He found the bridge shaped in a *half circle*. The big *figurine* turned out to be a huge rock, shaped like a nut. He said it was something like the Rock of Gibraltar and that it was well known in the area. The *key* was a symbol used on a building for advertising purposes. He also told me that the name, *Richardson* was very common in Tasmania. He also said that the *large stone structure with many windows* was located in a city called, 'Hobart', which is the *largest city* in Tasmania. There is also a large *castle* there, too. Quentin did not check Hobart. He said there would be a discussion with the family and other officials on whether or not there would be another search in the spring. To date, I haven't heard anything more.

*   *   *

There have been approximately four hundred cases in which I have been involved over the years—most of them using direct-voice over the telephone. In the chapter, **Psychic Detective,** I will explain how other law enforcement personnel nationwide were able to contact me and ask for my assistance. In most of these cases the officials were at a dead end and were looking for new leads, which they were hopeful I might be able to provide for them.

8 ▶▶

Atlanta 1980: The Panicked City

October 18th:

On this night, through visions that I had perceived in meditation—I would find myself involved with one of the highest profile cases in the world! One for which I was not prepared, emotionally, mentally or psychically.

There was just a small group of us that gathered that night for meditation. Besides myself there were Gene, Edie, Fred, Karen and Sue present.

"I believe these visions pertain to one of those missing children in Atlanta," I began. "I saw just the top of a head, from the forehead up, of what looked like a young black male child. And then I saw a cowboy hat, a shield or badge of some kind, and a grate in the ground. The next thing I saw was a large statue of Lincoln, and I kept getting an association of a Park or cemetery, or something. And then I saw something that is going to be very difficult to try and explain, because I don't understand it myself. There was this tall curved structure made out of stone or cement. I would have thought it was a dam, but there was no water. I really don't understand what it is—because there was a lot of red clay, dirt, not water. There was also a part of what looked like a black wrought iron fence, I think. And the word, 'Georgia', just kept coming to my mind."

"Hmm, I'm sure you'll find out what it's all about," Gene smiled, "you always do!"

"Yeah. You're probably right," I responded. "I'll wait and see for a while. If we don't hear anything, maybe I can call Bill Gavitt, or Sam, and they can make a call to one of the officials in Atlanta. If this is helpful, I certainly want to let someone there know about it."

266

"You just have to be patient, hon," Gene said calmly. "It usually takes within three to four weeks, and then you know."

*   *   *

Friday, November 7th:

"Hi, hon!" my husband yelled from the backyard, as I walked along the sidewalk. "Did you have a good day?"

"Oh, the usual, some kids noisier than others. Gee, the garage looks great! You must have worked on it for quite some time, huh?"

"Yeah. But it's getting a little too dark now—guess I'll finish it up tomorrow. Oh, by the way, Nancy called. She wants you to call her back."

"Nancy?" I asked, puzzled, as I watched him putting the large broom away. "Nancy who?"

"You know, that lady we met in Georgia."

"Nancy Ritter? We haven't heard from her in almost a year! Maybe she has some news about her husband. I'll go in and call her now."

"Hello," she answered.

"Hi, Nancy! How are you?"

"Pat! Is that you?" she asked excitedly.

"What's new? Have you heard anything about Larry?"

"No, nothing yet. I don't know why, hon, but I've had you on my mind all week. I just had to call and see how ya'all were doin'!"

"We're just doing fine. I've been busy and Gene has been cleaning the garage and stuff. It's been unusually warm around here for this time of year," I laughed. "Gee I was hoping you had called with some news about Larry."

"We haven't been able to search that area, Pat," she remarked, sadness very notable in her tone. "The location has really rough terrain. They can't get any planes to land there."

"I'm really sorry to hear that, Nancy," I murmured, tears stinging my eyes.

"I know you are, babe. But, I've got faith and I know the Lord's got His reasons. When it's time for me to know, I'll know."

"I'm happy to hear you talk like that. I feel the same way. And speaking of faith, I don't believe this call was a *coincidence*! Did Gene tell you about my meditation?"

"No, he didn't. What meditation is that, Pat?"

"Well, hang on a minute. Let me check my notes. I think it was on the eighteenth of October. Just a minute," I said, while I went and looked at my yellow pad. "Yes, that was the date. Here it is. I believe I received some information about one of the missing kids in Atlanta."

"Oh, God! Really, Pat? Tell me about it."

"I didn't know what to do. I didn't know if I should call down there myself, or maybe ask a police official from up here to call. I know that there was a psychic there already, so I figured they had enough help."

"Pat, honey, they need all the help they can get! I'll see to it that someone there in Atlanta, gets *your* information, don't you worry."

"Thank you Nancy. I'm sure you will. I'm not sure if there is such a place, but I do know that these visions were given to me for a reason. Please try and find out if there is a place called Lincoln—Lincoln Park, or cemetery, something like that. Also, I saw this strange structure, like a dam. What I mean is, there is this very tall curved stone or cement structure, but I didn't feel or see water—I really don't know what it is. It just reminded me of a dam."

"Hold on, Pat. Let me grab a pencil and paper. I want to write all of this information down!"

"Okay," I replied, as I waited for her to return to the phone.

"Okay. Go ahead. I've written what you've said so far."

"Well, I first saw the top of a black child's head. I saw a cowboy hat, a shield, or badge, and a grate. I got the impression that a child, or something belonging to a child was in that area."

"Why did you say, Lincoln? Lincoln Park or cemetery?"

"Well, I saw this huge statue of President Lincoln. I felt it was symbolic of a name. I also saw a lot of red clay, around that stone or cement structure, and also I kept getting the name, 'Georgia' in my mind."

"I'll certainly find out for you, Pat. I know the sheriff of Peachtree City, real well. I will personally visit with him later and I'll get back to you."

We exchanged good-byes and hung up.

*   *   *

Saturday, November 8th:

"I simply can't concentrate on my housework today," I muttered silently. "I wish Nancy would call and let me know how she made out." I recalled the conversation I had had with her, and the notes of my meditation, to my mind.

I took out the furniture polish and the dust rag, and began to clean the stereo cabinet in the living room when the phone rang.

"Hello."

"Pat. It's Nancy! I've got some news for ya," her perky voice exclaimed. "I didn't ride out to see, Don Skelton, our chief, but, I did speak with him over the phone. He isn't real sure about that area, Pat, but he thought he had heard of it. So I called a real dear friend of mine who was born and brought up in Atlanta—and guess what? There is a *Lincoln Park Cemetery* and it's smack dab in the middle of the city where those children are disappearing from!"

"Oh thank God," I sighed. "Do you think someone will go and check the area out?"

"Well, that's not all I have to tell you! I also phoned the Task Force and they said there was no such place! Can you believe it? I had to call them twice. After I spoke with Sonny, my friend, I called them back and said there was most definitely a place like that!"

"I feel so much better, now, at least I do know that the area does exist. I know they will find something in and around there, if someone will just check it out," I sighed.

"I'm working on it. I'll bug them to death until they do! They'll regret the day they ever heard of Nancy Ritter before I'm through!" she laughed.

*   *   *

Tuesday, November 11th:

Still no word from Nancy, it had only been three days since our last con-versation, but it seemed like an eternity to me. I wanted to call her, but I knew I had to be patient. The thoughts of how worried the parents of those children must be made me heartsick. I couldn't think of anything else. I whispered a prayer, "Please, help them. Guide someone to that area."

Supper was finished. Gene and I were chatting over coffee, our conversation focused on the possibility of my going to Atlanta.

"R-r-ring!" the telephone sounded. "That's Nancy! I know it is!" I yelled and jumped up to answer it.

"Hello!" I answered excitedly.

"Did you know it'd be me?" her cheery voice asked.

"Put it this way, we were talking about you and Atlanta when the phone rang!"

"I've got really great news, Pat, and some not so good news, too. There is a man from southern Georgia who needs help in locating his son, Melvin. Do you remember Doug—the man ya'all met here at my house last year?"

"Yes, I remember him. What's he got to do with this?"

"Just about everything. Doug called me last night. Cuba released some prisoners a while ago and Doug went to Ft. Lauderdale with the hope that Larry may have been among those prisoners. If, in fact somebody may have found him and turned him over to the Cuban Government. While Doug was there in Ft. Lauderdale, he met a man and they got to talking and Doug told him all about you. The man wants you to fly down here, Pat and see if you can help him locate his son. He's here at my house right now. Would you please speak with him?"

"Of course, Nancy."

In speaking with the man, I was able to give him very pertinent and helpful information concerning his son's whereabouts. He appeared very impressed by what I was able to disclose over the telephone, and the next thing I knew—arrangements were being made for Gene and I to fly to Georgia that Friday! Due to the nature of that case, I gave my word that I would not disclose the real names or specific details of this information publicly.

"Pat, I'm going to take care of all your flight arrangements and everything here. I've already checked with the airlines and you'll have nearly a three-hour layover in Atlanta before your flight leaves for Columbus, Georgia. You just leave everything to me. Sonny and I are going to check that Lincoln Park Cemetery out ourselves tomorrow. We will meet you at the airport and take you out there, and you can see it for yourself. I'm sure I'm going to find everything that you described to me over the phone."

"Everything is happening so fast! I just can't believe it!"

"I'll make so much noise that somebody will listen! You just leave everything to me, Pat. And thank you for offering your help to this poor man. His health is suffering over the mystery and possible outcome of his son's disappearance. I know in my heart that you'll help him."

"I'll do what I can, Nancy." I sighed.

*   *   *

Friday, November 14th:

"This airport is huge! Don't you think so, Gene?" I asked my heart pounding as we were walking the long corridor of the Delta terminal. "I wonder who is going to meet us here?"

"If I know Nancy, she'll probably have the mayor here!" he said giggling.

"We'll soon find out. We're approaching the lobby."

There was Nancy. Her gorgeous smile and pretty face stood out from the crowd.

"Hey there Gagliardo's! We sure have missed ya! Hey Gene! How ya'all doin'?" she asked, giving him a hug.

"Hey there, little person!" she laughed, bending over to hug me too.

"Hey Nancy," I smiled. "So were you able to get a hold of someone?"

"Oh crud! You just wouldn't believe the mess this city's in! Sonny and I went to that cemetery, Pat. The caretaker told us a body had been found in there! When the city councilman, Arthur Langford, heard about it, he had a fit! Mr. Langford said, there never was a body pulled out of that area, and then he started asking all kinds of questions about you and who you were. He became really enthused when I told him about your information, so he agreed to meet us here at the airport. Some other people are going to be in the Lincoln Cemetery area, too. And wait 'til you see that dam, Pat! I would've called it a dam, too. There isn't any water! It's just a big white curved wall. It doesn't serve any purpose at all!"

I could feel anxiety building inside of me. My heart was pounding fiercely now and the palms of my hands were clammy from perspiration. "Please help me, Lord," I whispered silently.

We went to the luggage area and picked up our suitcases and waited for Mr. Langford.

"Let's go and page him, Pat," Nancy said, grabbing me gently by the arm. "Time is wasting."

"I do hope he shows up," I said as we walked toward the information counter.

"He'll be here. He's interested enough, I could tell when I spoke to him over the phone. He's coming. I'm sure of it," she smiled.

"May I help you?" asked the gentleman behind the counter.

"Please page Mr. Arthur Langford. Ask him to meet us at the Delta Information, please. Thank you so much," Nancy said smiling at the young man.

The gentleman pushed the button to the page system. A peculiar look crossed his face.

"What's wrong?" Nancy asked.

"It's not working. That's strange. It was fine a few minutes ago," he commented, wrinkling his brow and frowning.

Gene shot me a look. It was that are-you-responsible look that he always gave me in these situations. I walked away from the counter.

"Paging Arthur Langford," the gentleman's voice echoed through the speakers. "Please meet your party at Delta information."

In just a few minutes, a nice looking man approached us. He was approximately five feet ten inches tall, and he was wearing a light brown colored suit. He also spoke in a very pleasant tone. Introductions were exchanged and then we were on our way to the Lincoln Park Cemetery.

Nancy pulled her car up directly behind Mr. Langford's car. There to our right was the wrought iron fencing—and then I *saw* it! There it stood—the huge stone structure! It was probably fifty or more feet tall, curved and just standing there with no visible purpose! We got out of our cars and headed toward the long dirt road, made of red clay.

There were a lot of people they're waiting for us. Mr. Langford introduced us to two of the officials.

"These two gentlemen are G.B.I. men, Georgia Bureau of Investigation—Mr. Fred Wideman and Mr. John Bascom," he said.

"Hello," I said, shaking both of their hands.

Another gentleman started to approach us; following behind him were two German shepherd dogs, on leashes. As we were about to exchange introductions, a woman with blonde hair and a man with a television camera walked right up to me. In her hand was a microphone, which she held right up to my face.

"I'm Jean Blake. Channel 5 news."

"Oh, I didn't realize the media was going to be here," I remarked a little on edge.

"The news stays with this story just about twenty-four hours a day," she replied. "If you would rather I didn't make anything public right now, I'll hold off," she smiled.

"Thank you. I really wish you wouldn't. At least not now."

"Fine. No Problem. But, I would like to verify your name and your involvement before you leave," she smiled. I just nodded.

"My name is Don Laken. And these are my tracking dogs, Hiney and Faulk," he said, reaching his hand out to shake mine.

"Pleased to meet you. I'm glad you have tracking dogs. I sure hope we will find something here today, and put an end to all this suffering," I sighed.

All of us headed up the long dirt road. As we walked a long distance and rounded a bend, I began to feel familiar vibrations. In my mind, the word, 'deacon' constantly repeated itself.

I stopped walking and looked all around the area. The cemetery itself was at a distance to our right. This area was very remote and secluded. And the vibration still continued, and the letter, 'J' came to my mind.

"One of the five children that are missing, one with the initial 'J', may I have an article belonging to him, please?" I asked, looking at Mr. Langford.

Mr. Langford took the dark green plastic bag that Fred Wideman was holding and as he searched in it he said, "That would be Jeffrey. Jeffrey Mathis." He took a small shirt from the bag and handed it to me. As I was about to take a deep breath and begin the psychometry, I saw a slender black man, wearing a suit, walking toward us. He was introduced to me as, *Reverend* Mitchell.

As soon as the shirt was in my right hand, a very sick feeling passed over me, and then the 'vision' and impressions that came made me fall down to my knees. My stomach was wrenching and I felt as though I was going to become physically ill.

"Oh my God!" I shrieked in agony, with tears running down my face.

Nancy rushed to my side and put her arms around me. "Pat, are you going to be all right?" she asked, a very worried and concern look on her face.

"Oh God, Nancy," I cried. "What's happening to these poor defense-less children is so horrible! It's simply horrible," I repeated, unable to stop crying from feeling this child's fear and his pain.

"Can you tell me? Tell us!" Jean Blake's voice pleaded. "Do you think they are being sexually molested?"

"No, no. Th-ey aren't being mo-lested—just—oh, God—please— please help them—please!" I cried.

"Pat, can you tell us, what is it?" Mr. Langford asked, his voice sincere and warm.

"Mr. L-Langford," I began, choking on my sobs, "I am going to tell you where I see two other children's bodies. Will you verify the information? I know that what I'm about to tell you hasn't been released to the public yet."

"Yes. Yes I will. Go ahead."

"A body of one child was found not far from here—I felt maybe a mile or less. The body was on an embankment, near a highway, right?"

"Yes. It was a girl. Latonia was her name. She was found about three-quarters of a mile from here."

"Another child was in either an abandoned garage or a school, is that correct?"

"Yes! How did you know that?" he asked, his face reflecting his astonishment.

"I can't explain it all to you now, I can only tell you that I 'see' images in my mind. It's like looking at a photograph, and sometimes like a slow moving video. Only I'd give anything not to have seen this! It's a nightmare! I need to speak to the child's mother. Will that be possible?"

"I'll arrange it," he said, and walked over to one of the men, and then came back.

As we turned and headed back down the road, Nancy, Gene and I gathered around Mr. Langford, and I spoke softly to him and Reverend Mitchell. I didn't want to have anyone else hear what I had to say to him.

"There was a car here last night, Mr. Langford," I began. "A very large older type of car, like a Cadillac. It was either a very light gray or white color. Two men were in this vehicle. A light skinned, short black man, with very short nappy hair. The other man was taller and very slender in build and had hair in some sort of long thin braids or something. It could have been a wig. This man I feel is responsible for at least three of these missing children. There is something about his wrist, I don't know exactly what, maybe a tattoo or something and his teeth; his teeth are bad. And just the word 'deacon', kept repeating itself in my mind. Also, I feel they were in this area, and in the trunk of the car I sensed a shovel and some junk. I'm positive they have something to do with these missing and murdered children, and there will be more. I believe he is connected with a green building, a home or a place that he frequents quite often. I need to verify some impressions about Jeffrey with his mother. I wish I had more time here. I will come back if you need me to," I smiled.

Fred Wideman and Reverend Mitchell both felt that they *knew* the man that I was describing and were going to take a drive to that *green building* later.

"I'll be in touch with ya'all," commented Arthur Langford, as we got into our cars.

We followed Fred Wideman to Jeffrey's house. I had perceived some impressions about the time Jeffrey had disappeared, the clothing he was wearing, and that they were at a grocery store that same day, close to this area. I felt that the shorter man was in that parking lot of the store, the same day, and may have seen Jeffrey and followed them to where they lived.

As we approached her home, I felt that same nauseated feeling in the pit of my stomach. I dreaded speaking with her, yet I knew I had to. I would feel her pain and anguish and more. I *knew* what happened to her son. I felt his pain, the physical suffering he had endured from the torturous way his young life was taken from him.

Our visit with her was short, just about twenty minutes. She verified everything I had asked her. My heart went out to her—a very pleasant soft spoken woman with her facial expressions twisted by fear, worry and anxieties over the disappearance of her son. She asked me if I felt that Jeffery would be found, I smiled and nodded. As we exchanged good-byes an expression of hopefulness now replaced her earlier look of sorrow and complete despair.

Time was against us now and we had to drive straight to the airport. I asked Nancy if she had the telephone number to the man in Dawson, Ga. She nodded. I asked her to please call if anything turned up in the Lincoln area.

Our flight landed in Columbus, Georgia. Melvin, the father of the missing man, greeted us, and drove us to our hotel in Dawson. It was approximately eight-thirty that night by the time we checked in. We made arrangements to meet with Melvin early the next morning.

About an hour passed, when Melvin telephoned our room and said that Nancy had phoned him and left a message for me to call her.

"Nancy, you called, did they find something?" I asked, when she answered the phone.

"They sure did, Pat! They found bloody clothing—a child's size twelve—tee shirt. A bloody windbreaker jacket, and sneakers!" she remarked.

"Oh Gosh, I just knew something was there. I feel there's more than that, too."

"Well, Mr. Laken and his dogs continued up that trail that we were on—do you remember telling me about the *grate*?"

"Yes. That was in my meditation."

"Well, there was one grate up there. It was very close to that grate that his dog, Faulk, began to paw at the ground. That's when they found the clothes."

"I'm sure they're connected to one of those missing children. I'm *positive* of it."

"Me too, Pat. The stuff is at the crime lab right now. The police aren't going to give any more statements until the report is back from the lab. I don't believe that information would've come out publicly if Jean Blake weren't there. Just like the locations you gave Mr. Langford about those two other murdered children. That shocked him, Pat! I saw the look on his face as you were talking."

"I believe I was given that information, so he would realize the gifts are real, and he could trust in them. He said he would be in touch. I hope so. I want to help all I can. Thank you, Nancy, for calling and letting me know. I have to get some sleep. I need to help Melvin in the morning. Unfortunately, I don't think he is going to be able to be reunited with his son. This is going to be so difficult for me to explain to him. I am so worried about his health. He isn't a well man, Nance," I sighed, calling her by her nickname.

"Your heart carries such a burden little lady. God Bless you, Pat. You'll be able to put his mind at rest. I believe he already fears the worst. He just needs to understand and know what really happened. The not-knowing is what is weighing so heavily on his mind."

"Yes, I agree. I'll ask God to help me with the right words to say to him. Tomorrow I'll be able to put all the pieces together, after the psychometry."

"Good night 'lil person. You sleep well."

"Thanks, you too, Nance. Good night."

When I got off the phone, I told Gene about the conversation and discovery in the area.

"Honey, you look exhausted. C'mon get into bed and get some sleep. I'm worried how much of an emotional toll all this is having on you," Gene soothed.

I started to cry. It was a release from all of my own conflicts that I was silently dealing with since we left Atlanta. It was very difficult for me to let go of the visions I had experienced while holding Jeffrey's shirt. Gene and I said some prayers together, and I asked God to please grant me peaceful sleep. And He did...

          *   *   *

We met with Melvin bright and early in the morning. He came to our hotel room and brought with him some personal items belonging to his son.

The missing man was a crop duster. He owned his own plane and his main livelihood was the income he made by dispensing pesticides from his plane for local farmers. In performing the psychometry, the information and impressions led me to believe that unfortunately he had become involved with some unscrupulous persons—drug dealers. I felt that the son had become a prisoner, a tortured prisoner, in Cuba, and the prospect of him ever seeing his father again was very slim.

Before leaving on our flight out of Columbus, I telephoned Nancy. We made arrangements to stay at her house that evening and hopefully meet with Arthur Langford again.

"I am going to try and meditate on the flight from Columbus to Atlanta, Nance. I am hoping to perceive some more information. If you can get a hold of Mr. Langford maybe he'll meet with us either tonight or tomorrow. Gene and I can fly out of Atlanta tomorrow night."

"Okay, Pat. I'll place some calls right now. He can come right here to my house if he wants too."

"Thank you, Nancy. See you soon."

On the flight from Columbus to Atlanta, I did perceive more information and details on the missing children. I received impressions of areas, locations and landmarks in and around Atlanta. These impressions included; Bolton, and an industrial park, Stone and a mountain, a barge (large boat) and Indian something, Boulder Park, and Valeland and Fulton.

Unfortunately, Nancy was told that Arthur Langford would be tied up in meetings all day on Sunday. We did not meet with him, or speak with him over the phone. I left the information with Nancy and I *know that it was given* to Don Laken and to Fred Wideman.

We arrived back at our home late Sunday night. The tape on my answering machine was nearly full of messages! Most of the calls were from the media from Florida up the whole eastern seaboard! The media continued calling the entire week. I answered most of the questions that I felt would not hamper the on-going investigation. Some of these networks included Cable News, Atlanta Bureau; Mark Picard WSC TV; Channel 5, Atlanta, and too numerous to mention radio stations and newspaper companies.

Nancy also called during that week and told us; "Pat, it came over the news today that a *black male and white male driving a 1965 or 1966 gray Cadillac* tried to abduct a ten year old black boy on Prior Street on his way to the bus stop! The boy started yelling and created such commotion when one of the guys tried to grab him, that they drove off."

"What is going on down there, Nancy? Isn't anyone looking into the information I left with you?"

"Pat, this city is in such a state! There is so much pressure and it is getting worse! George Harper and the Commissioner, Lee Brown, have decided there will be absolutely no info on the Atlanta cases from the Task Forces given to the media or released to the public in any way. He said that this was a very sensitive matter and investigation. News people are no longer allowed to enter the Task Force doors."

"I can understand the pressures, Nancy. I just don't understand why Arthur Langford isn't doing something about the information I left with you. He knows the information is credible—he should anyway, after what took place the first time."

"Pat, I talked with Don Laken, he wants you to fly down here again. He said the information you gave to me panned out. He also said that Reverend Mitchell was going to get a picture of that man with the rotten teeth and get it to you. He is going to personally fly you down here and work with you. Will you come back?"

"Of course. Just ask him to give me a call."

"I'll take care of the arrangements, Pat."

*   *   *

Friday, November 21st:

Nancy had made arrangements with Don Laken for me to return to Georgia. I would be leaving early in the morning, and I would be going alone.

*   *   *

Saturday, November 23rd:

Nancy met me at the airport and we drove directly to the hotel where Don Laken was staying. I met another gentleman there who was affiliated with the Task Force, John Bascom. Fred Wideman of the G.B.I. joined us a little later.

Don had in his possession many articles of clothing and various other items pertaining to what now totaled fifteen plus missing children. I wanted to get started on the psychometry of some of these items right away. I would only be here for two and a half days.

I searched through the plastic bag and took from it a small brown lace up shoe. Don said, "That belongs to Earl T."

I told Don I would take a pad and pen and go into the other room, where it would be quiet, and perform psychometry with it.

The visions and impressions I perceived pertained to area that was called, 'Redwine.' I also saw a shopping plaza, and the words 'Lake' and 'wood'. I envisioned an older large green vehicle, perhaps an Oldsmobile or Chevrolet. Two men were in this vehicle. I sensed one man to be black, and the other man to be white. I also envisioned the white or gray car again, and the man with the very bad teeth. I wanted to physically go and search some of these areas.

Don was on the telephone most of the morning. There always seemed to be some place he had to be. It was extremely frustrating to Nancy and me. Don took the notes and said, "We'll go out to that shopping center in a bit. I have to meet some people over at the Task Force Center."

"Well, call us Don," Nancy said. "I'll take Pat to my house and she can work on some more of those articles, okay?"

"Sure. Okay. She can take that bag and work on those items in it. They should all be marked with the names."

Nancy made a late lunch for us, and I continued to work on more of the articles. I can't begin to describe the horror that I experienced when I held one of the sneakers that belonged to one of the children.

In the bag was a small white sneaker marked, Christopher. However, when I held the sneaker, it kept coming to my mind that this sneaker belonged to a brother of this child, one with the initial T. I sensed that the brother was probably the original owner and then it was passed down to Christopher. The psychometry information I perceived holding that sneaker made me physically sick to my stomach again. The frustration that built over those couple of days was unbearable.

"Nancy have you had any luck reaching anyone?" I asked, walking into her kitchen. "I believe this one child is still alive! Somebody has to get to him before it's too late!" I cried.

"Pat, I can't tell you how many messages I have left, everywhere!" Nancy answered with an expression of sheer frustration on her face.

"I've got to get this information to Don. I feel he's in a school, it's abandoned I believe. I sensed him tied to a chair, near a blackboard; the word 'Milton' keeps coming to my mind. There is construction-taking place not too far from there. And when I held a shirt belonging to the child Patrick B., I kept getting that 'Lake' shopping center location. There is an area close to this shopping center, it's called 'red' something, like 'red' wood or wine."

"We've got to do something, I don't understand what's going on with Don, and why we haven't heard from him yet," she sighed.

"Why don't we try to find these places ourselves?"

"I thought of that Pat, but it's better if we have someone with us, for several reasons; one, we don't know the areas, and we need someone who does, and two, we need protection. There are killers runnin' loose!"

"I know," I sighed, "I just want to help find these kids! I *know what's happening to them* and it's making me physically ill."

"Let me call again to the Task Force, and see if Fred Wideman or John Bascom are around now. Maybe we can get this information to them."

Nancy telephoned again, and left more messages to have someone call us back.

Don telephoned that night, around eight thirty. Too late to do any searches!

Nancy was frantic when she spoke with him over the phone. "Don! Where have you been? I've tried to reach you all day. Pat has information on one of the kids that she feels may still have been alive! Take down this information, and maybe you can find and get out to the area!"

she commanded. She read the impressions from the psychometry report to him over the phone.

"What did he say, Nancy?" I asked, when she hung up the phone and we walked into the living room.

"He said he was working with the G.B.I., all day on some leads they were following up on. And he was tied up and couldn't call. He said he was going to give that information to the Task Force guys and he would see to it that someone checked it all out. He is going to call early tomorrow morning and we would go to some of those places together."

"Tomorrow may be too late for the child in that school," I sighed. "Is someone going to try and locate the area tonight?"

"I don't know, Pat," she sighed heavily, "He said he was going to pass the information on. I hope so."

Both of us spent a very restless night. I was awakened nearly every hour on the hour. I couldn't get the visions and impressions out of my mind. And the feelings of helplessness, frustrations and hopelessness increased.

*　　　*　　　*

Sunday, November 24th:

Nancy made coffee and some breakfast. Neither one of us could eat. We just barely got the coffee down. She called Don's hotel room, bright and early. This would be my last day here. In the morning I would be leaving for Connecticut. We were hoping for an early start!

It didn't turn out that way, however. Don had several meetings that he had to attend to first. He would meet us at noontime at his hotel. He also informed Nancy that everywhere he went, the media followed. He wanted to prepare us for that.

The media frenzy was overwhelming too. The city was in such a panic—and no wonder! Children were continually disappearing! Every channel on television and the radio were deluged with stories and events all pertaining to the missing children and their families! The pressure on everyone, especially the officials, was painfully obvious.

We arrived at the hotel at approximately 11:45. We saw Don's 'wagon' in the parking lot. Nancy parked her car next to it and we went up to his room.

"Hi Don. What's going on?" I asked, as he opened the door and let us in.

"It's a zoo. You can't imagine all the calls, and all the chases on possible leads, and the crackpots that are calling. I've got some maps here I want you to look at," he said, unrolling a large paper map that was secured with a rubber band.

"Look, here's that 'Redwine' area. Remember telling me about the 'Lake' something shopping center? It's right here," he said, pointing to an area called, 'Lakewood Shopping Plaza.' It's probably within one and a half miles from there."

"And what about the other areas? Something with the Stone," I asked.

"Yep, there is a Stone Mountain, it's a bit farther out. There's DeKalb County. I believe a lot of your impressions include areas there."

"Don, let's get going. I believe we can physically search ourselves. Maybe if I'm in the areas, I will pick up more information."

"Okay. We have to stop by the Task Force first. I need to get some more maps for those places."

Nancy and I exchanged glances. It was already 1:00. "Okay," I sighed heavily.

We rode with Don in his vehicle, along with the two dogs, Hiney and Faulk.

We stopped by the 'headquarters' and Nancy and I waited in the car. By the time we started to the first area, it was nearly 2:00. Don drove us to the Lakewood Shopping Plaza. I asked them to wait in the car. I got out and walked around the parking lot, in the hopes of picking up more impressions. And I did. I kept envisioning an old mill, and a river that ran along side of it. The word, 'Chattahoochee' kept coming to my mind. I sensed bodies in the water; at least two of them. And again I saw the large white or gray car. Back in the car, I gave the details to Don.

"There is the Chattahoochee River, I believe," he said. "I'm not sure about that mill, but I'll find out."

"Okay. Now I think we should go to that Redwine area. Maybe I'll recognize something physically and we can get out with the dogs," I sighed.

As we drove out of the parking lot and turned onto a main street, a media van pulled up behind us. The writing, 'Channel 4' was clearly visible on the side of the white van.

"Don, two of these children are going to be found fairly close to each other," I said, ignoring the vehicle behind us.

Don kept looking in his rearview mirror. Everywhere we turned, the vehicle followed. We were approaching the Redwine area. We drove off of the access highway and onto a marked road, 'Springdale'.

"We need to stop somewhere along here. I want to get out of the car, Don. We need to look into those woods, there," I said, pointing across the road.

"If we stop and get out, they will, too," he commented.

"Something is here. I can *feel* it, Don," I replied.

"I'll go back and get one of the Task Force people to ride out here."

He didn't stop the car. We continued to ride around on different roads in the Redwine area.

"It doesn't matter, Don, if the media is here, too," Nancy remarked after nearly three quarters of an hour, "We need to get out and be on foot."

"It'll be checked, don't worry," he said, "I'll come back here with one of the Task Force people."

"My time is very limited, Don. I'm leaving early in the morning you know," I said with a very frustrated tone in my voice.

"I know. I want to take you up to that Stone Mountain area. It's pretty wooded, but maybe you'll feel something there too."

We left Redwine and Don headed out onto another highway. After a few miles, the media van went another direction. I suggested that we go back to the Redwine area, and start to search. We didn't.

Don drove to DeKalb County. We drove around on several roads in and out of one area of the county. As it turned out, we were in the wrong section; we needed to be in North DeKalb. And again, we didn't physically get out of the car.

By the time we left the area and drove back to his hotel, it was nearly 6 pm. Frustrated, and hungry, Nancy and I departed, leaving Don with all of the information.

We drove to Peachtree, in silence. As we entered the Peachtree City limits, Nancy said, "I have a friend that runs a local restaurant. Let's go there, Pat. We can rest, and have a good meal. And 'lil person, cheer up. It's in God's hands now. You've done all that you can. There must be His reasons you know," she smiled.

"I am sitting here and thinking those very thoughts," I replied, trying to smile, "Or it's the work of the opposition. I have to rely on my faith. Thank you for reminding me of it," I smiled.

We spent another restless night. By the time Nancy drove me to the airport, I felt like I had been through a ringer. I was emotionally, mentally and physically exhausted. I couldn't help but cry nearly the entire flight home.

I received one telephone call that following week, at my home, from Arthur Langford. He was apologetic at first, and thanked me for my time, and then he said that 'the heat' from all of the pressures was making their jobs an impossible task.

Nancy and I stayed in contact by phone through the entire month of December. Nancy herself had made many phone calls and left messages for 'officials' who didn't return them. And still none of the areas that I had perceived had been searched!

A week after Christmas, with the city of Atlanta in full-blown panic, I returned one last time to Georgia.

*   *   *

January 7th through January 10th:

Finally, I thought, we were going to physically search the areas of Stone Mountain, Redwine, Boulder Park and Benhill, on January 8th. Those specific areas were perceived when I performed more psychometry with items belonging to three missing children; Lubee G., Darrin S., and Patrick B. However, around midnight on January 7th, Don told us that he had received a phone call threatening all of our lives. He told Nancy and me that a caller referring to himself as the 'Savior', and to me, as the 'eyes of Satan', and to Don and his dogs as 'the devil's advocates', said we would have to be annihilated if we were to 'show up' in any areas to search for the children. Don wanted to go to the headquarters *again*, this time to pick up bulletproof vests! He didn't want to put our lives, Nancy and mine, in jeopardy. Nor did we! Yes, we were frightened! As we were without any protection from officials—Nancy and I returned to her home. I completed the psychometry readings on the remaining items and left for Connecticut on the evening of January 10th.

The impressions I perceived on the morning of January 10th, concerning Darrin, once again pertained to the Stone Mountain area in a place called 'Lakeside'. I had also perceived a route, I-85, heading north, and an exit number 31 or route 31. I also 'sensed' that quite possibly this 'was yet to come', that is was in the future. I was also a bit confused as to why I felt that the perpetrator was on the 'strip' and getting off of the 'strip' of road and coming right back to the area again. It was later explained to me. I also suggested that the area of the mill and the river be patrolled. I *felt* that if it were being watched, a perpetrator would be caught disposing of the bodies of those poor, defenseless, slain victims.

*   *   *

February 18th:

Nancy, after much persistence on her part, and with her friend, 'Buck,' encouraged two of the FBI agents to meet with her at her attorney's office.

In her possession were typed written copies of my psychometry reports. This is the phone conversation I had with her:

"I believe I had a productive day today, Pat. I met with agents John H., and John M. in my attorney's office. I had typed a cover letter to John M., and a condensed version of what had transpired at the Lincoln Cemetery. We talked for an hour and a half. Both of these men were very attentive and nice, Pat. I am going to give you a capsule version of what took place earlier today. First of all, what soured agent John H. was all the hoopla around a psychic from New Jersey that came down here and stirred up everyone and screwed a lot of things up. After that, the word 'psychic' was a complete turn off to most of the officials. So then he asked me a couple of questions about you. First of all, he is a Christian, and he wanted to know where you thought your gifts came from. And then he said, 'I can't tell you how difficult it is to find someone in law enforcement who will believe in this. I can't tell you how many weird and crazy people have called; I mean hundreds,' he said. I told him I was working strictly as your mouthpiece, Pat, because you're in Connecticut and that you've been down here three times and that you worked solely with Don. I told him that we were under the assumption that Don was delivering your psychometry reports to people in the FBI, to which he answered, 'It's possible, but I haven't seen a copy of this before now.' He did say that he saw some 'scripture' verses, but that was all. Then I said to him, 'we should all be working together toward the same goal supposedly. I know that there are those fighting for political power, people not sharing information with other people, and in the interim innocent children are being killed everyday.' That's when he asked me, 'What's Patricia's interest in all of this?' He wanted to know where you were coming from. I told him that I had been going through this myself for fifteen months; Larry's disappearance, and I knew what the families were enduring with these missing children, first hand. 'Right now the priority is Darrin's remains that were found so his parents can put him to rest and grieve properly. Secondly, I want to see the killers caught, period. Now Pat is helping because her heart goes out to these people. She is using her gifts to help families with missing people. She gets many crank calls herself—people wanting lottery information, raffles, etc. She doesn't get involved with that—I am talking about a very quiet unassuming lady that has been given a gift and intends to use it in helping other people. She doesn't charge for her services, either.' So I think once he knew where we were coming from and we weren't interested in money, and show biz—he then relaxed totally with me. I went on then and spoke of what was in the typed words, not all of it, because I had it there for him in print."

"Nancy, were you able to impress upon him of the descriptions that I had given of the man, and that 'Mitch' felt he recognized him?"

"Pat, I told him this, that you had given Arthur Langford descriptions of the men, and a couple of vehicles, and them at least being responsible at that time for three of the missing kids. I told him everything; one of the men's hair description, his wrist, his teeth, everything. I told him how limited your time was here the first time and that I had to get you back to the airport. I told him when I had returned home, that Chief Skelton had phoned me to tell me the dogs had shown considerable interest and that they found the articles of bloody clothing in the location that you had given. I then said that Reverend Mitchell was going to obtain a photograph of the man that he felt you had described and send it to you for your perusal, which was never done. I then said, 'I personally went to the U.I.A.C., on the 22nd of November, and I asked Don if anything had been done to locate a picture of the man. I also gave Don the information on another area, which Pat had received. That's when Don suggested I make plans to fly Pat back down here, which I did. The copies are here in these reports of the extensive psychometry that Ms. Gagliardo performed on her visit here. On numerous occasions I have relayed information from Pat to Don. On January 7th, again she flew here to Atlanta and stayed through the tenth. She came here then to help with the disappearance of Lubee G. Those reports are here and attached as well. She also worked with each of the other missing three children's items and gave her impressions and visions. I have had many conversations with Ms.

Gagliardo, which is not typed here, but that I immediately contacted Don and passed on to him. It was my understanding that all of the information was given to the Task Force upon Major T's command.' Then he looked at me, Pat, and he said, 'I believe people do have psychic powers, but no one is going to read all of this.' I then told him what you said about Christopher's sneaker, whom you thought it belonged to, his brother with the initial T. He said, '*Timothy* is his brother.' And then I told him how you felt he was tied to a chair and that he was still alive, the school, the blackboard, everything, Pat. I told him about Lubee, the construction, the cranes, *Milton.* I told him about the Lakewood Shopping Center, Redwine. And then I added that you had not worked with any officials since your first visit here. I also told him that police officials in the past have always 'invited' you to help. I told him about your information on Darrin that you gave on January 10th and as of today, the eighteenth of February; no one has gone to the Stone Mountain area to check anything out! Then he asked me what page that information was on, and I said it's next to the last page. He flipped to the page, and his eyes got as big as saucers, Pat. He saw where you had said, *sledge* and *Springdale* and *lake side*, and he looked over at Buck and said, 'Lakeside, that's definitely in the Stone Mountain area.' Well that was about it, Pat. I left the reports with them, and he promised to go through it. I believe that they will."

"Nancy, you have worked so hard, I can't thank you enough. I just want to help. I pray that God will now intervene and these children will be found. God Bless you, Nancy."

"Don't you worry, 'lil person. I'll keep you informed. Bye for now. Give Gene a howdy and a hug for me."

"I will. Talk to you soon. Thanks again, Nancy. Love ya."

*　　　　*　　　　*

February 19th:

It was reported in the news that two more bodies were recovered in North East Atlanta *this morning*. In the *dense woods of North DeKalb*

County in Office Park, the skeletal remains of Patrick B., and one and a half miles from there, the remains of what is believed to be that of Lubee G.

*   *   *

March 14th:

I received another phone call from Nancy. She called to tell me of the latest developments. On the news of the previous evening, March 13th, allegedly the National Enquirer had paid for five psychics from all over the nation to go to Atlanta and offer their assistance. She said the news media was 'having a field day' and going bananas over it. She told me that the television news showed one psychic tearing her shoes off and asking everyone to feel the incredible heat coming out of her feet. She also told me that Don had phoned her, she hadn't spoken with him in five weeks, to tell her of *Exit 31*. He said to me, 'Do you remember where Pat felt, I-85 going north, and getting off exit 31 or route 31 and that she was confused about them getting back on the strip and going back the way they came?' I said, 'Yes, I sure do, Don.' Then he continued and said, 'Well that is what happened to Patrick. They got off of the *strip*, dropped his body on the embankment, got right back on the *strip* and came *right back*. And what's amazing is Pat got that information on the 7th of January, seven weeks before it happened!' And Pat, this is the most incredible! Let me tell you what was on the news last night. A friend of Patrick's called the Task Force the day that Patrick was snatched. I am not sure of that date exactly, but anyway, the friend told the Task Force that there was a *green car* and two men were in it. And the description of the green car was either a *Chevrolet* or *Oldsmobile*! Also a dental hygienist saw it too! That green car was in a parking lot, and then pulled out after the boys as they were walking by. The two boys took off screaming, and the kid with Patrick ran to a phone booth and called the Task Force and asked them to send somebody right there, but according to the news, no one showed up. At

that point, the two boys split up and of course you know what happened
to Patrick."

"Nancy, everything that is going on there is such a nightmare! Every
day I pray for the spirit world to intervene."

"Oh, Pat, it is such a mess. It's just God-awful. And do you remember
what you told us in strict confidence, about the possibility of 'rituals' and
the horror you felt and becoming physically ill over it? It got out."

"Oh no! What do you mean, Nancy?" I shrieked.

"Somehow someone got a hold of it and it went out over the AP wire,
late January or February."

"No wonder the news people continue to call me," I realized.

"I'm going to send you the newspaper article, Pat."

"Okay. Thanks Nancy. Thanks for everything. Please stay in touch."

"I will. Bye for now."

My involvement with Atlanta's missing and murdered children has left
a permanent wound in my heart. The frustrating lack of communication
and lack of corporation between all parties concerned remain an
emotional sore point for me. It was also brought to my attention some
time later, that at least two bodies were recovered from the *waters* next to
the *old mill*. I have tried to understand political motivations, pressures
and most importantly—God's Will. Being painfully aware of these
circumstances, I was relieved for the families as their victims' bodies were
recovered, and their anguished waiting, could now be put to rest. I know
that every thing that happens in life is a learning experience, and the key
is to do just that, learn and grow from it. I felt that the biggest one lesson
I had to learn was to protect myself emotionally as I was exposed to such
unfortunate circumstances, evils and problems in the world. I had to
realize that I was not going to solve or take away all the pain in every case;
that was only in His control. For me, reflecting on all of the teachings
and enlightenments from the Holy Spirit world, and trusting in faith,
despite the insanity, offered me acceptance and spiritual strength to
continue on my path.

9 ▶▶

Psychic Detective

April 1983:

I had just finished hanging some clothes out on the line and walked into the kitchen from the porch when I heard the phone ring.

"Hello."

"Hi Pat. How are you?" the deep, familiar, and cheery voice asked.

"Hi Andy. Doing fine thanks. I want to thank you and Jan again for the really nice time we had at your house last week."

"We had a good time too, Pat. We have to do it again real soon."

"I agree. This time at our house."

"Okie Dokie. Well, do you remember we discussed having that lecture, seminar, for the police and other officials? It's all set. Jan and I worked on it all week. We made the calls and put the word out basically nationwide."

"That's great, Andy. Where did you decide to have everyone meet, and when?"

"The last Saturday of this month. It will be in the afternoon, starting at two o'clock. And if you don't mind, Pat, I sort of left it open-ended. There will be people there from all around the country, and I'm sure some of the police are going to want to speak to you privately afterwards. Is that okay?"

"Sure. I'm hoping Gene will be off, too. If he isn't, maybe he can switch days with someone. Where will it be, Andy?"

"We've reserved the large conference room at the Day's Inn, in Mystic. There is an adjoining room, too, where you can speak in private afterwards and it will be quiet."

"That's a good idea. How was the reception? I'm curious on how you presented the forum, and what some of the reactions were," I interjected, with a little giggle in my voice.

"Oh, I'm sure there'll be a lot of curious-minded, and some really skeptical people there. Those are the ones I'm going to enjoy watching!" he laughed, "Especially when you raise the hair off their heads, like you did to me! My statements were short and to the point. I simply said that you're a very credible, and an honest person that has remarkable psychic powers, which can be a gift to law enforcement. I said you're a psychic detective of sorts. And that the lecture is to enlighten them as to how and what you do, basically."

"I see. The 'gifts' are abilities, not powers, Andy," I stated warmly, correcting him.

"Right. Abilities; I'll remember that. I'll be back in touch soon, Pat. Say howdy to Gene for me."

"I will. Talk to you soon. Bye Andy."

"Pat. Thank you. Bye for now."

Andy, Jan, Gene and I rode together to the Day's Inn. The drive took about forty-five minutes. We arrived at approximately one fifteen that afternoon. The front and side parking areas were nearly full. Andy parked the car and we walked into the lobby of the hotel through the front entrance.

Andy led us upstairs to a very large room with a seating capacity of one hundred fifty persons. There were approximately twenty gentlemen already in the room; some of them were dressed in suits, others in casual attire. There was a long rectangular table to one side of the room. It was draped with a white tablecloth. On the table were two large fifty-cup coffee urns with coffee brewing, and donuts and other pastries on trays. The adjoining 'suite' was comfortably decorated. It was warm, cozy and relaxing. With two wooden desks with several padded wooden armchairs around them, a leather couch, coffee table, recliner and two large chairs and a couple of end tables with lamps. We went out to the conference room, made coffees, and returned to the suite to discuss how Andy would introduce me. Within twenty minutes the conference room began to fill up; over a hundred officials attended the lecture!

Andy stood up and introduced himself to the crowd. "Before I introduce this very gifted person," he began, "I want all of you to know that she has been extremely beneficial in helping me to solve some very difficult cases. I can't explain to you how or what she does exactly, I can only tell you that it works!" And then looking at me and smiling, he continued, "Mrs. Gagliardo's clairvoyant and psychic *abilities*, I'm sure you'll find remarkable and amazing—just as I, and others have, that have experienced them first hand! Now without further ado, it's my pleasure to introduce to you, Pat Gagliardo."

Smiling and nodding at Andy, I got up from my seat and walked up to the front of the room. I glanced around and my eyes connected with some of the participants. As I began to speak, I sensed from the expressions on their faces, a mix of thoughts and emotions. Some were very curious, others uncertain and skeptical, and some wanted to speak to me as soon as possible with hopes of attaining information that would help solve cases for them.

"I would like to say, for those of you who are skeptical, that I can appreciate your curiosities, doubts and 'show-me-I'm-from-Missouri' attitudes," I commented grinning. I accomplished what I had intended, to make them laugh and produce a more relaxed and informal atmosphere. "I've been there and I can relate quite well."

I shared with them briefly some of my own previous skepticism and former views of the paranormal. I then explained to them how I discovered my abilities through meditation, and about direct-voice through Spiritual Guidance.

Then the audience began to raise hands and ask questions. At first, the questions pertained to general inquiries, such as: 'were you born with it? Are other members of your family psychic? How accurate is the information? Do you only get visions in meditation? Is everyone psychic?'

Then an officer from the state of Rhode Island posed this question to me. "I have a murder case, it's over twenty years old, and…"

"You're speaking of a woman, and she was found in a car, no, I believe it was a van or a larger vehicle, abandoned off of a highway road, access maybe, and a dirt road that runs along side of moving water," I remarked, interrupting him, as I had attuned to his voice and allowed the impressions to come to my mind.

The room was completely silent. You could've heard a pin drop. "Uh-yes, that's right," he murmured, shifting in his seat, with a look of amazement on his face.

"I will speak to you about it in private afterwards, if you would like. And I will help you as much as I can."

He just nodded his head.

His question sparked at least ten more questions of the same nature—missing, murdered, and various other crime related cases. After speaking for nearly two hours, I thanked everyone for coming and ended the forum. Everyone began clapping and stood up and many thanked me. Andy walked up next to me and announced that I would offer assistance in private in the adjoining room. He said it wouldn't be possible for me to talk to everyone that day, so he spelled out my name and gave them my telephone number.

There were at least ten officials that spoke with me in private. There was one particular officer, and one case that I would assist with that would reveal yet another aspect of my 'gifts'. The case came from Wheeling, West Virginia!

"Ms. Gagliardo, my name is Tom Williams," the gentleman said in a deep, but soft southern accent as he approached me. He was approximately six feet three inches tall, with brown hair and of large build. "I have been working on this case for about two months now, and I'm at a complete dead end. Two young girls came up missing after they were last seen in a Laundromat in…"

"There's a van. This man drove by at least three times. I'm on a main street. It's dark and late at night. I'm seeing a highway, and the numbers 8, 5 or 5, 8, a wooded area. Oh no, these girls are the victims of rape, and I believe murder." I sighed.

"Ms. Gagliardo, you're right. They were last seen around midnight. The Laundromat is in the center of town in Wheeling," he remarked, surprised at the rapid production of information.

"Do you have any photos with you?"

"No. I really didn't know what to expect," he smiled. "Can I call you on this?"

"Yes. Absolutely. I don't think they are that far away. It's possible a town or two. I'm sensing they are probably close together. It's a wooded area, and right off of the highway, not far in the woods, I believe up on the top of a knoll."

"You'll be hearing from me."

Over the next several months I heard from police officials virtually from all over the nation. I would give my impressions over the phone. Some called back and thanked me and would tell me the outcome of the cases, and others did not. I know that most cases were fruitful and that some of the police officials wanted to receive the credit and recognition of the 'collar' therefore didn't mention my involvement, which was perfectly fine with me. My motivation and intention was to help in any way that I could. During this time I was also contacted by Sergeant Robert Reder of the Morristown, New Jersey Police Department and I was invited to give another lecture there, which I did. That lecture also sparked many calls from other police officials and it was during this time that I learned that my name, address and telephone number had been placed in the police computers nationwide, as a resource.

I received the first of several telephone calls at my office from an Investigator Booth. He was calling from Dinwitty, Virginia. I asked him how he heard of me and his reply was, 'your name and number is listed in our computers, as a credible psychic.' I had assisted with several cases from

Investigator Booth regarding rape, robbery and murder. On the third phone call he made to me, he introduced himself as *Captain* Booth. During our conversation, I asked him jokingly, 'Captain, now, huh? Since you have never really given me any feedback on previous cases that I have helped you with, would you please tell if in *solving* these cases, was why you have been promoted to Captain?' In a very calm and matter of fact tone he said, 'Why, yes ma'am, it surely would. And thank ya so much.' And I remarked, 'Well, at least you told me the truth. And you're welcome. I will offer my help and do what I can for you any time.'

I had also heard from Detective Rainville again. He asked for my assistance with a local murder of an older gentleman at his home in Waterford. I was able to give him the description of two young men, the vehicle they were driving, and a connection with the state of Massachusetts. He called me back within a few weeks and thanked me, as the information provided necessary clues for the apprehension of the perpetrators.

In this same time I received my first phone call from Dan Teper. Dan was a trooper that worked with the Special Tactics Division in the city of Hartford. He asked for my assistance with a case of multiple arsons, which had the city of Hartford in a state of panic. Churches were being set on fire all over the city. Dan and I worked very productively together. I would work with him again on other cases, and including the serial killer, Michael Ross.

The months passed by and the year ended. It was now February, when I heard from Tom Williams of Wheeling, West Virginia, again.

"Ms. Gagliardo. This is Tom Williams. Do you remember me?" he asked, when I answered the phone.

"I'm not sure. Your name and voice sort of ring a bell."

"I met you in Connecticut. At the lecture."

"Oh, yes. Okay. How did you make out? I believe it was missing girls, right?"

"Yes. The case is still not solved. They haven't been found. That's why I'm calling. Is there any way you could come here? I'll personally take care of the arrangements."

"I'm sure we can work out something. What do you have in mind?"

"The first weekend in March. Will that be okay for you?"

"Yes. I will make some arrangements on my end too."

At that time my cousin, Ron, was driving for a nationwide tractor-trailer company. I mentioned to Ron that I would be going to Wheeling on the first weekend in March. As it turned out, so would he! When Tom telephoned again to finalize the plans, I told him that I would accompany Ron to Wheeling, and that he could make arrangements to fly me back the following Sunday. Ron and I would leave on Friday and when we arrived at a truck stop in Wheeling, Tom could pick me up there.

It was one of the most unsettling experiences of my life! It began with my ride with Ron and ended with the events that took place in Wheeling.

Ron was a very skilled driver of fifteen years, if he hadn't been, we probably would never have reached our destination. He had calculated the miles and planned on arriving at the truck stop in Wheeling between eleven pm and midnight on Friday. It would have given me a good portion of the night to sleep in the hotel and have a fresh start on Saturday. However, that's not what happened. It was very cold and there had been inclement weather for the past three days. In spite of the gray sky, and the blustery cold March winds, our trip started off very pleasantly. Ron made a stop just before we entered the state of New York. We used the facilities and picked up coffee and some snacks. Approximately fifteen minutes after crossing the border into New York and without any warning, we hit black ice! The trailer started to jack knife! I saw it swinging around through Ron's rear view mirror! Ron's swiftness and skill saved us from flipping over! I was scared to death and shaking like a leaf! Ron spoke softly to me and tried to calm me down. He explained that he could not pull off the highway as there wasn't an area large enough or far enough off of the icy road to safely pull over, but that he would travel very slowly and with his flashers going.

If he did pull over, then we would run the risk of having someone slide into us! He drove nearly a hundred miles at ten to fifteen miles per hour! I telephoned Tom at his home, to let him know what had happened, and that we wouldn't be arriving in Wheeling until early Saturday morning. We pulled in at approximately five thirty in the morning. I hugged Ron and whispered a prayer for his safety for the remainder of his trip. Tom took me directly to the hotel. I was exhausted and needed to shower and sleep. I thanked God that we arrived safely and then I drifted off into a peaceful deep sleep. I had no idea of what was coming next!

I telephoned Tom and he picked me up around noontime. There were three other gentlemen with him. As he introduced us, I sensed from one of the gentleman, Jim Wright, a strong skepticism. I took Tom aside and explained to him that even though I could relate and understand Jim's attitude, I felt it would interfere with my attunement. If he wanted him to join us that would be fine, as long as he rode in another vehicle. Tom complied. He and I rode together in one jeep, and the other gentlemen followed behind us in another jeep. If you've never been to West Virginia and you plan to visit, you won't get around if you don't have a four-wheel drive vehicle in the spring thaw! The weather was definitely not favorable. The skies were a deep gray and threatening rain at any minute.

I asked Tom to drive to the Laundromat where the young teenagers were last seen. Tom had in his possession several items belonging to the missing girls. There were bracelets, hair baubles and other varied items in a clear plastic bag. I reached into the bag and pulled from it a single gold colored round bangle bracelet.

"Tom, please focus your mind elsewhere," I said, looking at him, and placing the plastic bag on the seat next to me. "I'm going to hold this bracelet and perform psychometry in the hopes that we can trace the events of the night the girls disappeared. I don't want to pick up thoughts from your mind. So try to think of your family or some other distraction, okay?"

"All right. You just tell me what you want or need me to do, and I'll do it," he replied in his thick southern accent.

"Thank you. Believe me it's necessary. I want to make sure that all the impressions I'm perceiving are coming from this bracelet," I smiled, "and not any information from your thoughts, ideas or suspicions. We are sitting fairly close in this vehicle and I know that this case has been a torment for you for a long time, and I need to just pick up the energy from here," I commented, showing him the bangle clenched in my fist, "not from you as well."

"I understand. I will also let Jim know by the walkie-talkie not to call or disturb us, unless it's an emergency. Jim," he said picking up the black hand held device, "don't beep me unless you absolutely have too, I'll let you know what's goin' on up here."

"Okay," came the reply over the two-way.

I settled back in my seat, and cupped the bracelet in the palms of my hands, holding it close to my solar plexus area. I took a deep breath, closed my eyes and began the psychometry.

With my eyes remaining closed, I attuned to the energy and began to verbalize the visions and impressions...

"This girl is about eighteen, slender in build, and has shoulder length light brown hair. I believe she was sitting on a large rectangular folding table in the Laundromat and talking to another young girl. They are probably waiting for the clothes to dry. A dark green older van drives by. The driver is black, he sees the girls, drives up the road a bit, turns around and drives by again, very slowly this time, and I feel that he parked his vehicle just a little past the Laundromat. He is thinking. I believe he is planning a way to entice the girls outside; a pretext to lure them into the van. And he succeeds. I believe that he approached the door, smiling, and manipulated them with charm, maybe saying something like he had a lot of laundry and would they please help him bring it inside. If my impressions are correct, I believe their purses and other belongings are in your custody, they were left here in the Laundromat. You don't have to answer, Tom, just let me stay with this thread of information," I quickly added, not wanting to break the attunement. "This man is a little overweight, and has very strong arms and hands. He is swift in his actions, and I believe he either hit them with his fists, or grabbed something from inside the back of the van and knocked them unconscious, pushing them inside and closing the door. Tom, please start the jeep. I will direct you where to drive. He turns the van around and heads in the direction we are parked in. Drive straight ahead, please. He is driving nervously and constantly looking in his mirror. Soon you are going to drive over railroad tracks, on the right hand side, we are going to pass by large silver tanks, they either are oil tanks, or water tanks. A short way past here, you will come to an intersection. I believe there is a blinking caution light. You will turn right at that light."

Tom was not able to contain himself at this point. He was amazed that I was able to describe everything *before* he got to it, and he blurted out, "Here they are! The tanks and the tracks! They are large oil tanks, Pat! And I see the caution light up ahead!"

"Okay," I responded softly, "turn right. This road will be a bit winding, and it will eventually become dirt. We will probably need to stop along this road. He is looking for a place to stop, secluded."

"If it is dirt, it'll be red clay, and it'll be some rough driving in this thaw."

The road was winding and it turned into dirt, red clay. As we continued to drive along the dirt road, Tom said, "Uh-oh, we're on property that belongs to Reverend Moon.

See, look up on the hill, there is his mansion, and I see one of his people walking on the road. I'll just tell him we are passing through."

I opened my eyes at that point, and saw a young man about thirty, dressed in a long white garment with a belt and sandals, his hair in a long braid. Tom stopped the jeep, showed the young man his badge, and said we were just driving through. The man's expression remained solemn, and he never said a word. We continued, and the other men in the jeep behind us followed.

"This road will turn back into tar, not far from here. You will drive around a very sharp bend in the road, and a little ways further it will become tar again. Take another right turn, Tom. A very short way, maybe a little less than a mile, you are going to drive over a small bridge. As soon as you go over it, please pull off to the side of the road."

"Okay."

He approached the very sharp curve, and just shook his head. He continued for approximately a quarter of a mile and *the road turned back into tar*. He turned right onto the tar road and *approximately three quarters of a mile*, drove over the *small bridge* and pulled the jeep off to the side of the road.

"I need to sit quietly for a few minutes, and attune to this bracelet again," I stated, cupping the bangle in the palms of my hands and placing it up to the middle of my forehead, taking a deep breath and closing my eyes again. At this point, it had also started to rain quite heavily.

Tom sat very quietly, and I know that he was watching me, but he was trying to put his thoughts in another place, away from this case.

"Oh no! Oh no! Ow! Oh I feel such pain on the tops of my hands!" I cried, opening my eyes and placing my hands, palms down on the tops of my thighs. In my right hand, I held the bangle clenched between my fingers and thumb, resting on my thigh, while my left hand was stretched straight out, palm down.

I looked over at Tom and his face was as white as a sheet! He was staring at my hands and let out with a loud gasp, "Sh-ie-e-e-et! Look at your hands, Pat!"

I looked at the tops of my hands, *deep scratches had appeared! On both of them*!

"Oh my God!" I blurted, and instantly, right before our eyes the scratches disappeared!

Tom just sat there in a frozen stupor. This big burly giant, sweet and spiritual, was reduced to a stuttering and completely dumbfounded man.

And I was just as shocked and amazed as he was! This was the first time I had ever *experienced the actual physical events* that a victim had encountered!

We both just sat there quiet for a few minutes. I was emotionally and mentally exhausted and I definitely needed to rest. Tom picked up the walkie-talkie and tried to explain to Jim what had just transpired.

"You're n-n-not gonna believe this," he began, his voice stammering, "I've seen it with my own two eyes, and I still don't believe it. Pat had scratches appear on her hands and then they disappeared, real quick like. She has to stop for a bit. I'll explain more to ya'all later."

"Tom, when I felt the pain on the tops of my hands, I also perceived an area," I began, my body now calming down from the ordeal. "He pulled off the highway. I believe it to be outside of the city limits, and up a small knoll. You're going to find these two young girls in shallow concave graves, with debris covering them, and not too far apart from each other. He has brutally raped and murdered them," I sighed.

"It's raining so hard now, we won't be able to continue to search today," he remarked frowning. "And you need to rest up before you fly out in the morning."

"Tom, I know you'll find them, and you'll get the man too. You've had him in custody recently. He has been arrested on another charge. I don't know what it is exactly, but I felt it was a serious charge. Also, I believe the word 'beaver' may have a bearing on the location of where the girls are now."

"Pat, this has been quite an experience for me! I've never worked with a psychic before, and after everything we've gone through today, I've no doubt in anything you've said or done, thus far. I will personally devote as much time to this case as I can. And I can't thank you enough," he said smiling nervously and starting up the jeep. As he pulled back onto the road he picked up the walkie-talkie and said, "I'll meet ya'all back at the station. I'm taking Ms. Gagliardo back to the hotel."

We arrived at the hotel at approximately six forty-five pm. I was physically drained and very hungry. Tom pulled up to the lobby entrance and as I was getting out of the vehicle, he told me he would meet me in the lobby at seven in the morning to take me to the airport. "Sleep well, Pat, and thank you so much," he smiled and then drove away.

I ordered something to eat in the hotel's restaurant and then went up to my room. I telephoned my husband and told him of all the details that had happened. And then I fell into a deep sleep.

*   *   *

Three months had passed. I still hadn't heard anything from Tom Williams. During this time I received a telephone call from Lieutenant O'Connor, of the North Stonington, Connecticut Fire Department.

"Ms. Gagliardo, I'm Lieutenant O'Connor from North Stonington. I'm calling with the hope that you can help us out. Have you heard about the missing windsurfer, Whittemore?" he asked.

"No sir, I haven't. I don't read the local newspaper or listen to local news. I'm probably one of the least informed people you'll ever meet," I replied with a little chuckle in my voice. "It has to be that way. If I get involved with missing people or crime related cases, I can't have any preconceived ideas or information from other sources. It can cloud my impressions."

"I think I understand," he commented. "How much do you want me to tell you?"

"Nothing. I've already made an attunement to your voice. I believe you need to look in the water near the Mason Island area. I'm getting southwest of the island. There is long grass, a very sandy bottom, and I feel tall eel type grass. I'm sensing a small round area, perhaps a small island. You'll find him there, unfortunately. I believe he has drowned."

"I-uh, didn't expect this! I believe I know exactly the area that you are speaking of. We've already had divers out there, though. I don't know if I can convince them to go back in that area again."

"I've heard that before Lieutenant. I can only give you the impressions as I perceive them."

"I'll look into it. I know you've had many successes before, that's why I called you. Thank you."

Two days later, I heard from him again, and the news media as well.

"Pat. *He was there*! Thank you again! The divers in the first search were approximately twenty feet away from that area. When I told them what you said and where to look, I received a lot of flack. The *experts* said 'the way the tides and undercurrents run through there, he couldn't possibly be in the area she's described. It's just not *possible*.' But with strong conviction and insistence on my part, I got a couple of divers to go back out there. He was in the *tall eelgrass*, with a *sandy bottom*, near a *small island*."

"Thank God. I'm happy that the information was helpful to you."

"Well, I told everyone the truth on why we were searching in that area again. And that it was because of the information you gave me over the phone. I've gotten a lot of ribbing from some of the guys I work with, but after the discovery, I didn't hear anything more. I'm sure you'll be hearing from the media, if you haven't already. You're a very gifted person. Thanks again."

"You're welcome. And thank you for letting me know. I will pray for his spirit and for spiritual comfort for his family. And yes, several of the newspapers have called me, and some of the radio stations as well."

"I just felt it was important to give credit where credit was due. And other people that need help will know that you're credible."

"The credit belongs to God-consciousness, and His Spiritual Guidance. Take care and if you ever need help again, please feel free to call me."

"I will. Take care, Pat. Bye."

     *   *   *

It was toward the end of June, when I finally received a phone call from Tom Williams.

"Hello, Pat," his deep, gentle voice said, "how ya'all doing?"

"We are all fine, thanks, Tom. How are things going there?"

"That's what I'm calling to tell you. Actually there are two reasons. The first and main reason, we've *located the girls*. Pat, they were found exactly as you described! They were *across the county line*, near *Beaver Brook*, up on a *knoll* like area, and they were buried in *shallow* graves, covered by some *brush* and other *debris*. They were about *ten feet* from each other. Pat, the most incredible news I want to tell you is this; both of the girls had their *hands bound*, by some kind of *wire*, they're not sure, yet, if it's guitar wire or piano wire. Even though the remains now are nearly completely skeletal, their hands were bound in such a fashion that they were *crossed over each other*, but *top of hand* on *top of hand*, not palm crossing palm! I'm sure I don't have to tell you what that did to me! I remembered the scratches immediately that appeared on the *top of your hands*! And Pat, the perpetrator has been caught! He *was arrested* a month before those girls disappeared, on weapons charges. He was released. We found blood and hair samples that matched the girls, in the back of his *green van*. Lil' lady, I'll never forget you, and I want you to know, I'll never forget my experiences with you. Look for a package in your mailbox. It's not much, just a little something from me and the wife to show our appreciation."

"Tom, you didn't have to do that. I'm just so thankful that this case is finally over, both for you and the families of those poor girls."

"God Bless you, Pat. Maybe we can all meet again some time under more pleasant circumstances."

"Thank you, Tom. My husband and I would like that."

In a couple of days a small box arrived at my residence. Inside the box were two beautiful light blue wine goblets and a small wooden wall plaque with lovely birds painted on it and the words that read: 'What you are is God's gift to you; what you do is your gift back to God.'

These gifts from Tom and his wife touched me deeply. I know that the plaque had a two-fold purpose—a thankfulness yes, but more importantly and more profoundly it was a confirmation of Tom's belief that my 'gifts' were God-given and I was doing the work of the Lord.

*   *   *

Most of the people who live in the city of Norwich, and neighboring towns, I believe, had always shared the opinion that our area was a safe place to live, small quiet towns in which to raise your children, attend church, and share in family life activities…until Michael Ross decided to take up his residence in one of these towns!

Fear and terror ripped through our peaceful homes—as young women and teenaged girls began to disappear! The nightmare continued and seemed endless as the raped and brutally murdered girls bodies were being discovered.

I heard from Dan Teper again. Dan telephoned me and asked for my assistance when the last victim, Wendy B turned up missing. At the time, no one knew who the perpetrator was, or where he was from. I drove out to an area with Dan, just a short distance past the street where Wendy lived. Dan parked his car on the opposite side of the road and we proceeded to walk into the wooded area.

"Dan," I began, "he's driven past this place many times. He could be driving by us right now." I felt terribly uncomfortable as we continued to walk into the woods. I *knew* that the man was familiar with this highway.

We stopped for a few minutes and I told Dan that I wanted to try and *tune in* to the energy to see if that area might provide impressions or visions. I sensed a man, slight in build, approximately five feet eight or nine inches tall with wavy brown hair and wearing glasses. I also felt he was very intelligent.

"Dan," I said, after giving him the description and details, "this man is connected with the state of New York. I believe he lived there and probably has assaulted, raped and murdered young women there as well."

Dan listened intently. In working with me in the past, he knew that I needed to stay with the impressions, and he knew not to say anything, then.

"There is a blue car. It's an older model, compact or intermediate in size. I also see a small older ranch type house. It sits close to the road. I believe there is a small porch, very little frontage to the property, as the sidewalk appears close. He doesn't live far from here, maybe three to five miles or so. I believe he saw her walking as he drove passed her, turned around up the road, drove back by her, turned around again in the circle just below us and then pulled his car over up on the same side of the road a little ways ahead of her. He's a very sick and twisted individual. I believe he grabbed her and took her into these woods." We searched in the area of the woods for about an hour, and then we climbed over a stonewall…"I know she's here. I feel it! Or she was here, and he moved her."

"I'll have some people come in here to search more thoroughly, Pat," Dan said, looking up and down along the wall.

"This may sound a bit strange, but I keep seeing a broken, bent tree, an embankment and just a cigarette butt," I remarked, looking at Dan. "I know there is water by this embankment too. I don't think it's here though, in this area."

"Do you think that's a symbol that stands for something?"

"Yes. It probably is. Do you have something in mind, Dan?"

"Well, in working with you before, I know that you get symbols of things, that stand for something else. And when you said a butt, I thought of Butt's Bridge. It's not too far from here. There is an embankment, and water. I'll check it out tomorrow."

"Okay. I think that's a good idea. It's getting dark, I don't think we're going to find anything here now."

It was a warm evening that night late in June of 1984. On the ride back to my home, Dan and I talked about the five other victims, all females, two of them only fourteen years old.

"We're going to get him, Pat," Dan remarked. "You're right about him being a vile killer. When the bodies of April and Leslie were found up in the woods near the campground, I heard that one of the police officials got pretty sick after he discovered a rock that had writing on it in one of the girl's blood. It wasn't too far from where he left them. The words on the rock read: 'I love naked little girls.'"

"You're a good man, Dan…and very dedicated. I know that you'll get some help from up above," I said, trying to shake the image from my head.

"Thanks again for your time and help, Pat," Dan said, pulling the car up in front of my house.

"Any time, Dan. Say hello to your wife for me."

"I will. And I'll let you know if anything turns up."

Approximately a week passed by, when Dan telephoned.

"Hi Pat. I just wanted to let you know, Wendy has been found, and her clothes too. I believe that there is suspicion that her *body was moved*. She was found up near where we were looking. Also some of her clothes were found very close to a *broken tree*, some on the *embankment* and some down near the water…at *Butt's Bridge*."

"Thank you for calling and letting me know, Dan."

"Talk to you soon, Pat. Take care."

Michael Ross was arrested and convicted shortly thereafter, charged with the murders of four of the eight or so women. Gene read the article in the newspaper after his arrest, and he announced some of the facts to me. 'He was a graduate of Cornell University in *New York*, where they believe he is responsible for at least four murders there, he lived in *Jewett City*, (approximately three to four miles from where Wendy was found) was employed at a local insurance agency, and drove a *blue car*.

The residents of New London County could now resume some sense of normalcy back in their lives. However, the horrific and heinous crimes committed against our children, and the terror of having a serial killer haunting our once peaceful towns has left its scars.

10 ▶▶

Paranormal Investigator

It had become quite evident that my purpose in life was to utilize my gifts, sharing and helping others. At the encouragement of police personnel and friends, and a growing practice, I opened an office and hired a reception-ist full time. My office space was large enough to partition off areas to make more offices, which I did. I hired a carpenter and built two more rooms. One room was soundproofed for meditating. Another room was large enough to accommodate thirty chairs, which I used for instructing positive thinking/self-awareness and meditation classes.

Within a couple of months, I was to realize the gift of clairsentience— *clear sensing,* the ability to *see* and *converse* with spirits.

A gentleman called my office and left a message with my receptionist to 'please call him at my earliest convenience.'

I dialed the New London exchange and spoke with 'Matt.'

"Thank you for calling, Ms. Gagliardo."

"How can I help you, Matt?"

"Have you done anything with ghosts, or spirits?"

"In what way? Do you mean like hauntings, or earthbound spirits?"

"Yes. I know that we have something strange going on in our house. My wife, Sue, and I have experienced some very unsettling things here. We have a son, he's young and we're very concerned about this."

"I see. So you would like me to come to your home and investigate—is that it?"

"Would you, please?"

"I'll do what I can, Matt. Give me your address. I have your phone number, I will have to check my schedule and see what we can arrange, okay?"

"It's a little tricky to get to my house, if you aren't terribly familiar with New London. I could always meet you and you can follow me."

"Okay. We'll discuss all that, when we make the plans. I should come out in the evening, first. And I would prefer not to have your child present, okay?"

"Sure. I'll talk to Sue and we'll make arrangements. I'll look forward to your call. Thank you so much."

I telephoned Matt's home the following afternoon and I spoke with his wife, Sue. We made arrangements to meet at Hughie's Restaurant, seven pm, the next evening.

As Gene and I were walking to the car to leave for the drive to New London, he asked me, opening my car door, "Trish, do you have any idea—I mean, have you gotten any *guidance* for tonight? You've never done anything quite like *this* before. And we haven't had any time to really talk about it."

"I can only tell you this, hon," I said, as we pulled out of the driveway. "When I first spoke to Matt, I heard Vincent's words in my head, 'yes, offer your assistance and ask that the child not be present.' And then memories of Nancy's daughter came to my mind. You remember what happened in the group—through direct voice, right?"

"Yeah. Okay. I guess you'll be guided again, as always," he smiled.

We arrived at Hughie's Restaurant and Matt was waiting. We followed him to his home, which was approximately a mile or so from there. The house was very old and on a dead-end street, right across from the ocean.

We parked behind Matt's car and walked along with him, sort of getting acquainted as we proceeded toward the side and rear of his house. There was another home rather close to his and we had to walk between them. I stopped for a minute, and looked at the other home. I had attuned to the 'energy' already.

"Just a minute, Matt," I said, walking closer to the other house. "There's been a terrible tragedy here. Someone has died in this house, and you or your family is connected with it. Hot. I feel tremendous heat here."

Matt looked at me wide-eyed and said, "Yes. My *uncle* died in a *fire* in that house about five years ago."

I stood there for a few minutes longer, staring at the house, and then turned to Matt and said, "His name was Jack, wasn't it?"

"Yes."

"Okay. He is not here any longer, I don't want you to think that he is earthbound and causing any phenomenon in your home. I just attuned to the past here, nothing more."

"Okay."

We continued to walk approximately twenty feet, and then headed up a wooden staircase on the side of Matt's house.

At the top of the landing, Matt opened the door and we entered inside. To the right was a nicely decorated sunroom. To the left was a gorgeous kitchen. Matt had completely refurbished the house inside.

Sue greeted us in the kitchen. The house was an open floor plan. From the kitchen you could view the dining area and living room. To the left of the living room a spiral staircase led to the upstairs.

"May, I just walk around for a bit?" I asked.

"Yes. Please feel free to go wherever you want to," Sue answered, and Matt added, "Do you want us to tell you where and what is going on here?"

"No, please. Let me just see if I can pick up anything on my own," I smiled.

I walked away from them and headed into the living room. I could hear Gene talking to them and trying to explain my abilities. As I headed toward the spiral staircase coolness swept over me. I stood there for a few minutes, closed my eyes, asked for guidance and protection, and tuned into the *energy* that was present.

Mentally I asked, "Who are you? Why are you here?"

"*Paul. I am Paul.*"

I moved closer to the stairs, and as I started to climb them, I sensed a *different* energy...I reached the top, turned left and walked into their child's bedroom. As I approached the center of the room, the temperature seemed like it had dropped twenty degrees. I walked toward the window, and stood still, attuning to the energy there. I felt that this presence was female, older. She had a connection with this house, prior to Matt and Sue's ownership.

I went back downstairs and joined Gene, Matt and Sue.

"There are two presences here," I began. "I don't feel either one of them as a negative energy. Actually, the first energy I felt to be very troubled, male energy, and the presence upstairs, an older female, much like a grandmother, who has a connection with previous ownership. The name, 'Gladys', is associated with her. I would like to go down to the basement, all of us can go." I didn't mention the name 'Paul' at that point, as I felt he had a connection with the basement, and I was hoping to perceive more information there.

Matt led the way; I followed him, then Sue and Gene. We hadn't even reached the last step when I felt consumed with grief, anxiety and emotional pain. Matt continued to walk through the first room, which appeared to have once been a family room. There were now boxes and other items piled in it.

I walked only a few feet, closed my eyes and mentally attuned to the very evident presence...the same energy I had felt near the stairs...

"Forgiveness. I need his forgiveness. It was an accident, not intentional." These were the words that were *spoken* to me, and then in my mind's eye, I saw a motorcycle, I felt anxiousness and fear when I envisioned the motorcycle, and then I sensed a stupor, drinking and/or drugs.

"Matt, there is a definite male energy presence here, and I witnessed it upstairs. It is much stronger down here. The presence is named, Paul, and he needs your forgiveness, and there is a motorcycle associated with him, and I believe he drank a lot and possibly used drugs as well. Does this mean anything to you?"

Matt became so emotional; he couldn't hold back his tears. He just stared at me for a few minutes, then he looked at his wife, who was also crying at this point, and then he looked back at me. Sobs were breaking his words as he replied, "P-paul was my *brother*. He lived with us for a while. As a matter of fact, he *stayed* down here. He drank a lot, and we argued a great deal, and it got to a point where I didn't talk to him. Then he went out one night and *killed himself* on that bike."

"No, Matt, he didn't. It was an accident. He didn't kill himself. And he needs your forgiveness, so he can continue on his spiritual journey," I said empathically, and held his hand in mine. "You need to let go of any guilt you may feel, or any anger and resentments you may have, and forgive him and yourself. That is what is holding his spirit here."

"But when he left that night, he said..."

"It doesn't matter what he said," I interrupted. "It was an accident. He told me, Matt. I would like to come back with a couple more members of my prayer group, and say some prayers and ask that these entities be released from here, so that they may continue on their spiritual journeys. Is that all right with the two of you?"

"Yes. Yes of course," Sue said.

"In the meantime Gene and I will say some prayers now, and you both may join us. I hope that you will continue to say prayers every day for these spirits as well. You just need to encourage them to go to the light of Christ."

Gene and I began with prayers from our Catholic religion, and then via direct-voice from my spirit guide, Vincent, I was given other prayers to say.

As we were leaving, I told them I would make arrangements with members of our Unity, and get back in touch very soon. I also recommended that they place religious articles in the areas, the basement and the child's bedroom. A couple of nights later, Frank and Mary, Chris, Gene and I returned to their home. In our possession were Holy Water, prayers, faith and hopefulness in our hearts that these spirits would find rest in the spiritual spheres. Matt called approximately a week later. He told me that all was 'quiet' now, and he was continuing with prayers daily, and working on forgiveness for himself and Paul. He also told me that *Gladys* was a *grandmother* and she had lived in the house with her daughter and son-in-law many years previous, long before Matt and Sue purchased the home. Gladys had died in the home after suffering from an illness.

News of the events that had taken place in their home, spread like wildfire. I became inundated with telephone calls pertaining to earthbound spirits. I will share a few of the most remarkable and memorable encounters.

Barbara S. telephoned and asked if I would please visit her home in Bozrah, Connecticut. She and her husband, John, purchased a very large older estate home. They lived there with their two children. The entire second floor of this large estate was closed off. Their intentions were to refurbish each room, one at a time, over a period of time.

When Barbara first telephoned me, she told me of bizarre events that were taking place in her home. Lights would turn off and on, they could hear heavy footsteps going up and down to the second floor, she and her husband could hear voices, however they were inaudible, and at times there was a very unpleasant odor. Gene and I made arrangements to visit the house, again in the evening.

When we pulled up the long dirt driveway, uneasiness came over me. Gene parked the car near the porch entrance. When I got out of the car, *something* drew my attention to the far right side of the property. I walked over to the area, with Gene following close behind.

I sensed anguish, fear and hostility as I continued to walk around in a small perimeter of the area.

"Whatever is present here, is very unpleasant, Gene," I said, turning to look at him.

"Do you think it's evil?" he asked, as his eyes glanced around the property.

"There's a combination of energies here; some negative, and very uncomfortable. I'm not sure about evil, but we'll see what's present inside the house," I said, walking toward the porch entrance.

Barbara greeted us at the front door. We walked through a small entryway and into a lovely kitchen. It had been completely restored, but to it's original style and design of the early 1800's. We followed her through the kitchen, and into a living room area. Some of the very wide wooden floorboards were uneven. The living room was also restored to the original design and décor of the same time period. As we entered into the living room, that same uneasiness overcame me, this time, more intense. I looked to my left, and I saw a very large thick wooden door, which was closed.

"Through that door, do you go upstairs?" I asked her.

"Yes."

"And this is where you hear the footsteps, correct?"

"Yes. And my children have said they have heard 'breathing' coming from there."

"They aren't here tonight, right?"

"Right. I did what you asked, and made other arrangements, they're at a friends house."

"That's good. It's just that children are very susceptible to the presence of spirit energy, and I need to feel totally relaxed and not concerned about frightening them, or anything else. That's the reason I ask that children not be present."

"I understand. But they have both experienced things."

"I'm sure they have. As I said, children are very sensitive."

"Do you want to go upstairs?"

"Yes, in a minute," I replied, as I walked over to a lamp sitting on an end table, which I was drawn to. Examining the lamp, receptacle, and surrounding floor area, I asked, "This lamp goes off and on, doesn't it?"

"Yes. It sure does."

"Below this floor, there is only crawl space? Not a full basement, right?"

"Yes, again."

"Hmmm," I murmured, as I closed my eyes and attuned to the energy. My impressions indicated that people, many people had traveled through that area. I didn't know at that moment, when or who. But the fear, anxiety and hostility were strong, very strong. "May I just lead the way, Barbara?"

"Absolutely, Pat. Feel free to do whatever you have to."

"Okay," I smiled, and headed toward the closed door. I opened the door, and a wave of extremely cold air hit me. It wasn't a natural temperature, nor was it pleasant. I looked at Gene, with that 'say some prayers look' and I said aloud the protection prayer, as I continued to climb the stairs.

"Pat, there is only electricity in the first couple of rooms," Barbara said. "The first room has a flashlight in it—the room is to your left, a little ways down the hallway."

At the top of the landing and straight-ahead was a long hallway. There were at least four doors on the left and four doors on the right. There was only enough light to see that far. As I headed straight toward the first door on my left, a strong unpleasant odor permeated through the air. I turned to look at Barbara and Gene, both of them just nodded their heads; they could smell it too.

"I'm going to try and tune into this energy. Just be still please and silently say some prayers," I said, as I closed my eyes, repeated the protection prayer mentally and then attuned to the energy.

I became overwhelmed by the impressions and information that I received. I felt that slaves had been transported through this property. Some of the information led me to believe that young children were mistreated, physically, mentally and emotionally. I sensed there was an underground tunnel, which ran from the *right side of the property* right through the house and continued. Slaves were held in a room, a small room, and treated very badly while they were waiting to be transported to other places. Some of these people had died here, children and older people as well. I became very emotional and started to cry as I tuned into the energy of a young male child. This child was crying for his mother, they had been separated. I sensed that he was about eight years old. He was malnourished, frightened, and had been physically beaten. I also sensed the energy of an older man, a very *angry* older man. I believed that he had died there, very quickly—perhaps of a heart attack. And then via direct-voice, guidance from my spirit guide, I began…

"You are no longer of this physical life. I command in the name of Jesus Christ, Lord and Savior, that you leave this earth plane, and go toward the Light. I pray that you find peace in the Love and Light of Our Merciful Lord."

I then began to say the 'Lord's Prayer.' Gene and Barbara joined in. I asked Barbara if it would be all right to come back again with members of the Unity and to offer more prayers. She agreed. "In the meantime Barbara, I would put out some religious items, a cross, statues, etc."

"I have some in the boxes, I just haven't put them up yet. But I will immediately. I'm also going to check through records and see what history I can find out about this house and property."

"I would also inquire with some of your neighbors," I said. "I believe if you talk with your neighbors a couple of miles up the road, I believe the house is like a barn-red color, you'll get some information from the older gentlemen that lives there."

She looked at me inquisitively and asked, "How do you know about that red house up the road? Did you go by there before stopping here?"

"No. I sensed it, when I felt that underground tunnel. I know that the tunnel continued at least up that far, maybe even further, but that's as far as my impressions led me."

"Well' you're right. It's up on the same side of the road, and it's about a mile and a half from here. I will stop up there," she smiled.

"I'll be in touch very soon, Barbara," I said, walking down the stairs. "I hope we will be able to put these tormented spirits to rest."

We made arrangements the following Friday night. This time along with Gene, Chris, Frank and Mary, Jim and Kathy also accompanied us. Just as with Matt and Sue, we continued with prayers and the sprinkling of Holy Water throughout the entire house, and on the grounds. I haven't heard anymore from Barbara concerning anymore unsettling events in their home. She did call to tell me that she spoke with the *older gentleman* that lived up the road in the red house. He told her of stories that his father had passed on to him. 'Yes there were *slaves that were transported*, and in his father's day, some of the *underground tunnels were discovered*.'

*   *   *

This next experience was a bit unnerving, especially for my brother-in-law, Jim. I had received a telephone call from a woman in Norwich who had purchased an older historic home. It was over two hundred years old and had at one time belonged to a famous historical family. The home was located across the street from a convalescent home, and was close to a school. The woman, who asked that she be identified as Margaret T. telephoned to tell me of 'strange occurrences' and the discovery of some bones that were found by her husband in their basement. I asked if it would be all right if I had at least four or five other individuals accompany me on the first visit. She agreed.

Normally I would go the first time alone, or Gene and I together, but this time, I felt a need to have some group members accompany me. I am glad that I did.

It was early evening, about seven pm, when we drove up along the sidewalk in front of the house, and parked the cars. Gene, Chris, Del and I were in my car—Frank and Mary, Jim and Kathy were in Frank's car. There was very little front yard, and the house itself sat very close to the sidewalk, and had a very short tar driveway. There were a couple of small hedges on either side to the entrance of the house.

Margaret greeted us at the front door. Introductions were exchanged and then she escorted us to the basement. As we walked down the stairs to the basement, I felt dampness, and a web like substance pass over my body. I hadn't experienced this before; this was a first time, but certainly not the last! Part of the basement had a dirt floor, and the walls were like crushed stone and cement in structure. She led us into a smaller room, also with a dirt floor and similar walls, and it had a peculiar odor in it. It was almost like the scent of an animal's urine, like that of a cat.

"Sh-h-h-h," I said, putting a finger to my lips. "There is a presence in here. Please all of you mentally begin the prayers, and let me attune to what's here."

The group knew exactly what to do and formed an energy circle, each taking a hold of one another's hands. Chris took Margaret's hand on her right, and Gene took her left hand in his and so on until a circle was formed. I began with the sign of the Cross, and the Unity followed. I began with the protection prayer, and it *angered* the *presence* in the room! The odor became stronger, and it made Kathy nauseous. She prayed louder, as we all did. Then something very strong, but not visible, hit me behind my right knee, making me lose my balance and nearly fall to the floor. In my mind's eye, I envisioned a heavyset man, approximately six feet tall, with shoulder length hair pulled back. It was a hairdo that reminded me of the soldiers in the time of George Washington, and I felt this man was, in fact, a soldier. I felt that the hairstyle was symbolic of that era. I sensed that he had murdered two people; there in that area. The energy of one of those spirits was that of a young male, approximately fifteen or sixteen years old. The other was an older man, maybe in his thirties. Both died at the hands of this once heavyset man. I began to command this spirit to leave the earth plane, and to ask for mercy from God-consciousness. As we prayed for his spirit, the energy became more enraged. Then Jim winced out in pain, and his left ear was bleeding! There appeared to be a bite mark and two teeth marks on the lobe of his left ear. We prayed louder and more fervently. Margaret was praying too and she kept her eyes closed. We kept the prayers going continuously for about an hour. The odor left the room, and there were no subsequent occurrences.

Before we left the premises, we said more prayers and again sprinkled Holy Water throughout the house. Margaret telephoned about a month later to tell me that they found out some information about the property. Some of the 'stories' confirmed soldiers of that time era, and the bones were being analyzed to determine if they were human or animal.

*   *   *

This next experience was not only remarkable, but also pleasant, uplifting and a relief for a woman, who had anguished over the death of her mother. She had many questions and concerns about her mother's death and needed answers that only her *mother* could provide.

Mary Lou Warren had been a client for about three years prior to the death of her mother. About three months after her death, Mary Lou phoned for an appointment. In the course of conversation she asked me if she could bring a photo of her mother. She wanted to know if I could 'pickup' any impressions about her. I told her to bring her mother's photo with her, and we would see what happens.

I set Mary Lou's appointment two weeks away and in the evening, six o'clock. In her possession in a five by seven inch brass bordered frame, was a picture of her mother. I sat behind my desk and Mary Lou sat across in front facing me. She handed me the picture frame. I took a deep breath, closed my eyes for a few minutes and then opened them and stared at the face of her mother.

I continued to stare at the photograph, and then my energy attuned to her mother. I began speaking to Mary Lou, never turning my head to look at her. I had made a connection with her *mother's spirit* and began...

'*How I so enjoyed our visits at the beach. I don't know if I ever really told you just how much I enjoyed them. And it was him you know, there. He helped me. I was afraid at first, but then I saw him, and he helped me cross over...I told you I would find out the truth one day...I know all about Ben Franklin...And my sister, Helen, she was there. And you do remember my neighbor—Anne, she was there too. I don't want you to feel guilty about anything. You have no reason to. I am happy and pain free and at peace.*'

Her connection left, but I remained attuned to the vibration, and then I began to perceive visions and other information. Still focused on the photograph, I said...

"There is a lovely small light gray house, it is very quaint and appears to be on a street that has houses all of the same architecture and style.

These houses are very close together. This small gray house has an absolutely gorgeous flower garden that runs the entire length of the front of the house, separated by a short sidewalk. There are a few steps that go up to a small porch."

Mary Lou began to sniffle and then she broke into sobs, as I continued.

"I am inside of this house, it is decorated so lovely. The kitchen has lots of light blues, and pale yellow and I think some light peach colors. It is small and leads into what looks like a small type of library or sitting room. There are many books in shelves on the wall in here. There is lots of water around this house, I can't see it, but I sense it very strongly. The ocean. Yes, that's it—it's the ocean. I'm now outside and there is a tan colored house across the street, same style as this house—Anne. It belongs to Anne."

Mary Lou, unable to contain herself any longer said, "Pat, you have described my mother's home, which is on the beach in *Nantucket*, to a tee! And what you said about Ben Franklin—that did it for me! I know it was *my mother* that gave you that message! She and I had numerous conversations about Ben Franklin. My mother has said to me, 'If there is life after death, I'm going to find Ben and have a talk with that man.' Pat, I can't begin to tell you what this reading has done for me. I've anguished so much over her death—feeling guilty. I don't anymore. Thank you so much!"

We were both crying at this point. I stood up from my chair and walked over to Mary Lou and we hugged each other.

This final encounter begins when a friend, Bruce Christie, joined us for dinner, and ends with an investigation on a piece of property where a man was murdered.

We were standing in my kitchen talking. I was on one side of the center island, and Bruce was across on the other side, facing me. As he was talking to me, I felt the presence of another energy close to him. Bruce's lips were moving, but I didn't hear him, as I had attuned to the energy. I closed my eyes and envisioned an older woman, her name, and how she would have looked in her physical life.

"Bruce," I interrupted, "who is Beatrice?"

"What? Wow, where did you get that from?" he asked, bewildered by my question.

"Before you answer me, she says, 'mother is fine, and you're not responsible.' Do you know what that means?"

Bruce just stood there for a few minutes in silence. By the look on his face it was apparent that what I had said caught him completely off guard.

"Beatrice was my choir director a very long time ago when I was a kid and sang in the church choir," he answered solemnly.

"Her spirit is around you. I'm not saying she is your Guardian Angel, but she could be. In any event if you've been carrying an emotional burden, she is trying to help you."

He stood there just staring at me for a couple of moments, and said, "We've never talked about my *mother*. On the day she died, I had a terrible argument with her earlier that morning. I left angry. Then she died. If I didn't argue with her, she might…"

"Bruce. You're *not responsible*. She was ill, and it was her time," I interrupted, walking over to him and giving him a hug. "It would have happened whether you were there or not, regardless of the argument," I said empathically.

Bruce shared some personal stories and we chatted for about two more hours. By the time he left, he had a lot to think about. And I had hoped his emotional burden had been lifted. We haven't discussed that night since.

Three or so weeks had passed since that evening, when I received a phone call from Bruce. He had been looking to buy a house for a couple of months. He called to tell me that there was a house for sale in Waterford that he was going to look at on Saturday. He wanted to know if I could meet him there…

"Pat. This house in Waterford that I want to look at—somebody was murdered in it. I was hoping maybe you could meet me there and sort of walk around the property and in the house itself and see if you feel anything there. I can tell you that…"

"Bruce," I interrupted, "please don't give me any details. If I'm going to meet you there, and if anything is present, hopefully I'll perceive any impressions or entities then."

"Okay. I've made arrangements through the realtor and I have permission to go there on Saturday and look around. Is noontime okay for you?"

"Yes. It should be fine. Give me the address and I'll meet you there."

On Saturday, Gene, Frank, Mary, Chris, Del and I drove to Waterford. The house was located at the end of a dead-end street. I pulled the car up and parked in front of it. All the windows were boarded up, and the house itself was in need of some repair. There was a small yard in the front and a little larger yard to the right side.

We got out of the car and walked up onto the front yard, where Bruce was waiting. Introductions were made and then I said, "I'm going to walk around the outside first. If any of you want to come with me, just stay a little behind, okay?"

All of them followed staying about fifteen feet behind me. As I walked on the right side and heading toward the rear of the property, a very uncomfortable feeling came over me. My first impressions indicated that the man that had lived there was older, late sixties or seventies. I was about halfway in the yard, across from the side door of the house, and I stood still. My impressions were that this man allowed destitute, homeless and some unsavory people in and out of this house continuously. More impressions were of sadness and then of fear.

"Bruce, we need to go inside the house now," I yelled to him.

The side door was sort of hanging crooked and Bruce had to jiggle it back and forth to open it. It led into a kitchen, and it was quite dark. On the table inside was a large flashlight, which Bruce picked up and turned on.

"Just a minute. Please stand right here and please be silent. Bruce, would you please turn the light off?" I asked, closing my eyes and tuning into the very present energy.

"Who are you? Why are you here?" I asked. There was no response, nothing for a few minutes. I walked toward what I had thought was a hallway that was to the right of the kitchen, and I repeated, "Who are you?" The name 'Henry' came to my mind. I walked in further and realized it was a narrow room and the pipes in the ceiling were exposed. As I reached the center of the room, coolness swept over me, along with a very uncomfortable feeling. Everyone was right behind me.

"He died right above this room. Upstairs. Oh no, this poor man was sleeping, and another man appears in his bedroom. He was awakened. He was trying to get away. He leaves the bedroom, next to the room, right above us. He was beaten, choked, I believe stabbed, a hole, there is a hole," I said becoming emotional. "Henry, you are no longer of this earth plane. Go to the light. Find peace and rest in the Love of Jesus," I said aloud.

I was about to begin the prayers when we heard a truck pull up outside. It was Bruce's brother. Bruce left and went outside. As soon as he walked out of the door, a blue ball of mist, about the size of a basketball appeared above our heads, right next to the exposed pipe. All of us witnessed it. The group held hands and began to pray. "Henry, leave this earth plane. You are no longer of this life. Find rest and peace with Jesus," I pleaded and began the Lord's Prayer. We were saying other prayers when Bruce returned. We continued for a half hour longer. As we were saying the prayers, I had perceived more information from Henry. He had a daughter living in South Carolina that he had not spoken to for many years. There was dissension and animosity between them, and had been for nearly thirty years. We would somehow pass the information on to her, to please forgive her father. The energy presence left. We offered prayers of thanks and we left.

Bruce telephoned a couple of days later. He was talking to a man where he works and told him about the experience at the house in Waterford. It turned out that the man was Henry's brother. He told Bruce that Henry was *sixty-eight* years old, and that he had *people in and out of his house* daily. The man that murdered him was a *homeless man* and killed Henry over twenty dollars. There *is* a daughter in South Carolina; they hadn't spoken in *thirty-three years*, and yes the information would be passed on to her.

Did Bruce buy the house? No. Was he upset that he did not see the spirit of Henry? Extremely!

Afterword ▶

I continue to receive telephone calls, letters, email, and packages from police, government and private persons, asking for my assistance. At the encouragement of personnel and friends from the New London Police Department, I opened an office. The space was large enough for my practice, as well as for me to instruct meditation/self awareness classes to groups of twenty-five persons.

I have hosted my own television and radio talk shows, 'Insight', WTWS 26, with coverage over five states, and 'The Pat Gagliardo Show' radio show, WSUB, Groton, Connecticut. Aside from my appearance on **PM Magazine**, I have been a guest on the **Good Day Show**, and most currently I did a taping on the **Sally Jesse Raphael Show**. I was a radio guest, taking calls from listeners, with Theresa Berry from WBMW, Ledyard, Connecticut, from October 1998-October 1999, every Monday, Wednesday and Friday. I continue to appear as a guest on other local radio stations.

I am a lecturer of fifteen years with audiences in private clubs and organizations, fundraisers, and corporations. Recently the main focus is geared toward college students. I very much enjoy the eagerness, willingness and enthusiasm that I receive from the students. The forum that I offer to these wonderful young people is a mix of question and answer, participation in Aura and ESP exercises, and positive mental and mind energy stimulation—for retention and memory recall. I have lectured extensively on the East Coast however, a recent feature article about me has appeared in the college magazine, **Campus Activities**, which has a circulation of thirty-eight hundred colleges nationwide. This will broaden my areas of travel within the United States and possibly abroad.

Having these wonderful 'gifts' and the Love and Enlightenments from my beloved Spiritual Guides, despite the trials, tribulations, and opposition have enriched my life more than words can express. Speaking of opposition, as I *started chapter 6*, I developed a very serious tendonitis condition in my right arm, which continued throughout the writing of this book. Prescription—'stop typing'—I didn't. *Coincidence?*

*   *   *

In Love and Light,

Patricia Gagliardo

About the Author ▶

Patricia Gagliardo is a practicing, intuitive clairvoyant counselor, author, and lecturer. Over the past twenty-two years she has gained the respect of law enforcement, federal and government agencies and private persons, aiding with her clairvoyant abilities in locating missing persons and assisting with various criminal cases nationwide, and as far away as Australia. She first received national acclaim in 1980 when she worked with the State's Attorney's Office, in New London, Connecticut and led officials to a location which recovered the body of a missing Coast Guard Warrant Officer, Richard Eastman. The story received nationwide coverage via the National Enquirer and the AP newswire.

In the early 90's, she had hosted her own television and radio talk shows. Her live television show, 'Insight' WTWS 26, covered a viewing audience of five states, and 'The Pat Gagliardo' radio show, WSUB, Groton, Connecticut. Most recently, she has worked with Theresa Berry, of WBMW, Ledyard, Connecticut, and continued to astonish call-ins with her remarkable clairvoyant abilities. She offers her intuitive counseling, via phone, through her website, www.patgagliardo.com.

For the past fifteen years she has lectured to audiences in private clubs and organizations, and corporations. As of this past year, her main focus is geared toward college campuses. Ms. Gagliardo enjoys the eagerness, willingness and enthusiasm she receives from the students. She has lectured extensively on the East Coast, however, in February of this year, 2000, a recent feature article about her has appeared in the college magazine, **Campus Activities**, which has a circulation of thirty-eight hundred colleges nationwide and has broadened her areas of travel.

Patricia Gagliardo resides in Norwich, Connecticut and lives close to her son and his family. She is a proud mother, and grandmother. In her spare time you will find her wherever there is a BMX track, watching the light of her life, her grandson, Michael, racing his bicycle.

And what does Patricia Gagliardo say of herself?

"When I look in the mirror, I'm amazed at the reflection of the woman I see. I thank God that I have evolved into this secure, happy and fulfilled human being. I've embraced my position and purpose of this life, and no longer ask why. In helping others, I have found myself."

Appendix ▶

Meditation Exercises

The following pages will outline some of the meditation exercises that I have found to be valuable tools in tapping into my 'higher' self. There will also be a section on recognizing spirit energy, and some do's and *please* don'ts.

*   *   *

• Basic Preparations:

I am going to share the process that has worked best for me. You may have to work with these basic outlines to find out what is best suited for you. First and foremost, be patient, positive and consistent. Let's start with the 'room' that you will designate for your meditations. It should be a room that you enjoy being in. The atmosphere should provide relaxation, happiness and comfort. You will need to choose times of the day that you can utilize this room without disturbance or interruption. Personally, I have found that approximately one half hour after rising in the morning provides excellent results in meditation. I recommend that you meditate three times a day, however, twice is also very beneficial, and for a period of at least twenty to twenty five minutes. Next is the location in the room— whether you will face north and south, or an east and west direction. The reason for this is to encourage an 'energy' balance between your magnetic force field, (located in your solar plexus area) and the energy source of the planet. After you determine where magnetic north is located, (which is easy to determine by use of a compass) you can then experiment with sitting or lying down. In either case, be sure that your hands and feet are not crossed and that your back and head are straight. A small flat pillow is okay to rest under your head if you're lying down. I prefer to sit facing north, my back straight and obviously toward the south, with my feet flat on the floor and my hands resting on the top of my thighs, palms up. Some people prefer a yoga position; I would only recommend this if you practice yoga regularly. Proper diaphragmatic deep breathing exercises are also a must in helping to relax your mind and body. Please be sure to perform these deep breathing exercises properly. I strongly recommend that you get yourself informed on proper breathing techniques before applying them, as not to become hyperventilated. When you're ready to begin your meditation process, you should only do *two* of these breathing exercises. First inhale *very slowly* through your nose, mentally counting to eight, saying 'one thousand one, one thousand two, one thousand three, etc.' and breathing in from your diaphragm, much like blowing up a balloon, feeling your abdomen expand, and not inhaling from your upper chest cavity. When you reach one thousand eight, then hold your breath and mentally *count to four*, then exhale through your mouth just as slowly using the same counting method to eight. You may also want to insert a positive suggestion when you perform the second breathing exercise, such as 'I'm breathing in all positive and calming energy' and when you exhale, you may want to suggest, 'I'm releasing all negative energy and thoughts, and I will relax.'

*   *   *

• Helpful Tools:

You may want to set a timer or an alarm clock. Have a tape recorder, writing tablet, pens and pencils, for logging your experience. If you choose to have music as an aide to help you relax, you will need a Tape or CD player. It should be new age or instrumental type music, no lyrics, and barely audible in the background. I also recommend having religious articles—visible in the room, a written or typed protective prayer and live plants or flowers. Certain gemstones, such as quartz crystal, have vibrational properties. You may want to have them in the room as well.

*   *   *

• Purpose of meditation:

Prior to beginning your meditation, you should have a clear purpose of why you are starting this exercise. What is it that you would like to achieve; spiritual attunement, serenity, peace, more self-control, patience, self-confidence, self-awareness or tapping into your 'higher self?' Knowing what it is that you're seeking will help you to stay focused. I recommend that you make one choice and meditate on that same choice daily for at least three to four weeks, and then make another choice and so on.

*   *   *

• Mantra, Chant or Visual Technique:

Okay, now you're ready to begin. Your room is prepared, your clock or timer is set, and you're either lying down (on your back) or sitting up, and facing either north or east. Before you do your deep breathing exercises, you will need a focus for this technique. A Mantra is simply one word that you can recall to your mind, to replace an incoming thought. You should choose a one-syllable word, such as *love*, *peace* or *joy*. A chant should also be a one-syllable word and said in a monotone rhythm. The most common chant that is used is 'Ohm'. The most commonly used visual technique is a flower, one rose. You may choose any flower that you like, but be sure it is only one. Close your eyes and try to picture it in your mind, using all of your own creativity and imagination. See it or sense it as clearly as you can.

*   *   *

• Guided Mental Visualization Technique:

I began with guided mental visualization exercises, which initially worked the best for me. Guided mental visualization techniques, or guided imagery, are particularly helpful for beginners. A tape-recorded voice counts the listener down into a state of relaxation and gives verbal cues and instruction for the listener to follow in the meditative state. The voice then guides the listener back up for full alertness. You may want to visit a new age bookstore, or perhaps check the Internet to try and purchase audiocassettes or CD's offering Guided Mental Visualization meditation techniques.

*   *   *

• Silent Meditation/Contemplation Technique:

This exercise is followed in the same manner as the above instructions, omitting music in the background, or the use of any guided meditation mental visualization tapes or CD's, chants or mantras. Your only focus would be to picture a flower in your mind's eye and recall it to your mind when other thoughts enter in.

*   *   *

• Helpful Hints:

First and foremost, relax. Do not analyze your meditation—let it happen. With practice and consistency, the object is to dull your natural senses and attune to the 'higher' senses of sight and hearing. Your goal is to have mind, body and spirit in harmony. Your emotions prior to meditating should be positive and calm. Prayer before beginning will provide a peaceful atmosphere. Negative emotions may block any success to your meditation. Remember you can also experiment with positions (sitting or lying down) and direction (North and East) and the times of day that you choose.

*　　　　　*　　　　　*

• Protection Prayer:

"Lord as I enter into this meditative state, I ask for Thy Protection of my mind, body and spirit. Encompass me in Your White Light and protect me from all that is unholy and impure. I ask for Thy protection from evil spirits, evil thoughts and evil deeds. I ask of Thee while in this meditative state for Guidance, Wisdom, Patience and Knowledge that will help me to achieve harmony of mind, body and spirit. I ask for my three selves to become one and attuned to Your Love and Light so that I may attain spiritual growth. And I ask this in Thy Holy Name. Amen."

*　　　　　*　　　　　*

• Recognizing Spirit Energy; Positive and Negative:

In the past nearly twenty-two years I have investigated numerous 'haunted' houses, properties and possessions. First, you must eliminate any natural causes to the phenomenon. For example, if lights are being turned on and off, is there a faulty switch? If you open a cupboard door and food or dishes come flying out, are the items jammed in—is the shelf slanted? Another possibility, and I have found this to be the case, is someone playing tricks on you? If spirit energy exists, there will be telltale evidence that will remove *any doubt*. After all other possible natural explanations have been eliminated; then you may look for unnatural signs, such as these:

*　　　　　*　　　　　*

1. Is there a significant temperature change where the phenomenon occurs?
2. Is there an odor? Is the fragrance sweet or offensive?
3. Is there anything visible where the phenomenon is occurring? A mist, a shadow, a glowing ball of mist?
4. If this phenomenon is taking place in a residence, have any of the occupants experienced a web-like sensation pass over any parts of their physical bodies, such as their arms, hands, face or hair?
5. Has an occupant of the house when sleeping, been abruptly awakened in the very early morning hours—between one am and three am? What was the experience—did this person *feel* something touching them, hear a voice, have a dream, and what are the details of the dream? How often is this person encountering this experience—are the details always the same?
6. Are there young children in the residence—if so; has the child spoke of an imaginary or invisible playmate? What are the conversations, and or actions between the child and the playmate? Has there been a *very noticeable* difference in behavior or attitude of a child?
7. If some or all of the above apply, please pay close attention to the following:

*   *   *

• Do's:

1. Contact a reputable expert in the field of Parapsychology/Paranormal. A suggestion would be to search the Internet to locate a reputable and credible association.
2. Contact a minister, priest or member of the clergy and ask to have your home blessed.
3. Place religious artifacts throughout every room in the home and in plain view. I would also recommend putting Holy Water in open containers, such as small plastic bowls, in every room.

4. Do some research of your property. Did anyone die on the premises—if so; how and when?

*   *   *

• Please Don'ts:

1. Use a Divination Board and try to *contact* the spirit or spirits.
2. Have a séance.
3. Try to exorcise the spirit or spirits yourselves.
4. Choose a psychic, medium, tarot reader, etc. out of the telephone book, or choose one at random. *Investigate credentials thoroughly.*

Spiritual Poems

I hope you will find some comfort and peace from these prayer poems that were given to me through automatic writing. This poem was given to me within a week after the death of my cousin Crystal, my sister and my best friend.

The Spirit's Journey

There needn't be a long or lonely night...
Reach for My Hand, it is near, hold tight.
I've reserved a place that is special for you...
A place here on earth and in the heaven's of blue,
Be not sad and give into despair...
For you hold onto riches, none else can compare.
The spirit's journey of this physical life;
Is here to experience, grow in faith and then to rejoice,
In the Kingdom of God with all of the faithful;
The spirit renewed, cleansed and joyfully grateful.
Begin each new day with a hymn of praise,
'Glory to God on High,' for He lights the way,
In times of trial and tribulation;
Seek His Comfort by prayer and exultation.
Keep close to your heart, His Love and His Truth;
The power in prayer and abiding faith will soothe.
When your physical life comes to an end...
Remember the soul's journey is to be with the Father once again.
Amen. Amen   September 27, 1999

A Plea From the Soul
Who is Triumphant in the Lord

Help them oh my God; they who mourn for me,
Give them of Your comfort...
That they may know my peace;
Touch their hearts with Your Wondrous Love...
That they may know that I am fulfilled;
Give them of Your Strength...
That they may feel Your Might;
And endure my physical loss,
but know that I am whole.
Give them of Your Joy...
That they may know that I am Yours.
Give them of Your Love...
That they may know that I am content;
and that I have not left, but returned.
Tell them I am here, painless and complete,
and will watch and guard over them;
until we are together again.

Amen.

Blessings

Bless me, Heavenly Father, forgive my erring ways;,
Grant me strength to serve Thee, put purpose to my days...
Give me understanding, enough to make me kind,
So I will judge all people, with my heart and not my mind...
And teach me to be patient...in everything I do,
Content to trust Your Wisdom, and to follow after You...

And help me when I falter;
And hear me when I pray;
And receive me in Thy Kingdom
To dwell with Thee some day.... Amen

Grace

Man can find many descriptive words and phrases to depict the word; Grace. However, the one description and most important message for man to under-stand for the word Grace, is this: Grace is a virtue that is given by God in time of temptation in order that man realizes that he alone is powerless to the attacks from Satan, and to the corruption of the flesh and the world. If man falters; falls from faithfulness (Grace), and commits sin, upon asking for forgiveness; once again he is given Divine Grace, which is freedom from the sin—Spiritual Freedom. Divine Grace is a state of being that releases one's spirit from the binds of physical corruption, continuous sin, anger and malice. To be in the State of Grace is to experience true inner peace, spiritual wisdom, inner beauty and true love of self.

I saw Jesus up in the heaven's looking down at the earth, and then he was standing on a huge cliff overlooking the ocean and I felt as though I was standing next to him and this was the *message* I received....

Jesus' Plea

I stood atop the hill,
I could smell the ocean below;
And though He whispered,
I heard Him still...
'In the beginning this was beautiful—unstained by man.'
These were His words as He gestured with His hand.

His outstretched arm moved in circular form,
Tears were in His eyes—as He glanced all around.
'Man must see the error of his ways;
For the destruction is great—and there is more to come,
And in so many ways...
But if each does his part and reaches out to each other;
The ONE that reigns now will succumb to the Master.
An attitude change must be desired by man,
He must look into self and see when it began;
That he chose the path filled with deception and sin;
Then ask for My help, for a new start—a place to begin.
Faith is a Grace, given only by God.
The asking is easy—the rules and tests they are hard.
But man must be faithful and make a change of heart;
Only then can we achieve a new start.'

Thank you for taking the time to read these inspired poems and enlightenments. If these words have brought you peace, given you food for thought or put a smile in your heart—goal achieved.

May God Bless You and Grant you peace and happiness.